BRUCE GROBBEL...
AN AUTOBIOGRAP...

Bruce Grobbelaar, goalkeeper for the presti-
gious Liverpool side, is undoubtedly one of the
most outstanding keepers in the world game.
He is renowned not only for his extrovert
personality but also for his unorthodox and
frequently spectacular style of play.

Grobbelaar was born in South Africa and
brought up in Rhodesia where he did two
years' National Service before leaving to play
first in South Africa and then in the North
American Soccer League for Vancouver Whitecaps. He was lent by Vancouver Whitecaps to
Crewe Alexandra in 1980 where he quickly
came to the notice of Liverpool who followed
him back to Canada and signed him as cover
for Ray Clemence. After just three reserve
games for Liverpool, Clemence transferred to
Spurs and Grobbelaar took over, becoming a
colourful and invaluable member of the team.
BRUCE GROBBELAAR: AN AUTOBIOGRAPHY is
an entertaining look at one of the most likeable
figures in football today.

About the author

Bob Harris, who collaborated on the book with Bruce Grobbelaar, began his career as a journalist on a Birmingham weekly paper and then spent the next 20 years as chief sports writer with Thomson Regional Newspapers before joining *Today* as chief football writer and athletics correspondent. He co-wrote both Graeme Souness's and Steve Coppell's autobiographies as well as BOBBY ROBSON'S WORLD CUP DIARY and several publications on behalf of the Football Association.

BRUCE GROBBELAAR: AN AUTOBIOGRAPHY

With BOB HARRIS

CORONET BOOKS
Hodder and Stoughton

Photographic acknowledgements

For permission to use photographs reproduced in this book, the author and publisher would like to thank: Associated Sports Photography; Steve Hale; Tommy Hindley; Craig Johnston; Sportsphoto Agency; Sport and General; and Bob Thomas.

First published in Great Britain in 1986 by Willow Books William Collins Sons & Co Ltd

Coronet Edition 1988

British Library C.I.P.

Grobbelaar, Bruce
[More than somewhat].Bruce
Grobbelaar : an autobiography.
1. Soccer players—South Africa—
Biography
I. [More than somewhat]II. Title
III. Harris, Bob, 1944-
796.334'092'4   GV942.7.G7

ISBN 0-340-42645-4

Printed and bound in Great Britain for Hodder and Stoughton Paperbacks, a division of Hodder and Stoughton Ltd., Mill Road, Dunton Green, Sevenoaks, Kent. TN13 2YA. (Editorial Office: 47 Bedford Square, London WC1B 3DP) by Richard Clay Ltd, Bungay, Suffolk.

Contents

Foreword by Bob Paisley

1 African Youth
2 Jungle Man
3 In the Bush
4 Making my Mark
5 In Reserve
6 In at the Deep End
7 The Treble
8 Good Luck Charms and Witchdoctors
9 Goalkeeping: My Style
10 Hooliganism: Football's Shame
11 Brussels
12 From Paisley to Dalglish
13 Looking Ahead
14 The Double

DEDICATION

To all my friends who died in a needless war

Foreword

by Bob Paisley

It did not take a lot to persuade me that Bruce Grobbelaar was the goalkeeper I wanted at Liverpool as cover and eventual replacement for our England International Ray Clemence. He was recommended to me after our scouts had watched him put up the shutters for bottom-of-the-table Crewe against promotion-chasing Portsmouth. I followed it up by going to watch him against Doncaster Rovers and I could have left even before the kick-off!

I saw enough during the kick-about to confirm those initial reports. Bruce stood on his line with one of his team-mates blasting the ball at him from little more than 6 yards. He not only stopped everything – but caught it. Unfortunately, before we could make an offer he was off to Canada but, having made up our minds we were not to be put off, and we crossed the Atlantic to watch him twice more. We could see his agility and raw talent. He had the right approach and desperately wanted the chance to play for Liverpool and, daft as he sometimes is, I knew that the 'Kop' at Anfield would take to him. That was an important factor for the supporters behind that goal have a passion for good keepers and their applause has been known to lift opponents to outstanding heights. They would not change their ways even when the late Bill Shankly tried to stop them because of this.

What we did not know when we signed Bruce was just how soon he would be taking over from Ray Clemence. But I had no fears. We would not have gone all the way to Vancouver for a comedian; there are plenty of those on our own doorstep in Liverpool. Despite his lack of experience he did not let us down as he helped us to maintain our remarkable run of success. Certainly he had his wild moments and was caught out once or twice in the process but now, despite some criticism, he matured into a fine goalkeeper and, what is more, he has every chance of becoming even better. As he gets older he realises that he does not have to break his neck for every save and he is learning to read the play much better. Of course, he will continue to make the odd mistake but that is due to the tremendous amount of work he does for his defenders and he is often blamed for their errors.

There is, however, a wild, untamed streak in him and that will never change because it is an essential part of his character. I, for one, will accept those wayward moments in return for his qualities and I would not change him for any goalkeeper in the First Division, Peter Shilton included. Had he not been committed to Zimbabwe I am sure he would have eventually taken over from Shilton in the England goal.

Bruce Grobbelaar is one of the game's true characters. Everyone who watches the game knows of his skills and the colourful side of his personality. There is also another side to him. He is a deep, caring young man as this book will show to his many fans.

1

African Youth

So many of my family have had legs amputated that they used to call us the 'Hopping Grobbelaars' back in South Africa. My great-grandparents had fought on opposite sides in the Boer War and my grandfather had played saxophone in a circus band. With a background like mine is it any wonder that I was attracted to the art of goalkeeping for, after all, aren't we all supposed to be crazy? But even that was not certain and instead of becoming an international goalkeeper I might easily have become a one-legged 'Hopping Grobbelaar' when, aged four, I tried to stop a bicycle by sticking my foot through the spokes of the front wheel. However, I survived to go on and play football for my adopted country Rhodesia, which then became Zimbabwe. I also had the necessary qualifications to play for South Africa, the country of my birth, England and even Wales. A change of passport, a new ruling by the Zimbabwean Football Association and an old ruling by the international governing body of the game, FIFA, means that I am now a stateless person as far as representative soccer is concerned.

Complicated? That is the story of my life so far which
began for Bruce David Grobbelaar on 6 October 1957 in
the maternity ward of a hospital which backed onto
Greyville Racecourse in Durban, South Africa. Trust me to
be born in a country that was to be excluded from
international sport because of its apartheid policies! Not
that my mother, Beryl Eunice, was to know at the time.
She was of good British stock while my father, Hendrik
Gabriel, was born in the Transvaal, a true Boer in every
sense of the word and one of thousands of Grobbelaars
spread throughout Southern Africa. I once tried to count
my cousins in Johannesburg alone but stopped at 75. Some
family tree, it looks like a weeping willow. Even my
surname played a joke on me because, translated from the
original Dutch, it means 'clumsy'.

My claim to British citizenship came about because my
maternal great-grandparents were in Cape Town Castle,
which was a British stronghold during the Boer hostilities
and therefore designated as 'home' soil, when my grandfather, Edward Ernest Banning, was born. His father was a
member of the Welsh Fusiliers and his mother had been
born in the Lancashire town of St Helens. Grandad clearly
did not relish the idea of following in the family's military
footsteps for he became a wandering musician, playing the
sax in that circus band.

The wanderlust had a strong grip on the Grobbelaars as
well for my father was on the move in more senses than
one from the moment I arrived. He was on the road
working as a driver of a double-decker bus and, before I
was two months old, my parents, my two-year-old sister
Jaqueline and I were on our way, travelling north to
Rhodesia where a one-horse town called Sinoya became
home. One of Sinoya's few saving graces was its caves
which drew the tourists to view a bottomless pool of still

blue water. It also had a railway passing through which provided my father with a job.

We didn't linger too long in Sinoya for, just four years old, I packed up my toys and set off once more, this time heading for the Rhodesian capital Salisbury with the latest addition to our family, an African houseboy called Lummick, a poor man's au pair. To a British family it may sound like black slavery in the southern states of North America, especially as a family's wealth was often judged by the number of houseboys who lived at the bottom of the garden in accommodation built onto the garage. It was an accepted way of life. We had no garage and could only afford the salary of one boy, Lummick. We weren't all that poor as Dad still worked for the railways and Mum brought in extra income as a book keeper with a local firm. We lived in a nice little semi-detached house in Baker Avenue, which is now the main street in the renamed capital Harare. Lummick obviously did not mind sharing our house with us as he stayed for 16 years, becoming part of the family. In those days his chores would consist of taking my sister to school and me to nursery school, cleaning the house, doing the washing, working in the garden and then, at night, babysitting.

A couple of times a year Lummick would disappear, leaving us to fend for ourselves while he returned home to Sinoya to see his wives and growing number of children for a fortnight. He would give his two wives the money he had saved and work on the house he was building as well as sowing the seeds for the further extension of his family. They all lived together in a hut on the Rural Tribal Trust Lands which was built out of mud, branches and had a thatched roof. His pride and joy was his new house built of mud bricks which were made by his wives and its corrugated iron roof and proper windows. Lummick would return home after his holiday and say to my mother: 'Madam, the grass in the house is still longer than the bricks.' It took him seven to eight years to finish it but his pride and determination would not allow him to permit anyone else to help build it.

From a distance and with no knowledge of the circumstances it may sound unjust but Lummick looked on us as family and we all loved him, though I must confess that I sometimes had strange ways of showing it. I still flush with embarrassment when I recall the day he came to pick me up from Tree Tops Nursery School. Of all things I had been cast in the role of the Angel Gabriel in the school play and, apart from the wings and halo, I was still in my costume when Lummick lifted me onto the crossbar of his bike. When we reached home I wanted to jump off and run up the front path, impatient to tell my parents all about the production but my minder insisted that I stayed with him while he took the bike around to the back of the house so that he could keep an eye on me. It was at that moment that I almost lost a foot and became one of the 'Hopping Grobbelaars' for my four-year-old mind told me that the easiest way to get what I wanted and stop the bike was to put my little foot through the front wheel's spokes. We both tumbled to the ground and Lummick, though battered and bruised from absorbing most of the impact of the fall, picked me up in his arms, abandoned his precious machine and ran 17 blocks to the casualty ward of the local hospital. His reward when we returned home to concerned parents was for me to blame him for the crash.

What made it worse was that, even at that tender age, I probably believed he was at fault for racism was taught early and was part of a white man's, and particularly an Afrikaner's, education. Inevitably it played a large part in my life as I grew up in a country where white superiority was firmly established. However, I had no hesitation in playing for all-black sides in sport, if I thought the standards were higher than the whites could offer, or later, to room with a black player, Carl Valentine, for two years in Canada when we were best friends and almost inseparable. Maturity and travel have now removed the blinkers but I am sure it would cause a lot of anguish if my daughter Tahli ever wanted to marry a coloured person, as it surely would to black parents if their child were in the same position.

To appreciate this clash of ideas you would have had to grow up in the same sort of environment that I did, moving backwards and forwards between Rhodesia and South Africa and then seeing the Rhodesian Government declare UDI, and become Zimbabwe with black and white almost reversing roles. I make no excuses and offer no apologies for my early attitudes, simply because I did not choose to be born in South Africa any more than I had a say in whether I should be black or white. In Rhodesia the damage was done long before Ian Smith, who did far more for the black community than the British ever did, came to power. We were taught that there was a fundamental difference between black and white from the first years at school. We were told that we were superior and this was perpetuated because there was one school for the whites and another for the blacks with much higher educational standards in the former. This had been the case for many, many years with the blacks coming from the north to gain the sort of education they would not have been able to get in their own tribal lands. Naturally, though, it meant that the better jobs went to the better educated, and so the wheel turned. Of course, it went · deeper. Young white boys, myself included, would treat coloureds and blacks as inferiors and no white adult would offer as much as a reprimand. It meant that I could happily play with Lummick's two sons

Funwerre and Gordon, as a six-year-old, without even thinking to ask why the only decent shoes and clothes they wore were my cast-offs.

The situation was considerably worse in South Africa than in Rhodesia as I grew up but, looking back, it was unacceptable in both. Africans were not welcomed in the white man's bars and though they could go into certain hotels they could not eat in the same restaurants. In cinemas a black could show you to your seat but could not sit in it himself. He had even to clock in at his job so that police could keep a check on movement and enforce the curfews when they were in operation. Transport was the same and, in Rhodesia, the whites would sit at the front and the blacks at the back. This was a real problem because, being a superstitious race, the Africans thought the back seats were unlucky and would try to sneak to the front, provoking fights with the black drivers who were afraid of losing their jobs for not enforcing the rules. It is significant that when Rhodesia became Zimbabwe in 1980 the roles were completely reversed and the whites now sit at the back of the bus.

The segregation in trains was even more marked with four classes and the train divided completely in two. Next to the engine were the fourth-class benches followed by the third-class sleeping benches. These compartments were for the blacks who were served by their own tea boy while we whites had second and first-class accommodation with restaurant and buffet cars. As a train pulled into a station there would be a seething mass trying to get on at the front and peace and order at the back. It was all very colonial and, it must be said, a normal and everyday thing to black and white alike. It was drummed into us at home and in school, that black and white do not mix. If you did it was a sin — unless it was for sport and, in particular, if you were representing your country together. Circumstances like this make you wonder whether the boycotts, both by black and white, are the right way to tackle apartheid for it was competing together that helped to break down the barriers as far as I, and many of my friends, were concerned, even to the extent of risking imprisonment if caught consorting with a coloured member of the opposite sex.

Admittedly we whites still thought we were a cut above the black man even in sport. They might have had the skill but we were harder and more competitive. After all we had the boots while they played in bare feet! The older generation was horrified when we played multi-racial soccer and baseball and particu'arly when we formed a mixed boxing club and actually swam in the same pool together. This, of course, was Rhodesia rather than South Africa but even there taboos remained strong with black men unable to play in the Rhodesian Open Tennis Tournament while only a very, very talented negro golfer could play in the Rhodesian Open. Indians played cricket but did not mix socially after the games though, maybe somewhat surprisingly, there was mixed sport at school level. But the changes were coming and there for everyone to see. The black breweries, with plenty of cash behind them, were importing white sportsmen from Great Britain to lift standards and improve knowledge long before full integration came with the change from Rhodesia to Zimbabwe.

Whether black or white it was a healthy life for a youngster under the African sun and, though we were by no means well off, we were not short of anything. I went to good schools, was well fed and genuinely enjoyed those early years, though there was a major upheaval when my father decided it was time to be on the move once more and we all went off in search of his roots in his home town of Benoni in the Transvaal where he had been offered a job in his old trade as a wood machinist. Lummick was not allowed to travel with us as it was in South Africa. He cried when we left and we were all equally sad. The remarkable sequel to the story was that when we moved back to Rhodesia, Lummick somehow knew and instantly rejoined the family as though we had never been parted.

It was the third time we had moved in the space of two years and the loss of Lummick was offset by the tantalising prospect of seeing the sea for the first time. Unfortunately I didn't get a chance to see it as we moved, not to the coast, but to the mountains. There was no sea but I looked in wonder at snow for the very first time and we were able, in the middle of July, to build snowmen. Another advantage was that we had so much more space. Gone were the cramped semi-detached houses and two-bedroomed flats of the city, here we had room to move, three bedrooms and, more importantly for a youngster, a garden with fruit trees and places to play.

Sport was an inevitable part of my life even at that early age with my father, in those days a dashing, athletic man, playing football, baseball and cricket while my mother was good at hockey, softball, tennis and badminton. After the regular Braai Vleis (barbecue), I would be off playing the sport according to the season while my sister was more of a bookworm. It was around this time that I first showed signs of being a goalkeeper like my father, who helped me by building goalposts in our back garden and, before long, I was playing in teams with boys three or four years older than myself.

Although Dad was happy playing for the railway club he was good enough to play in goal for Rhodesia against Malawi at the Glamis Stadium in Salisbury. He was a great incentive to me as a sportsman but he wasn't just a good goalkeeper and a fine catcher at baseball, he was also good looking and charming with an eye for a pretty face. His extra-curricular activities eventually led to my parents' divorce. Dad, after a series of operations, was later to have his left leg amputated below the knee. He suffered from something known in South Africa as Burgher's Disease. He was told what would happen if he did not stop smoking and drinking, but he still carried on. Dad was the third in the family to suffer an amputation though Uncle Willie lost his leg after falling down a mine shaft. Brave old Uncle Willie carried on riding to work on his bike with a fixed wheel. Gangrene finally took my father's life in December 1981.

It was not long before we were back in Rhodesia and the David Livingstone School where I put my new-found goalkeeping skills to the test with the second team. I was no more than eight when I had my first taste of what to me was the big time and I decided then and there that I liked it. The Rhodesian National Coach Danny McLean came to our school for a coaching session and asked me to go in goal so that he could demonstrate the art of taking penalties. He placed the ball, turned to the other boys and said: 'This is how to score from the penalty spot,' and promptly lashed the ball to my right. I threw myself at the shot which was so powerful that it spun me around, but I kept it out. The Rhodesian National Coach was not impressed and ordered me to stay still while he blasted the next shot past me. I did not mind. I had made my point. I soon moved up to the first team and even helped them to make a final which we lost, would you believe it, to a penalty. There was no stopping this one which was taken by a young Scot named Graham Shearer who eventually became one of my best friends. Much later the two of us were even invited over to England for a trial with an

English manager named Brian Clough. I actually saw the two air tickets that were sent for Graham and me but the manager of the team we played for said that our education was more important and he and his wife used the tickets for a visit to England.

Africa, whether it was Rhodesia or South Africa, was a great place for school, particularly if you liked the outdoor life. I played every sport possible and, as a result, became captain of my house, but as for schoolwork I had a deep aversion to homework, and would catch up with my prep by cribbing off my mates in the morning before lessons. It must have been hard for my mother to cope with such a wilful little boy, especially after my brother Mark Edward was born when I was ten, and before Dad left home. It helped when we moved to a flat not 100 yards from school until my Mum remarried when I was 14 to a man named Denys Davies. I was well aware that my Mum and Mr Davies were very friendly and it was generally assumed that they would marry. However, when they did one day it took me completely by surprise as I arrived home from cricket to be told: 'Meet your new father.' My sister Jaqueline was more fortunate as she was in the house when the spur-of-the-moment decision was made and was able to attend the ceremony. Just think, with my middle name of David and my Welsh background, I might well have been known as Dai Davies!

My stepfather was a strong influence. He was a very fair man who tried to impose the discipline I had lacked since my father left. But for his arrival on the scene I could have easily gone completely off the rails. I was a regular for the strap at school and was constantly gated by the headmaster, Old Pop Lawrie, for failing to do my homework, talking in class and doing sport to the exclusion of all else. I was in particular trouble if the headmaster caught me outside the classroom during lessons. That was sure to mean the strap or even being banned from games. If I heard footsteps after being dismissed from a lesson, I would frantically find somewhere to hide and once went to the extreme of climbing out of the window and hanging onto the ledge by my fingertips.

However, Old Pop Lawrie could be a kindly man as well. Once a bout of glandular fever threatened to keep me out of a big cricket match against our local rivals. I felt recovered enough to play but my mother put her foot down and said no. It was the headmaster who sorted it out by driving me to and from the game without her ever knowing. But he banned me from so many other events that when I attended the fancy dress party at the end of grade five, my mother dressed me in swimming costume, school blazer and cap with sporting colours, football boot and sock on my left leg, white sock and cricket pad on the right leg, a tennis racket in one hand, a hockey stick in the other and a cardboard gate over my shoulder. When the intrigued Mr Lawrie asked me what I was supposed to be I simply replied: 'Gated.' I won the prize for the most original costume though, more, I suspect, for cheek than for style.

Being an over-enthusiastic all-round sportsman might have been a disadvantage in academic terms but I was discovering that it helped a great deal in other respects. Goalkeeping was not the only quality I inherited from my father, I also had an eye for the girls and, because I was considered a top sportsman by my contemporaries, I fared quite well. I was into my first year as a teenager when I willingly lost my innocence to my sister Jaqueline's 16-year-old friend, who offered to look after me, and did, while my mother and sister were out. Such was my interest in the opposite sex at that early age that I even decided against the option of an all-boys school, which would have enhanced my sporting prospects, in favour of going to a co-educational college along with policeman's son Douglas Cannon. He used to rave about how good Mount Pleasant High School was with all those lovely girls and I reckoned that, as he wasn't the prettiest of boys, with his glasses kept in place by a piece of string around the back of his head, I must stand a chance even if it did mean a five-mile ride to and from school twice a day (four times if I went home for my favourite lunch of sweetcorn and poached eggs on toast.)

When I arrived at the school, I set off in hot pursuit of the Grove twins, Jill and Jenny, who used to send me up something rotten because I could never tell them apart. There was also the lovely Felicity with the big blue eyes and the dark hair who lived so far out of town that the only chance of a quick kiss and cuddle came at the end-of-term dances when we boys would try as hard as we could to get the girls behind the curtain on the stage or up against the vaulting horse in the gymnasium.

All this hardly helped me improve either my schoolwork or my general behaviour. I even ran away from home at one stage, packing a bag and slipping out of the house at midnight to hitchhike the 175 kilometres to Inyazura where my father was living with his new wife and my little baby brother, Mark. My mother made no attempt to bring me back for she knew all along that I would return. She was right. I stayed for three months before both my brother and I went back. Everything was fine with my father, as I was doing so well at sport, but I did not get on with my stepmother. My father had boasted about my football prowess and I was invited to play for the local black police team in their seconds. Their pitch was right next to the bush and some 100 yards from the nearest mud huts, so we all changed on our opponents' bus. The lazy, summer afternoon was suddenly interrupted by a shrill scream and a deep roar. We all stopped and turned to see an African nanny emerge from the tall elephant grass at the edge of the bush carrying her baby and glancing fearfully over her shoulder at a fully-grown lion which was casually following her. The football was forgotten as we all raced for the protection of the visiting team's bus and the game was abandoned as we waited for the animal to be captured.

Back at Mount Pleasant High, when I was not pursuing Jill, Jenny or Felicity, I was developing my talents at cricket as a wicket-keeper batsman; at rugby in which I became the youngest fly-half to play for the first team; and also at cross-country running and high jumping. There was no football team but there was a ground nearby which I was able to use if not chased off by the groundsman. I was there one day having footballs blasted at me from all angles when a car pulled up in the road outside while the occupant looked on at our kick-about. Fears that he might have been a policeman about to arrest us for trespassing were dispelled when the driver came over and introduced himself as Dave Russell, coach of a local team who were in need of a goalkeeper. Was I interested? I explained that I was keen enough but that I would have to seek permission from my Mum first and that obstacle was overcome when Mr Russell offered to pay my club fees and promised that it would not interfere with my studies.

This was not only a new step for me but it was also my introduction to multi-racial football for though my new club, Salisbury Callies, was all-white and virtually all-Scottish, we played against the crack black teams. Although, in those days, I still considered myself a cut above the coloureds and the blacks we played against every week, at least the barriers began to be broken down as we mixed socially after the games and, when no one was around, would even take our rivals to the Hellenic Club next door for a swim in their pool, even though the adults frowned on this and accused us of flouting tradition.

I was having a wonderful life as I not only enjoyed and made progress in soccer but was also doing so in other sports, widening my horizons with regular trips into South Africa. My swashbuckling style with the cricket bat and my safe hands behind the wicket earned me a place in the Rhodesian 'Fawns' for the games against the young South African teams in the Under 13s, Under 14s and as twelfth man for the Under 15s. It was a great adventure taking two days to reach the North Transvaal, though I always needed to find a sponsor to pay my way. We would also make the long trip to Umtali by train three times a year for matches. The only problem for young tearaways like us was boredom and I still break out in a cold sweat when I think of how we used to relieve the monotony by crawling along the top of the speeding train James Bond style. Never mind being a 'Hopping Grobbelaar' I was close to becoming the first of the 'Bouncing Grobbelaars', deceased!

Baseball also gave me the opportunity to travel around Southern Africa and enabled me to represent my country against the Springboks at junior level. My father had also played the game to quite a high standard and I teamed up with an old opponent of his from Northern Rhodesia, Rod Partridge, and his sons Reg, Roy and Roddy to win everything in the 'Little League' on Sunday mornings. I was keen to move up to play with the big boys in the major League on Sunday afternoons. My stepbrother Barry, who was six feet five and four feet wide, was reputed to be the fastest pitcher in the whole of South Africa and I wanted to be like him but my Mum, who had given way to me over football, put her foot down and said that it was far too dangerous for a boy to play that particular sport with the men. She was probably right, she usually was. As a junior I did represent my province and then Rhodesia in a mini series against the Boks and, as far as I know, I still hold the Under 16 record for the most strike-outs with 19 from a possible 21 and only two making it to first base. I was so wrapped up in baseball that it could easily have superseded soccer as my chosen sport. I was later to come very close to accepting the offer of a baseball scholarship from North Adams State College in Massachusetts.

I am not so sure that North Adams State College would have been so interested in me had they checked my academic record. Things had not improved at all on that front and my new headmaster, Mr Lambert, only put up with me because of my prowess on the sports field and he frequently warned my mother that I was in danger of expulsion if I did not pull my socks up. Every Monday morning my name would be read out at assembly as one of the sinners of the previous week and I took as many cuts of the strap as was allowed by the teachers' union and, on one notorious occasion, received even more. I had received four cuts from the headmaster in the morning for playing football instead of doing my homework and then, later in the day, I took another half dozen from the deputy head for leering and winking at a pretty female student teacher. It was only when the entry was made in the punishment book that it was realised that I had taken the day's count into double figures — and that was against the rules! Having been on the carpet and in serious trouble I suddenly found myself the object of fawning apologies and was given a 'reward' of two weeks without the strap.

I was almost as bad at home even though my mother and stepfather worked hard to keep me under some sort of control. They knew that the best punishment was to stop me playing whichever sport was in season but, even then, I would hide my gear in the dustbin in the alley and sneak out. Mum once banned me from playing football because of a broken finger. Again the dustbin came to my rescue. It was five years later that I owned up and, even then, my mother was annoyed because I had been deceitful and I had to apologise. That was also the hiding place for my crash helmet for my illicit rides on the Partridge boys' motor scooter. This was more serious than playing football when forbidden and it was not long before my parents found out and caught me red-handed, sitting on the bike at the traffic lights. That weekend was spent locked in my bedroom.

It was the last thing my long-suffering mother needed for even my studious sister Jaqueline was causing her problems as she was going out with a long-haired hippie named Joe Roy whose lifestyle did not go down well with my straightlaced family. I wasn't too keen on him myself until, one Christmas, I was knocked over by a big African boy and Joe stepped in to defend me, saying: 'We might be family one day – we have to look after each other.' Joe was in the army and was a bush Mormon which meant he smoked, drank and swore and went to church when he felt guilty. He eventually had to marry my sister for the oldest reason in the world with everyone nodding their heads and muttering: 'I told you so.' However, the story has a happy ending for Jaqueline and Joe settled down to a very happy marriage and Joe is now a deacon in the Mormon Church.

I was making good progress with Salisbury Callies and when the number one keeper, Edinburgh-born Walter Lowrie, a former professional with Hibs in Scottish football, was injured I found myself plunged into first-team football at the most crucial stage of the season. I played four successive matches for Callies as we won 3–1 in the quarter-final of the Cup competition; lost 2–1 in a League game; won 2–0 in the Cup semi-final and 1–0 in the League. I was on top of the world especially as my best friend Graham Shearer was also in the team as we prepared for the big final, against a black side from Bulawayo called Mashonaland United, in the Rufaro Stadium, Salisbury. My place in the BAT Rosebowl final looked a certainty when Lowrie turned up for the final training session in a suit but, having watched us work out, he declared himself fit. We all took our club suits and kit to a local hotel on the eve of the big game only for Graham and me to be told by the manager that we were dropped because he considered our inexperience could cost the club the cup. To say that we were amazed by the decision would be an understatement and when we took our seats in the Rufaro Stadium, which is opposite the capital's main graveyard, it was in a bitter frame of mind. The 50,000 crowd mainly comprised blacks and Graham and I must have stood out like a sore thumb as we sat in the white block behind the club sponsors, players' friends and wives and the club officials, for we rowed with the Chairman, shouted abuse at our team-mates and cheered on Mashonaland. It wouldn't have been so bad but our rivals won 2-0 and one of the goals scored by Gibson Homela, who later had trials in England with Millwall, crept in at the foot of the post past Lowrie. I couldn't have been more delighted.

I was still behaving like a spoiled brat at home, school and at the football club and something had to give. It was me. The headmaster had given me enough chances and he quietly told my mother that if I did not leave the school I would be expelled. Clearly, after the Cup Final business, I could not expect to carry on with Salisbury Callies where I was now a schoolboy professional. It was decided that I should catch a train south to join my parents, who had recently moved to Bulawayo, that very night. In fact, it had only been with great reluctance that my parents had allowed me to stay behind and pursue my professional football career, and I had been living with friends, the Partridge family. So quickly did things happen that by the next day I had enrolled in Hamilton High School, Bulawayo.

Callies put me on loan to Matabeleland Highlanders, a black side which predominantly consisted of members of Joshua Nkomo's Ndebele tribesmen. They had a Scottish centre-half named Martin Kennedy playing for them and he laughed when I told him that I had signed on at my last club for a meagre $10. He told me to go for the big one so when I negotiated with the manager Silas Ndhlovu, I took a deep breath and demanded a massive $100. Silas, who was later imprisoned for embezzling post office funds, raised an eyebrow and said: 'Is that all. We thought you would be wanting at least $500.' As it was we negotiated a win bonus of $35 a game and a scaled-down payment for a draw, depending on the opposition, with nothing for a defeat. He gave me around $450 signing-on fee which, somewhat suspiciously, arrived in used one and two dollar bills in a brown paper bag!

I had also made up my mind that it was time I grew up and started to behave myself at school. I was looked on as one of the senior pupils and gave no one any trouble at all. I even captained the house for one season and represented them at cross country running as well as at soccer. The football was particularly successful. The week before I arrived Hamilton had lost to Morgan High, a team of coloured children, 11–1. A few weeks later, with me in goal, we won 1–0 and I was an immediate hero.

It was a good time for me. Financially things were comfortable. Mum owned a couple of shoe shops, one for men in the African part of town and the other for women in the European sector, while my new Dad was one of the country's leading diesel mechanics working for Rhodesian Railways. For a schoolboy I was very well off as my football was paying so well. It was unusual for a schoolboy to be a professional footballer, though not unknown.

Hamilton High was a boys only school and that undoubtedly helped me to concentrate on my studies a little more, though there was still the distraction of the girls' school next door. My status as a wage-earning schoolboy did my reputation no harm in that direction, either, as the girls would come and support our soccer games. My particular favourite was a pretty girl named Theresa Wyley whom I used to walk to school, carrying her books, and take out to the Marisha Cocktail Bar which was owned by the football club chairman.

Despite my poor reports and threats of expulsion at Mount Pleasant High in Salisbury, I left with good passes in English, mathematics, science, Afrikaans, geography, woodwork and technical drawing. I failed miserably at cooking (I didn't mind that, but I wasn't at all keen on needlework which formed the second part of the syllabus), and was not too good at history or social studies. I was quite pleased with myself and thought that with the extra effort I was putting in at my new school, I would get several examination passes. Who was kidding who? My first report changed all of that. Although older than most of the kids in the class, I came twenty-seventh out of thirty. The report, which I kept, was somewhat repetitious telling me to work harder, make a greater effort to catch up and to concentrate. It was not until the sports section that there was anything complimentary. It said: 'An outstanding goalkeeper for the 1st XI'. This was echoed by my form master who wrote: 'He has made little effort to catch up. He must concentrate on his schoolwork rather than his football', while the headmaster added: 'I have admired his goalkeeping. However, he is wasting his time in the classroom.'

I took the remarks to heart. If this was the sort of report I was going to get when I was on my best behaviour and working hard, what was it going to be like when I slipped back into my old ways? There was only one answer and that was to leave school and concentrate on making football my career. Surprisingly I met with no objections from home where my mother had all but given up hope of me being a child prodigy. I was legally entitled to leave and Mum thought that it would help me become my own man.

There was certainly some indication that I could make the grade as a professional footballer for, while still at Hamilton High, I came second in the National Castle Soccer Star of the Year awards, only losing out to the outstanding Dynamos player George Shaya. It was no disgrace, certainly not for a 16-year-old beginner, as George was the acknowledged master and could have played to English First Division standard except that he would never have been able to work outside his native environment and he would have never survived a Liverpool winter! As for me they said: 'You can take Bruce Grobbelaar out of the bush but you can't take the bush out of Bruce Grobbelaar.' I can't argue with that, either.

The only other white person among the selected XI for the awards that year was Billy Sharman who played for Chibuku, a black brewery club from Salisbury. Tastes in beer differed dramatically in Rhodesia and the beer that made Chibuku most successful was called Shake-Shake, because you had to shake the cardboard carton it came in to make the yeast rise to the top so that you could chew it while you drank the beer. The rival black brewery was called Rufaro and their main product was an equally evil liquid called Mhamba which meant, simply, 'Go'. There was no question of contravening the Trades Description Act for, if you were brave enough to miss out on the more familiar European beers, it certainly gave you a run for your money, reaching the parts that all beers reach, only a lot more quickly.

It was Chibuku who came in with a timely bid for my services at the time I was ready to finish my schooling. They agreed a fee with Callies, who still held my registration, and then came to me offering a choice of jobs at the brewery. It satisfied everyone; my family were pleased that I had walked into a steady job; I was happy because it was an opportunity to move back to Salisbury with good wages and high win bonuses; and, not least of all Salisbury Callies received a record fee for a teenager of $3,500 which funded a brand new cocktail bar at the club. When I go back to Zimbabwe now, I like to go for a drink at the club as I feel I helped build it. Time has helped smooth out any ill feelings over my sudden departure. The only people not happy with my move were the supporters of Matabeleland Highlanders. They identified with their local brew and thought me a traitor to abandon the Ingwebu beer; whenever I played in Bulawayo I would be roundly abused. It was as bad as moving from Liverpool to Everton.

Chibuku Shumba were a big company with almost unlimited resources and few prejudices. It was a fully-integrated team with four or five whites, a couple of coloureds and the rest black. There was, however, growing racial tension in the country and to get to work at Stainless Steel Industries, who made beer tankards and toilets, I had to pass through the volatile Seke Township and that was not always good news if there had been any problems the night before. But, once more, I was lucky. Part of my training involved acting as production manager for the brewery and I noticed there that when a 12-pint carton of Shake-Shake was damaged, the whole lot was thrown away. I thought that, at 10 cents a pint, this was a bit extravagant, so I began loading up the bad cartons in the back of my Mini and selling them in the Township for 8 cents a pint. This proved to be a shrewd move for not only did it make me popular at the social club, because I put the takings into the club's drink kitty, but also in Seke Township where I became known as the footballer with the cheap beer and when there were riots on the main road to Victoria I was waved through without being stoned.

The manager of the Chibuku team was a cigar-smoking Englishman named Jack Meagher who had arrived from Wankie, a team based around the largest coal mine in the southern hemisphere, bringing with him a black goalkeeper named Posani Sibanda whom he had rescued from a car washing job. Jack's idea was to annex the two best young goalkeepers around and corner that particular market. His judgment was promptly confirmed by the then Rhodesian National coach Bill Asprey who picked both Sibanda and me for the National squad's tour of the country, which was designed to build up team work, morale and confidence. We travelled to places like Umtali, Bulawayo, Gwelo and Salisbury and the manager told us that Sibanda and I were to share the goalkeeping responsibilities between us. I made my international début against Dynamos in the Gwanzura Stadium right in the heart of the black township of Harare, which was eventually to give its name to the capital.

It was a memorable début to say the least. We were leading 2–0 midway through the second half when I threw myself at the feet of a striker and took a kick which spread my nose all over my face. I was whipped off to hospital in an ambulance, still in my goalkeeper's kit, and told to fill in a form and wait for the doctor. By the time he turned up my whole face had ballooned and my eyes had closed up. The doctor looked at the x-ray and told me that nothing was broken and to go home. Home, of course, was the team hotel and Chibuku club-mate Billy Sharman took one look at me and said: 'Here they have very good doctors and very bad doctors. You have just seen a very bad doctor. Even I can tell you have a broken nose.' It was no consolation as I flew home to Bulawayo where my mother picked me up and packed me off to bed. It took me a full hour to prise my eyes open the next morning and I immediately went to the local hospital where they confirmed 'Dr' Sharman's diagnosis. They had to rebreak the bone to set it. But such is the resilience of youth that within six days I was playing baseball for the provincial team.

I was also ready for the start of the season and we began as one of the favourites to take the League title and, had I been content to accept the number-two position behind Sibanda, I have no doubt that we would have won it. My presence kept my rival on his toes but when I left he was not the same. He took to the Shake-Shake, got the shakes and let in too many goals. But he was popular with the local black community as well as the manager and my appearances were limited to three games apiece for the first and second teams. I had been with my new club for barely ten weeks when I played my last game for them and, according to livid manager Jack Meagher, my last game for anyone in any grade of football. It made my departure from Callies look like the tearful farewell of a lover going to war.

It was a hot July afternoon in 1975. I had been dropped again and found myself in the reserves playing in the curtain-raiser against my old club Salisbury Callies, and all the lads I had grown up with in junior football. One of my team-mates was my baseball pal, Gary Clarke, a big Manchester City fan from England who felt that he was able to play in a better side than the Raylton Club. I had persuaded Chibuku to give him a trial. Like local derbies the world over, it was a tough, physical match from the kick-off but it got out of hand when our coach John Garatsa, who was playing left-back, hit the Callies' young right-winger so hard that the lad skidded halfway under the metal perimeter fence. He was in agony as the Callies' coach, Tommy Pettigrew, tried to pull him out and punched Garatsa in the face, while he was at it. Instant pandemonium broke loose, not only on the pitch but in the stadium as well. I thought that the best thing I could do was to stay on the sidelines and, as I leaned against my goalpost, Gary Clarke wisely sat on the ball in the centre circle watching in amazement. I remained remarkably calm until my former junior captain Ian Noble ran past my goalmouth, hotly pursued by two large, black Chibuku defenders and, as one of them tripped him over and the other jumped on his head, I decided it was time to abandon my neutrality and join the fray. Two against two would have been fine but my whole upbringing made me rebel at seeing a white friend being beaten up by two blacks – even if they did play for my team.

Having helped sort out that little fracas, I took off my boots and made my way to the dressing rooms in disgust. Billy Sharman, the first-team skipper, patted me on the back and told me that I had done the right thing but a furious Jack Meagher asked me what the hell I had thought I was doing. With steam coming out of my ears I told him that if this was his idea of football he could keep it and that I wanted no part of fighting, especially when it put my mates in physical danger. I agreed to go out for the second half but told him it was the last game I would play for the club. I walked back out in time to see Jack Garatsa and Tommy Pettigrew sent off and the rest, with the exception of Gary

Clarke, booked. As order was restored Gary rose to his feet, picked up the ball and passed it to the referee, who promptly took his name. Gary shook his head and said to me: 'I think I'll stick to the Railway Club.'

I was determined to keep to my promise even though I realised that if I walked out on the football club, I would also be walking out on my job. I packed all my belongings into my car, told Stainless Steel Industries I was going and left to drive the 400 miles to Bulawayo with Jack Meagher's words that I would never kick a football again as long as I lived still ringing in my ears. I had ample time to contemplate my actions as my faithful little Mini had a blow-out on the way back and, without jack or spanners, I had to stop passing motorists until I had enough help to lift the car onto bricks and effect the repairs.

Once more my poor old Mum was taken completely by surprise as I walked into her shop, Bothwell's Shoe Store, on Abercorne Street in Bulawayo. She had to sit down in shock when I strolled in unannounced and she waited until we returned home before we talked it through. My mother quickly regained her composure and suggested that as I was due to be called up for my National Service at any time, I might just as well go and get it over with then and there. That is exactly what I did and that same day I went to Brady Barracks in Bulawayo and spoke to the officer in charge who told me that there was not another new intake for three months because the next lot were due to sign on the next day. 'Why,' I asked, 'couldn't I go with them?' 'No reason,' he replied and the next day, 7 July 1975, I enrolled with C Company, 147 intake. Bruce Grobbelaar was in the army.

2

Jungle Man

I will always remember my two years of National Service. How could a 17-year-old forget seeing his best friends killed? How can he forget killing a fellow human being? The simple answer is that he cannot. Even now, years later, I still have nightmares in which I hear again the screams and see those frightened faces, before waking up in a cold sweat. After having experienced border raids, drugs, delousing, having to eat beetles because you are out of rations, and tracking terrorists, football hardly seems to be a matter of life and death. Losing a semi-final is not a tragedy and missing a match because of a groin strain is not the end of the world. If war teaches you anything it is an appreciation of being alive and I will never apologise for laughing at life and enjoying my football.

However, you are not concerned with such weighty matters when you first join up. I went through a crash course in becoming a soldier from my brother-in-law, Joe Roy, who had already done his bit for his country. It was before the escalation of the war when Joe did his spell and the instructions were not so much about dodging bullets and bayonets as keeping clear of the regimental sergeant major. Urgent matters, for instance, of not reporting to Llewellyn Barracks with your parents in case you were branded a 'mummy's boy', a stigma that carried its burden long and hard unless you arrived on your own in the special bus from the town hall. He also offered practical help and advice, lending me his pair of specially-polished boots for inspections, a set of extra utensils, which were always to remain spotlessly clean because they were to be unused, and a travelling iron to smooth the pimples out of the new boots instead of using the traditional hot spoon. Joe also tipped me off about getting a short haircut from a reputable barber so that the army would not butcher me on arrival. Joe's last piece of advice was to take as little of my own gear as possible and I quickly discovered why after going through the medical when we visited the quartermaster to be kitted out.

Those raw recruits who had not had the benefit of an old soldier's words suddenly found themselves carrying their two suitcases full of clothes plus all their army gear, including their mattresses. I was immediately able to ingratiate myself by offering a helping hand to my new-found friends as we were ordered to our billets, on the double. We were given two days to polish our brasses and bone our boots before our first major inspection. I sorted out my black batman, Thomas, and gave him my iron. He was delighted at the prospect and it soon became obvious that Thomas and Bruce were two of a kind. In no time at all we had lined up ten other recruits who paid a dollar each for the highly skilled artistry of Thomas with my iron. He was perfect, making sure that the iron never went within a millimetre of those nylon stitches which would soon have fallen apart and caused endless problems. He also used the iron for laundry and, between us, we earned a nice steady income.

Thomas was also indispensable when it came to the midnight inspection for which we had to change from our number-one kit into our physical training gear and back again under the threat of 28 days' confinement to barracks if the creases in our trousers were not as sharp at the back as they were at the front. Thomas would stand outside the door while we passed him our number-one slacks for ironing as we slipped into our PT kit. The extra money, allied to Thomas's influence within the officers' mess, meant that we were never short of drink and cigarettes. I had so many that when the other chaps went short they would come to me for a beer and pay me back with interest, in beer of course, when they were in funds. I could go for nights without having to buy a drink and by the time we moved to bush camp I was owed so many drinks that the others paid me back by carrying my kit and doing other duties. One fellow, Jan Vermaak, must have owed me a dozen or more beers and he settled his debt by carrying my kit, as well as his own, on a ten-mile hike.

Another problem during this first phase that brother-in-law Joe had warned me about was never to receive more than a couple of letters a week from my Mum, otherwise I would be branded as 'missing Mummy' and suffer accordingly. Even after this warning I got into trouble when it was noted that, apart from billets-doux from my girlfriend Theresa Wyley, I was receiving mail from a certain Mrs Davies. I had all sorts of difficulties explaining that the letters were from my mother and that I was not carrying on with a married woman.

My best pal, Stewart 'Stooge' Ayre, was not so fortunate. His girlfriend insisted on writing to him on coloured, perfumed notepaper. The instructors did not feel that this fitted in with the army's macho image and poor stooge was forced to climb the flagpole and shout 'I love you darling' for every letter that was handed out. The scented letters soon stopped. We also had problems with a Portuguese-speaking soldier in our group who had extreme difficulty with the language and, in particular, with the word 'corporal' which always came out 'corp', earning us many five-mile hikes in full kit. Anyone else would have been beaten into line but this gentleman carried an evil knife and was reputed to have been a mercenary. In the end we found out that he had been no more than a cook in the Mozambique Army and, indeed, he finished up in our cookhouse where he could put the knife to good use peeling potatoes.

I had no complaints over our phase-one training for, just as it had done at school, sport came to my rescue. It was the rugby season and I was asked if I would organise a team. It was no problem as we had several good rugby players and, as those who made the side were given weekend passes, so many applied that we had to have trials. We did well, too, particularly in our home games at the barracks where the whole troop would turn out to cheer us on and would not be adverse to joining in if an opposing winger happened to be silly enough to run too close to the touchline and a willing foot. It was hardly surprising that most of our games were played down the middle.

Even when the rugby season ended there was baseball to take its place and another good team. I was the pitcher while the regimental captain was the catcher. It was a good arrangement so far as I was concerned though the captain complained of raw hands now and again. I also managed to take the odd Saturday night's absence without leave to visit a girlfriend, by hiding in the back of an instructor's car. It was worth while but the risks were high. If I had been caught by the military police it would have been 28 days' detention which was much tougher than spending the same period in civilian prison because of Sergeant-Major Pretorious. He was the company's heavyweight boxing champion who liked to keep in shape by sparring with the prisoners in his charge. It also meant 24 times up and down the assault course before the 5 a.m. breakfast.

I managed to elude those diligent men over that occasional indiscretion and with the rest of the platoon in our barracks did my best to make sure that I stayed on the right side of the army's strict rules. By this time we were on our camouflage and concealment course and I was one of six training corporals in our barrack room. We always made certain everything was perfect for our inspections by the RSM. Our quarters were spotless with covers, blankets and pillows arranged at the required angles, lockers immaculate and even our ribbons on the mosquito netting met every demand. Everything was ready except for the very first man in line, Private Griffiths. I was tenth along but, looking out of the corner of my eye, I feared the worst when the RSM did a doubletake and ordered each of us officer hopefuls to march up in turn and look behind Griffith's left ear. It was camouflage cream and, to make it worse, we had not been out on exercise for two days! The dirty private earned us two successive nights of midnight inspection, and sleeping on the floor to ensure the beds were always ready. How we made Griffiths suffer. His punishment was a tub of ice-cold water and a scrub down with yard brooms, wire brushes and Vim. He hardly had any skin left by the time we had finished with him, never mind any surplus camouflage cream. It didn't do him a lot of harm for he not only turned out to be the cleanest fellow in the platoon but also a fine soldier who would do anything for anyone.

Our platoon was proving to be pretty good at the art of camouflage and tracking, so good, in fact, that we were set a very special task by our instructors who ordered us to kidnap a coloured fellow from Llewellyn Barracks and lock him in the bottom of one of our empty cupboards. We suspected some sort of wind up as the instructors all used the same bar. To ensure that it wasn't to catch us out of bounds in the coloured soldiers' section we sent Thomas, my batman, over to the target, Arnold Jeffries, to tell him that C Company had some 'whacky tobaccy' to sell and if he wanted some of the finest smoking marijuana, to see Corporal Grobbelaar that very night.

Two of our boys were stationed up a fir tree to make certain that Jeffries wasn't followed and the moment he entered our barracks he was in the locker before he knew what had hit him. Then came the catch. We also had a snap midnight inspection and while there was panic in the other camp over the missing soldier, the CSM was more than curious at the banging and hollering coming from our lockers. It was left to me to explain and though our CSM accepted the story, theirs did not and we had to run a gauntlet of rotten fruit from the coloured soldiers when we were ordered to report for our punishment. It was all short lived as the coloured soldiers always reckoned they were greater lovers than fighters.

The army were doing their best to prepare us for the escalating war outside but the prospect of death seemed a long way off, even when we got down to the nitty gritty of bayonet training. The more aggressive they tried to make us, the funnier we found it. They had us screaming things like: 'I'll kill you, you black bastard' as we stabbed the bag. At the time we thought that the most likely use for our weapons was to open our ration can but if we were caught making fun or not taking the whole matter in deadly

earnest, we were made to run around the assault course
with our rifles above our heads. It all became too much of
a strain for one of the boys who suddenly cracked and,
instead of stabbing the bag, hit the mouthy instructor with
his rifle butt. We sensed the seriousness of the situation
and the prostrate sergeant could obviously feel our mood
as he picked himself up, dusted himself down and said:
'That's what I want to see — raw aggression.' That was the
end of our bayonet practice.

The worst drill in those balmy days was chipping our
boots on the parade ground. It was all a bit of a game for
a gang of 17-year-olds still wet behind the ears. We knew,
of course, why we were there. We knew that our country
was being threatened by terrorists and that the black
political leaders opposed to Ian Smith and his Government
were over the border in countries like Mozambique and
Zambia, where they were backed by the Soviets with their
troops being trained by the North Koreans and others.
There were so many of them: Mugabe and his ZANU PF
party; Muzorewe and ZANLA; Sithole with ZIPRA and
Nkomo with the ZAPU. The war had already been going
on for a long time as the black guerrillas fought for the
land that they believed was theirs. To us they were
terrorists but, no doubt, they regarded themselves as
revolutionaries.

Sadly bombs don't pick sides or targets, especially when
they came in the form of land mines which were buried in
dirt roads used not only by soldiers of both sides, but by
black and white civilians as well. This was suddenly the
harsh reality. Training was over and we quickly discovered
what fighting was all about as we emerged from the
protection of our camp into a war that was growing in
intensity with death becoming a part of everyday life. Our
briefing was to police the Mozambique borders, maintain

order, and stop the regular incursions of terrorists attacking the white farms and spreading anti-government propaganda among the blacks in the Tribal Trust Lands. We were told to make contact with the local Frelimo Army across the border, to exchange cigarettes, chocolates and, somewhat more importantly, information.

It sounded straightforward enough as we were shipped out to base camp at Umtali before joining the rotation that took us out to the bush and our camp at an old school in the Chimanimani Mountains in the eastern Highlands by a river which marked the border. We were told by 10th platoon, whom we replaced, that you could actually see the terrorists from the school roof while the Frelimo troops warned us that they had received word of increased enemy activity. Neither were wrong and I spent Christmas Eve, 1975 digging in while our Christmas present was a massive mortar attack. Fortunately for us they seemed to believe that we were all suspended a foot or so above the school judging by the aim of their mortars, and we were in more danger from people running around indiscriminately with buckets rather than from the terrorists' attacks.

It was not exactly a transition from buckets of beer to buckets of blood but it was, all the same, a sobering lesson that this was the real thing and we all felt pretty sorry for ourselves in that we were spending Christmas under fire instead of with our families. What made it worse was that, before the attack, we were told that the local farmers and their wives would be driving up to our camp with traditional festive fayre but there seemed little likelihood of that when 25 December dawned wet and miserable. But, to our amazement, a rhino anti-mine armoured vehicle strolled up with a woman dressed as Father Christmas handing out beers. There were a dozen beers apiece and, just as welcome, a whole pig for our Christmas dinner. It did not matter that we had to erect old tarpaulins to roast the animal nor that the beers were warm. Never has wet, broiled pork tasted so good with the accompanying knowledge that the local people held us in such regard as to delay their own celebrations and risk death to deliver gifts to a bunch of unknown soldiers.

We learned from our commanding officer, Major Taylor, that our posting was a picnic compared with the Zambezi Valley and we settled into our routine in the Eastern Highlands for three months, getting to know the area when, without warning, we were summoned back to base camp in Umtali. It meant a stiff ten-mile march to the pick-up point where we were told that something big was happening and we were to be flown out. All we needed was to be taught how to jump 10 feet from a hovering helicopter without breaking a leg. The crash course in parachuting presented no problems as we jumped off boxes and dangled on the end of elastic ropes to teach us how to jump, fall and roll. What they had failed to tell us was that we would be dropping out of the sky at midnight — into a game reserve! The aircraft could not land because of the animals and the torrential rain. We were not so much worried about dropping into the open jaws of a man-eating lion, because we knew the noise of the helicopters and our Dakota would scare the animals away, as of landing in the tall trees surrounding the Gonarazu Game Reserve and we were grateful that only two of our platoon were snared in branches and came out with minor injuries.

Our immediate task was to ensure the safety of a pop group called 'Four Jacks and a Jill' who had a chalet in the reserve but by the time we arrived we were told by the game warden that the Selous Scouts, the crack SAS-type regulars, had already escorted them out. Not that this mattered a great deal as we were preoccupied with the prospect of being the first independent company to be used as a 'Fire Force', replacing regular soldiers. We made camp and prepared for our drivers who arrived with the equipment in the early hours of the morning. As a Fire Force my group of four men, called a stick, was on constant alert, ready to run the operations' room, pick up grid references and fly out by chopper to the area we were needed to patrol. This was a bit different from the Eastern Highlands. For a start the elephant grass made the going a lot harder, the patrols were longer and often we were only able to move at night through the Tribal Trust Lands. We not only had to worry about terrorists, who would kill us on sight, but also the wild animals, particularly the elephants, who would come and investigate if you got on the wrong side of the wind. It meant climbing up the nearest tree or scrambling to the rocky ground above where they were reluctant to follow.

The situation was now very serious. You could tell that by the Canberras and Hunters which screamed overhead and the practical use of our camouflage and concealment training. We were the guinea pigs and we knew it. The commanding officers were watching carefully just how a company of national servicemen coped with the work of regular soldiers who, in turn, were needed where the fighting was even heavier. At least we impressed the American and South African pilots with our map reading, so much so that they even let us navigate. We found out later that it was indeed a test and had we failed the regulars would have been back and we would have been relegated to the supporting role of 'walkers'. Sometimes I think that it would have been better had we failed. War can do strange things to people who have never come close to death, especially if they are only 17. Mortars and mines are a different matter altogether to facing your enemy eyeball-to-eyeball. You know it is kill or be killed, but that doesn't make it any easier when you take a human life.

The moment of truth for me came when we had a call at first light to go into the tribal land of Sengwe next door to the Gonarazu Game Reserve where, judging by the activity on our radios, there was a lot happening. We responded to our Five-three Bravo call sign, scrambled into the fighter-escorted helicopters and headed for the Mozambique border and a terrorist stronghold in the village of Pafaru. You don't need your passport when the order is to sweep through the camp and kill anything that moves. It was an unnerving experience going through the heavy jungle with the closest man five yards away on either side and snipers likely to be anywhere. The stench of the dead and charred bodies burned by the Frantan incendiary bombs was stomach churning, as was the sight of the lifeless forms. There was no time to feel sorry for them as, only 20 yards away, Stephen Japp, a superb tennis player with a brilliant future ahead of him, was shot in the back as he passed a huge anthill. The bullet nicked his spine, permanently paralysing him from the waist down. Tim Kemp, Japp's machine gunner, turned round and emptied his full clip of 40 into the black terrorist.

One of the regulars with us took three bullets, one in the leg, another in his stomach while a third went through his mouth, shattering his cheekbone. That could have done a lot of damage to us raw recruits but we were given new resolve when the soldier, through broken teeth and spitting blood, screamed: 'Go kill the f . . . s!' It was soon afterwards that I killed my first man. I felt nothing but relief that I shot him before he shot me and, strangely, that he was wearing camouflage gear and was not in civilian clothes. That would have been hard to take. It all happened in an instant as a group of the enemy broke cover and made for the sanctuary of the Limpopo River, firing at us as they went.

Stooge Ayre and I were badly shaken by the events but our machine gunner Doe Herbst was revelling in the action. He was a farmer who had already suffered family bereavement and other troubles at the hands of the terrorists and he was wreaking revenge. Doe cut an awesome sight. He was a big man who was 'boss' even when he was without that machine gun. At home on the farm he would lift bags of maize in his teeth to impress on those around him his strength. Doe began that day to carve notches in his machine gun for everyone he killed and as if that was not enough he would cut off an ear and put it on a string until he returned home to his farm where he would keep them in a jar. It is not surprising that I still suffer from nightmares about these experiences.

We managed to drive the remaining enemy back towards the Limpopo and as suddenly as the action had started, it finished leaving the sort of deathly silence that only exists in the jungle. We swept on up to the stores which had already been stripped and looted by the Selous Scouts, leaving us to collect souvenirs like flags and bayonets along with the odd bottle of cheap wine. While we were doing this, the orders came in for the regulars to move on to the next skirmish and for us to shift the dead bodies of both sides by loading them, 30 at a time, into a big net slung underneath a chopper. It was while we were pulling what was left of the bodies from the crocodile-infested Limpopo that a major from the K Car ordered me and my stick to lay an ambush and await the inevitable return of the terrorists to the camp.

I was ready to mutiny and walk my stick back to Rhodesia if necessary but, fortunately, as I contemplated the inevitable court martial that would await me, the mad major was overruled by the colonel. The relief was short lived, however, when the colonel informed us that it would take the helicopters two hours to refuel and return to collect us. Our grisly duties with the corpses completed, we sat down to share a bottle of the looted wine, ears and eyes alert to every sound and movement. We then heard the distant rumbling and with sheer terror spurring us on, we dropped our booty and began to race in the direction of the Rhodesian border — some 4 or 5 kilometres away. We had run about 200 yards when the noise of what we had taken to be enemy trucks turned out to be helicopter rotor blades. It was our own men but we were so shaken that we asked them to do a complete reconnaissance of the surrounding area before we crept back to pick up our souvenirs and clamber aboard the life-saving chopper.

I never did get used to killing other men—even if they were hell bent on doing me as much harm as possible. I still dream about another encounter which happened shortly before the end of my first year while we were supporting a Dad's Army Unit (made up of 35-55-year-old reservists) when we were fed the information that a dozen terrorists were close at hand. We selected the killing ground and laid our claymore mines in the rocks and then set our two sticks of four in ambush positions. The mines killed the first three and the rest we caught in a lethal crossfire.

There was just enough moon for me to see the white teeth bared in horrific screams that still ring in my ears when I have those awful dreams. Four or five days later, the same patrol was laying another ambush in the middle of night when we disturbed a spotted hyena. Now these animals may look funny in a zoo but they are not the best thing to meet at night high up in the Inyanga region. Doe warned us to zip our sleeping bags right up to our chins as we took up our separate positions. That hyena must have been mighty hungry for he came back and dragged the terrified Stooge some 400 yards in his sleeping bag. We could not fire a shot because of the close proximity of the enemy and it was left to Stooge to smash the animal's teeth with the butt of his gun to drive him away. He told us that we were lucky that the smelly creature was on its own rather than in a pack. We would have had to open fire under those circumstances and I, for one, would rather be shot than be eaten.

Nightmares really are made of that sort of stuff as my wife and a few footballer room-mates will testify having seen me wander around in the middle of the night before a big game. Our first Fire Force base at Gonarazu Game Reserve was eventually taken over by the Territorial Forces, who were recalled National Servicemen, while we moved to the other side of the Tribal Trust Land and another airstrip. This one was not so well served and it meant a two-mile drive simply to pick up fresh water from the railway water tower. The road needed to be patrolled regularly and on this particular night we were designated a listening brief. We made our camp underneath thorn bushes so that we could not be seen from above or from the road some 20 yards away.

We dug in, protecting ourselves as best as we could from the frequent rain showers and attaching a length of string to each other so that we could keep in contact without breaking silence. It was around 3 a.m. when the black District Assistant tugged on the strings to warn us that something was happening and, as we listened, we could hear digging in the road just a few yards away. Our first reaction was to get ready to fire but that would have given our own position away. Instead we waited till they had finished and when we heard a distant mine explode we called in our engineers to conduct a minesweep while we set out to track the terrorists. Although we were rather short of rations we set off after them, meeting another stick led by Farnie Cloette on the way to give us a full tracker unit. We trailed them for 75 kilometres, gaining all the time. They must have been aware that we were following for they kept splitting into groups and coming together again before they separated into twos and went in different directions. Our two-day ration supply had run out by then and we were living on roots and berries. Doe, being the outdoor type, knew exactly what to eat and what to leave alone and we had many tasty meals consisting of green Mapani worms which live on the leaves of the Mapani tree, and stalks that taste like potato when you squeeze the inside out and fry the shell in butter. Other favourites were the big, juicy flying beetle and fried flying ants. Snake steaks were also a luxury we relished! We managed to stave off starvation and keep the enemy in sight until, weakened through dehydration, we were replaced by Selous Scouts. We had done our job so well that, only five hours later, there was a pitched battle in which one Selous Scout and five terrorists were killed.

We, of course, were unaware of the fight at the time as we were told to head for a pick-up point ready for return to camp. We met another group on the way back and, relaxing after the tension, we decided that instead of sticking to the bush and doing a dog's leg around the District Assistant's office we made directly for it, knowing that we could rest, have some decent food and some fresh water. But as we rounded a rocky ridge two grenades went off and I was hit by a piece of shrapnel in my right arm and my mate Stooge was hit in the leg. The injuries were not serious and the skirmish lasted for no more than two minutes. We assumed that it was either some of the group we had been tracking or a couple of guerrillas working for

Rhodesian Railways who had spotted a chance of retaliating. We were badly shocked but asked base whether to follow the new spore or to continue. The colonel told us to keep going and we limped on for another half an hour until, in sight of the DA's office, we heard machine-gun fire, mortars and mines. By the time we arrived, the scene was total chaos with eight injured lying on the verandah where we had planned to rest up. They had been hit by the blast of a mortar which had come through the roof and were suffering from varying degrees of shrapnel wounds.

Julian Linson, a Cockney, was in a bad way with a kneecap blown away. Julian was already a morphine addict and needed three shots instead of the normal one. He was so high that he simply got up and walked away. Perhaps walk was the wrong word – he was flying. No one took a great deal of notice because drugs were a major part of army life and not at all difficult to obtain. Marijuana, known locally as dagga, was readily available. Just as in Ethiopia and Jamaica it is part of the local religion. If we were going into action we would smoke some to take our minds off what lay ahead. The use of marijuana was so prevalent that it was even grown in the main base camp at Umtali despite the severe penalties for anyone found indulging. A blind eye was turned in the bush, however, where it was appreciated that anything that calmed the nerves was helpful. From what I understand it is nothing new among combat troops whether they were Americans fighting in Vietnam or Russians in Afghanistan. The danger lies in moving on to the harder drugs such as LSD and morphine, like my Cockney friend who, when last I heard, was back in Soho alive and kicking, though not too hard with that injured leg of his. As a sportsman I was aware of the harm that the use of drugs can cause, but when possible death awaits you at the end of every patrol I was able to understand why the soldiers took it. I honestly believe that it helped, unlike drink which could have been a real killer if you had been drunk or hungover when on patrol.

Enemy fire and drugs were not the only dangers we faced. There were also the animals and not just the hyenas! Stooge and I were delighted when we were sent to a camp at Lake Mcilwaine for a refresher course in tracking under the top instructor Corporal Bonnias, a captured and reformed terrorist, who was just about the best in the business. As the camp was the closest to the capital Salisbury there was limited terrorist activity and we had the comfort of the Selous Scouts' quarters while they were away fighting. The spores were laid overnight and, as an incentive, there were prizes for the team who could cover the track the quickest. We were with a tall lad named Palmer, whom we called the Kalahari Kid, because there were miles and miles of nothing. He was going at it enthusiastically until the corporal asked us what the hell we were following. It turned out to be chipembere, or a rhino, and it was quickly decided that we should continue following this unexpected spore. We reached the rocky ground where we found a heap of dung and while we stopped Stooge was sent on, head down into the grassland. Bonnias wanted us to tell him how old the 'find' was by rubbing it between our fingers. It was fresh, so fresh that the black Bonnias went pale as he looked up at Stooge standing frozen 100 yards away between two snorting rhinos. Before we could react Corporal Bonnias was yelling at us all to climb trees while he distracted the shortsighted beasts' attentions with his hollering and arm waving, not scampering up a tree until he was sure that the shaken Stooge was safely up one too.

A couple of days after our experience at the DA's office I was on easy guard duty at base camp when a lion, attracted by the smell of the food, boldly wandered into the operations room. Instant panic ensued as one of my fellow soldiers, high on marijuana, began to let fly with his rifle. He could not have hit a barn in his condition but while the radio operator and I looked on in open-mouthed amazement, the lion took the hint and loped off back into the bush.

While I was away in the bush there was trouble brewing at home. Unbeknown to me, my sister and her husband Joe had been desperately trying to have another child. Having had Shane when Jaqueline was only 16, there did not seem to be any problem but miscarriage followed miscarriage until eventually a daughter, Natalie, was born. Jaqueline and Joe were overjoyed as their Mormon faith encouraged large families. But Natalie was born prematurely, complications set in and she was dead within the week. Jackie, understandably, was distraught and she was put in a psychiatric ward, just one step away from being committed to an asylum. Her sickness manifested itself in her believing that everyone she was close to was dead unless they could physically prove to her that they were alive and not ghosts. With me being away and fighting in a war I was the focal point. But I did not find any of this out until I was handed a telegram from my aunt, Pam Archer, saying: 'Sister gone insane. Believes you are dead. Come as soon as possible.' I received it five days after it had been sent and I discovered that for two days it had sat in camp even though I was back. Fuming, I stormed into Major Taylor's office to ask what the hell was going on. He took me completely by surprise when he replied: 'We need your tracking ability and knowledge of the area for one more patrol before you are on a pass.' I was amazed at the heartlessness of the situation and, knowing there was a vehicle leaving, I threatened to go absent without leave. I got my pass.

I must have presented quite a sight when I jumped on

that lorry heading for the relative civilisation of Umtali. Duties meant that I had had no bath for four days and the run to Umtali took two days with another to get to Salisbury. A seven-day pass left me with exactly two days to convince Jackie that her brother was alive and well. It was not as simple as it sounds and, in the end and running out of time, I took her to the recreation room to play table tennis where I continually let the ball hit me on the chest, proving to her upset mind that I was flesh and blood and not a ghost. The story has a happy ending for Jackie began to come round a few days later and, in 1982, she gave birth to another son, David, who became the focus of attention in that loving family. They also adopted Debbie and Tracy Lee, the product of our father's second marriage, which had also ended in divorce.

Going back to camp was no great hardship as it was only a question of seeing out the remaining days of my statutory year's service. There were only 25 days to go as I sat with the army drivers listening to a forces' broadcast when, suddenly, it was read out that, because of the intensification of the war, military service had now been extended to 18 months. It was bad enough for us but it was even worse for Intake 146 who had just two days of their tour remaining. As if that was not bad luck, six months later it happened all over again and this time hapless 146 had given all their kit back to the quartermaster's store only to have to pick it all up again for a further six months' active duty.

I matter of factly accepted that there was another 24 weeks to do, more bush raids and more hair-raising moments to come. But I had reckoned without Lieutenant Jones of the regulars who wanted to experience some action with the best stick and was assigned to us. He was bad luck from the start. On our first call-out we were dropped as close as possible to a relay station which was under heavy mortar fire. We landed on top of the hill, and as we dived out of one door, Doe Herbst hurtled out of the other to give us covering fire with his machine gun only to fall down a crevice and break his leg. Our new gunner was a Boer named Sarel Vermaak. He had a lot to follow in Doe but he had already proved himself every bit as tough. Sarel began his active duty as a cook in base camp where all had gone well until a group of the tough SAS Scouts decided that the first come, first served principle in the canteen did not apply to them. They wanted to join the queue at the front but our chef wanted them at the back where they belonged. The soldiers told him quietly that if he persisted in his old-fashioned ideas they would break off his arms and beat him to death with them.

Sarel took off his hat, rolled up his sleeves and came round to our side of the counter where we made sure that the odds would be no longer than one against one. It took one punch from Sarel to settle the argument and resulted in one flattened regular with a 6-inch gash above his right eye, a group of regulars at the back of the dinner queue and Sarel Vermaak applying to join up with the fighting soldiers. Who was going to quarrel? Sarel had flat feet but was a good walker and he joined our stick with almost the same attitude as Doe's for killing his enemies. He also relished the opportunity of revenge for what they had done to his farm and relatives. Poor fellow must have wondered about the wisdom of leaving the cookhouse when our new Lieutenant Jones decided that our experience counted for nothing and we would do everything by the book which meant two hours on and two hours off for two at a time instead of one of us doing one hour on and three off. As a supreme gesture he offered to take the last hour from 5 until 6. We lay awake and, sure enough, ten minutes or so into his hour our good Lieutenant was fast asleep and snoring his head off. We quietly took his boots and rifle and moved back 20 yards into the shadows and sat there until 6 a.m. when we threw small stones at him to wake him up.

He awoke with a start and promptly went berserk. He wanted to charge us with all manner of crimes until we gently pointed out that falling asleep on guard duty was far, far worse than anything he could accuse us of doing. Lieutenant Jones saw sense and we got our way. To be fair he became quite a good leader and came out with us quite often to get in his bush mileage. His only lasting fault was his persistence in wearing long trousers instead of the standard shorts. He was asking for trouble. Ticks were a big enough problem without offering them their own breeding ground. The most hazardous of them all were the ticks in the game reserves for they would jump from the animals onto the long grass and then onto us as we brushed through. They would make for the warm moist areas between the legs or under the arms and you needed both powder and cream to stop them burying their heads in your skin unless, of course, you were a macho man like Doe who would burn the little blighters off with the end of his cigarette.

It wasn't just the discomfort the ticks caused but also tick bite fever which left you with swollen glands between your legs, a high temperature and the feeling that your bladder was full of roughly-ground glass whenever you relieved yourself. It was important to know who your friends were when you returned from patrol looking for someone to delouse the regions that were hard to reach!

3

In the Bush

I had intended to be a good soldier but somehow you tend
to lose a little enthusiasm when the Government scores an
off-side goal in injury time to force extra time and then
does it again in the replay. You begin to think that the
odds are stacked against you or, at the very least, that the
referee is a little bent. The result is that you start breaking
the rules yourself and the problem there is that you cannot
win that way either. It did not help that we were in an
outpost called Silver Streams, a white settlement which
consisted of a bottle shop, a co-operative store and a
butcher's. With only ten days' leave every six weeks, we
had to work hard to make the most of them, hitching lifts
from the four-and-a-half ton lorries taking the injured back
to Umtali or jumping aboard empty storage tankers. Even
so it often left only a couple of days to see my girlfriend
Theresa Wyley and my family. So, when one of the lads
invested in a large American Cadillac which could transport
eight of us in comfort to Bulawayo in less than half the
time, we were naturally delighted.

The only problem was that the green monster drank

petrol faster than we could drink our beers and, to make
matters worse, all the local petrol stations closed at night
for fear of attack. We either waited until morning, and lost
a day's leave, or we did something about it. I stood watch
while the driver syphoned petrol from the armoured car
bowser at the back of our barracks. Unfortunately he was
caught by the military police and I was instantly implicated
so, instead of setting out on our ten days' leave, we found
ourselves under close arrest awaiting Major Taylor's return
from the bush to supervise our court martial. The sergeant
major marched us into Major Taylor's office individually
and when the driver came back smiling and whispering that
he had been fined only 60 dollars, I thought we were going
to get away with our pilfering. I was not so lucky, however.
I was found guilty and though fined the same amount, I
was also told to hand over my stripes which the Major
immediately put in his drawer. It meant that on my next
bush patrol I went out under a new stick leader, who was
a full corporal named Evans. He was a disaster and when
on one occasion I pointed out that he was putting us all in
danger, we had a violent punch-up which ended with me
threatening to blow his stupid head off.

My army career looked distinctly uncertain as I was
marched into Major Taylor's office for the second time in
two weeks but this time I came out smelling of roses as
Evans lost a stripe, being demoted to lance-corporal, while
I was handed back my stripes. What was more Doe Herbst
was in action again having recovered from his injuries and
the team was together again, back on fire force and based
at Chapinga airstrip. There were sixteen of us altogether
which allowed for two sticks on duty; one on stand-by and
the other resting, which in other words meant getting high
on marijuana or drinking beer.

It worked well until, one day, there was a serious

engagement between two of our patrols and the Maken-
dangas (the local terrorists). It was serious enough for
Corporal Cloette's stand-by stick to be called out; which
immediately put us on full-alert status. Within two hours
the radio crackled back to life and we were told that the
chopper was on its way back to carry us out to the action
some 13 kilometres away. There was immediate panic and
with one of my men still drunk and another high on
'whacky tobaccy', we had just enough time to run them
under a cold shower before the helicopter arrived to whisk
us away to the battle. It was quite some battle. We killed
three of the enemy as we landed in a cultivated fir forest
where the branches of the tall pines started some 13 feet
off the ground, offering no cover at all. We swept through
the bare area into the tree line where we were pinned
down by a rapid firegun until Doe's mate, rifleman Crewe
and his stick, led by Smith-Rainsford and supported by
Toland and our old friend Vermaak on the machine gun,
arrived to help us out. Eventually all 16 of us were in line
and ready to sort out the snipers but, as we began to move
forward, we were met by a hail of bullets. A bullet went
straight through Toland's rifle magazine and into his
stomach; Vermaak took a flesh wound; Smith-Rainsford had
a toe shot off; and Crewe was hit right between the eyes.

We looked around for support only to see another of
the sticks had also lost a man and, to make it worse, we
hadn't a clue where the shots had come from. We felt
highly vulnerable until Doe, anger welling up at the loss of
his best pal, suddenly turned his machine gun upwards
towards the trees and instantly one dead terrorist fell to
the ground followed by another, who was injured but still
alive. The episode seemed slightly unreal to me, almost as
if the events were happening somewhere else and I was
just an onlooker. Doe threw down his gun and, with a

dreadful yell, ran to avenge Crewe. By the time we
recovered and chased after him he had already cut off the
terrorist's genitals. We held him until he quietened down
but the moment we let go he raced back again and slit the
throat of the man who had killed his best friend. The war
was not getting any easier and this was emphasised when
Doe had his court martial dropped after the inevitable
report on the incident. It was some weeks before we trailed
back from the bush, arriving at Chapinga on Independence
Day, 5 November 1976, relieving the Rhodesian African
Rifles and being put on stand-by. What a state we were in.
We had not bathed or changed out of our shorts (we didn't
have pants or socks), camouflage jackets and webbing for
three weeks. We showered and rinsed out our few clothes
but the unperfumed carbolic soap could not rid the stench
of the bush battles.

Undeterred we headed for the bar for a few chabulies
and, to our great surprise, we were invited by the President
of the Independence Ball to join the festivities. He caught
one whiff of our distinctive aroma and allocated us a table
near the band, by the waiters' hatch, and well away from
the guests. Despite our smell we proved to be popular
guests for, as well as having all our drink free, other guests
kept coming over and dropping money on our table for us
to buy more. We were soon very merry and when the
hired band took their break we volunteered to fill the gap
to rousing cheers. We were fortunate in that my mate
Stooge was a good guitarist and his close friend Mark
Torrington was an even better singer. Lieutenant Jackson
filled in on the double bass and I attacked the drums like
'Animal' from the Muppets. It must have sounded good for
we soon had more people rocking and rolling than the
professional band had and we did several encores before
finishing with Mark's favourite, 'The Wizard' by Uriah

Heep. We went back to our chabulies to a standing ovation with Stooge and Mark wrapped in each other's arms.

Two short weeks later Mark was in Stooge's arms again but this time there were no smiles and laughter, only tears, for Mark had been picked off by a sniper and had died in Stooge's arms. Mark's parents gave his guitar to Stooge and when I was asked, some years later, to be godfather to Stooge's daughter Kelly I knew that I was only second choice. It was a cruel war for a bunch of kids, for that was what we still were even though we had been forced to grow up so quickly. It was around this time that we had heard that in all probability our 18 months was likely to be extended to two years and a few more took to the 'whacky tobaccy' or went a step closer to insanity. Colin Frost was not the only soldier seriously to contemplate suicide as a way out rather than endure another six months of fighting in the bush. They should have spotted the way he was going when it took him less than an hour to complete a trip which normally took closer to two. He went through the pass in the Chimanimani Mountains like a bat out of hell with his passengers clinging on to whatever they could. Two of them lost their rifles and that was serious because it meant paying for them out of your own pocket.

Fortunately the missing guns were recovered but Frosty had to pay for the damage done to the jeep when Lieutenant Jackson drove in front of him to stop him going over the cliff. The glass house would have probably caused him to go off his head but Major Taylor was a flexible and humane man who, instead of giving him 20 days in the guard house, gave him 20 days' leave, sending him for a holiday to the seaside in South Africa.

We all thought that was the last we had seen of our driver but the Major had a sixth sense about these things and Frost returned on the right day, fully recovered. It was not the only time the Major impressed us with his second sight for, on five separate occasions he moved camp, days, sometimes hours, before it was subjected to a big hit which invariably took lives. When the rumours were confirmed that our original year had indeed been stretched to two, we were setting off for what we had hoped was our last stint in the hottest place of all, the Honde Valley, where you were guaranteed sun and action every day. The platoon leader gave us the news before we heard it announced over the radio but there was little reaction from the saner members who had anticipated it. There was, however, an unexpected new diversion with the introduction of women volunteers into the army. In traditional forces' style, these unfortunate girls were quickly nicknamed 'the groundsheets' or 'sleeping bags' for obvious reasons and I must say that some of them tried hard to live up to their reputations while others were unashamedly looking for husbands, particularly among the officers.

There were not too many ladies about in the Honde Valley where we patrolled the increasingly busy eastern side which took in the Grand Reef Airstrip, which was the only one servicing Umtali. Major Taylor decided that it was imperative that we installed an observation post on top of World's View, which, as its picturesque name suggested, entailed a long climb up, particularly with full pack and radio through the dense bush on the lower slopes. It took Cloette's stick two days to climb the 4,000 feet to the top. It was hardly a record but they arrived completely exhausted. Imagine their annoyance when it was decided that too much time was being wasted doing it this way and our stick was flown in by chopper! I must say that I have never seen a more beautiful sunrise than that from World's View and, on a clear day, you could see the Indian

Ocean. That, however, was not why we had been sent there and we were soon admiring and using Doe's sharp eyesight for he could somehow manage to pick out land mines in the far-off dirt roads. I am sure a lot of it must have been guesswork but even his guesses had an unnatural accuracy as he would tell you which aircraft was about to be attacked or which vehicle was going to be blown up by a land mine.

From World's View we went, somewhat poetically, to World's End, just 10 kilometres away from the famous Troutbeck Hotel in Inyanga. There was nothing very beautiful about our surroundings this time as we were airlifted to join an action where we trapped some 14 terrorists in a crossfire between sticks. We killed seven of them before the rest escaped into the bush where they were followed by the other stick, leaving us to clear up the debris once again. One of our less pleasant duties was making a body count, moving the corpses together and then guarding them overnight. It was cold on top of those hills at night and, because we had moved out quickly, some of the lads were without even the basic comfort of a sleeping bag. It meant we shared guard duty and even had to double up two to a sleeping bag, taking three hours on and three hours off to keep an eye on the stiffs. It was an eerie business and not helped at all by our old friend Griffiths who, at the end of his watch, woke all of us up as he tried to prod his replacement awake. It was only by the light of a torch that the poor man discovered that he had been trying to wake up one of the dead terrorists. It was also strange to listen to Radio Mozambique and hear a report on our contact with the enemy. According to them we had lost a dozen men to the freedom fighters near Troutbeck Hotel. We did not, in fact, have a single casualty and, presumably, propaganda was the reason for us guarding the bodies of the men we had killed.

When we returned to Grand Reef there was a pleasant surprise awaiting me. The Rhodesian Air Force were using the base more and more and it resulted in my stepbrother, Barry Davies, being posted to Grand Reef as an air traffic controller. The authorities reckoned that Lieutenant Davies was the youngest qualified air traffic man in Africa and quite possibly the world. He carried the burden well and liked a beer as much as the next man. We were soon going to each other's mess and such were the extent of the family celebrations that finding our way back to our quarters from the other side of camp could be quite hazardous. Barry, on one occasion, finished up in front of his superiors after walking straight through the fence instead of past the guards.

Barry was also interested in anything which flew and, before long, he was conning the helicopter pilots into giving him lessons, surprising them with his aptitude, particularly in the difficult art of landing. It was during one lesson that a call came through to pick up a high-ranking officer from the police camp in Umtali. It was too late to change pilots and when the chopper landed the lieutenant-colonel jumped straight aboard before Barry could switch places with the real pilot, leaving him to fly back and the pilot to man the machine gun. In the circumstances nerves got the better of Barry and he finally landed with quite a jolt, prompting the officer to remark: 'You must be one of the newer pilots.' My stepbrother, needled by the remark, could not help but retort: 'It's my first time up in one of these — I'm in air traffic control.' The officer went rather pale and shakily got out of the helicopter to report both Barry and the unfortunate pilot to their commanding officer. They were severely reprimanded.

It was probably a good thing that I was soon separated

from Barry or we might have got each other into even deeper trouble. As it was my platoon was hastily shipped out to the Kateya Tea Estates which were now under threat. They were an important part of Rhodesia's economy and had to be guarded against attack from the surrounding hills. We were dropped in by a competent helicopter pilot and as we sat at the roadside a jeep drove past with two beautiful girls sitting in the back. It was a sight for sore eyes after so long in the bush and we could scarcely believe our luck when the vehicle came back, this time driven by a gorgeous blonde who introduced herself as Jean MacDougall and her companion as her younger sister Mhiri. They had also brought a box of cold beers and some magazines. This vision in jeans told us to leave the empties and the books at the estate offices but Stooge, his eyes popping and his mouth watering, would not hear of it and insisted on returning them to the house which the elder girl told us was just round the corner. We rested and left an hour before last light to give us time to return the things and set up our observation camp. We rounded the corner and, sure enough, there was the estate and the big house no more than a kilometre away, but as the crow flies! We cursed Stooge all the way for a good 5 kilometres before we arrived to meet the girls' parents and their third beautiful daughter called Laura.

Mr MacDougall insisted that we join the family for tea and scones and told us not to worry about the time as he would drive us to our post in his jeep. Only one thing spoiled an otherwise perfect afternoon and that was the family pet dog, a huge Rhodesian Ridgeback who took an immediate dislike to me. The only way I could walk through the gardens was with an escort and once in the house I dared not move. It was nothing I had done and I can only imagine that the animal could read my mind and my lustful

thoughts towards the 17-year-old Jean. We all became
good friends, though sadly not the way us boys had in
mind, and the MacDougalls provided me with one of the
most pleasant interludes of my entire two years in the
army. The three girls all went to school in Umtali and we
were regular visitors to both their town flat and the house
on the estate. We were the envy of the platoon when we
went out to the local discos with these girls on our arms,
even if the girls stubbornly refused to stop off at the Wise
Owl Motel where you could skinny dip in the pool and
rent rooms by the hour rather than by the day.

With our time in the army drawing to a close and certain
in the knowledge that there would be no further tour of
duty, the farewell parties began in earnest, particularly
among the fire force. The boys recruited a few bad girls
but Stooge and I thought we would like to show off with
the prettiest girls on our arms and I went to the
MacDougalls to ask permission to take their daughters to
the disco. What I did not tell them was that the party was
at the Grand Reef Airfield and as we drove past the Wise
Owl, where the usual disco was held, and through Christmas
Pass into bandit territory, the girls began to think that they
were being kidnapped.

It was only when we had driven some 25 kilometres
that we revealed we were taking them back to base and
that, for safety's sake, they should lie on the floor in the
back of the jeep while Stooge and I rode shotgun with our
rifles poking out on either side of the jeep. The party was
a wild affair with the usual streakers and drunks, but I had
to leave early to get the girls back home. I arranged with
Farnie Cloette, who was also seeing a girl home, to meet
up on the way back so that we could help protect one
another and I could drop off the jeep. However, I missed
the deadline by some margin as I had spent so long saying

goodnight and it meant a long drive back on my own. As I approached the dangerous Christmas Pass I reached in the back for my rifle only to get it stuck between the roof and the seat. Panic began to grip me and, as I struggled to release the rifle, I took my eyes off the road and ran the jeep into a ditch 4 feet from the cliff's edge. I had hit my head against the windscreen and was still dazed as I surveyed the jeep perched at a precarious 45-degree angle and totally immovable. I was contemplating the long and fearful walk back to the Wise Owl and the nearest police presence when a car screeched to a halt beside me. Incredibly it was my lift! Corporal Farnie Cloette had taken even longer saying goodnight to his escort than I had with mine.

It was not long after that when we left the bush behind and returned to Adams Barracks, which was increasingly becoming the target of mortar attacks. More patrols were needed as the terrorists even recruited young schoolchildren to do their dirty work for them in the town. After the nerve-racking 18 months of non-stop action in the bush, laying ambush by a border fence in the town represented total and utter boredom and the prospect of four months' messing about like that did not inspire me at all. The occasional explosion usually turned out to be nothing more than a baboon treading on a land mine.

The night watch of 20.00 to 05.30 was the worst and, wet and cold, the stick decided that it needed some army initiative to break the monotony. Unfortunately Stooge's girlfriend Jenny lived on the other side of town but a few dollars to the driver persuaded him to make a detour and drop us off within tracking distance of Jenny's, so that he didn't know our exact destination, with an arrangement for him to collect us from the same spot at 05.30. When we arrived at Jenny's, I would radio to base and request radio silence because of our closeness to the border fence. We would then call up first thing in the morning, speak personally to our driver and confirm in code the time that we were to be picked up by the fence; the garden fence. Our camouflage training served us well and to make doubly sure we were not caught we hid under a tarpaulin until we were back on the recognised route. Until now that was a secret between the four of us and our well-paid driver. Sorry lads! The border fence may not have been as secure as it should have been but Jenny's little house was about the safest place in town, protected by us sleeping in the kitchen with our rifles at the ready and with a direct link to the barracks close at hand. We rarely strayed further afield than Jenny's apart from our trips home and it often seemed to me as though the purpose of the exercise was to debrief us after so long in the bush. There was certainly no way that they could extend our service for a third time but they did not want to send a bunch of wild animals, who lived on their wits, back into civilisation.

I was already leading a more normal life with longer at home on leave and plenty of time with the lovely Theresa Wyley. My thoughts even turned to football, though I was more surprised than anyone when, completely out of the blue and not having played top-grade soccer for almost two years, I was called up to join the Rhodesian National squad. What made the offer even more unbelievable was that the team was now being managed by none other than Jack Meagher — the very man who had told me that I would never play professional football again in Africa. Sport had, naturally, been greatly disrupted as the war escalated and football suffered more than most. Meagher's team, Chibuku Shumba, had been one of the early victims as the multi-racial teams were first to suffer while the white and coloured teams were unable to play because so many of their players were, like me, on active service. However, a distraction from the troubles and it was decided that the National team should be reformed to play against the might of South Africa.

Meagher still had not forgiven me but was forced to swallow his pride and not allow his personal prejudices to come in the way of the international team. He was quick to tell me that if I had been playing in England I would never have played again but, due to the exceptional circumstances, I was being let off. Jack was probably right but this was certainly not England and it was unreasonable even to try and compare the two countries. Soccer in Britain is a vicar's tea party compared with Rhodesia with its politics, fiddles, back stabbing and unprofessionalism. I have to say that there was more dishonesty in the game there than anywhere else I have come across in all my travels.

Even so the proposed match was unlikely to arouse world interest as both Rhodesia and South Africa were banned by the International Football Federation, FIFA, at the time because of apartheid. Meagher received permission from the army for me to transfer to the military training camp just outside Salisbury, in what had been a holiday resort before the war, and we were billeted in an agricultural college well away from the city centre so that we would have no distractions while preparing for our test series against the all-powerful Boks. I turned up armed with my pass from Major Taylor and under strict instructions to report back to camp no later than 06.00 on Monday, 15 July.

Jack Meagher was so shocked when he heard that I had not touched a football for two years, that I couldn't imagine what he thought the army and the terrorists were up to in the bush around the Mozambique border. Perhaps he thought we organised games. The upshot was, with the

pride of the country at stake, he decided that not only
would I not play but that I would not even be on the
bench. I was to be third of three goalkeepers. I could hardly
argue with the decision and, in any case, I was delighted
to be away from army surroundings. It also threw up
another interesting possibility as Graham Boyle, my former
captain in the Callies' Under 16 side and now an officer
instructor in Gwelo, had told me on arrival that Durban
City were interested in me playing for them in South
Africa. Colin Addison had tried to get me out of the army
after 12 months and, according to the message, the club
were still keen. I spoke to Jack Meagher about it and he
agreed that I should leave the squad to go to South Africa
ahead of the team to try my luck with a trial. I could still
watch the game and make it back to Adams Barracks before
my pass ran out.

A few telephone calls later, I was on my way out of the
country heading for a trial match at the New Kingsmead
Stadium for Durban City reserves against Pine Town. We
won 3-1 and the team coach Harry Weir was interested in
signing me as soon as I had finished my extended National
Service but the chairman Norman Elliott, known to all and
sundry as the Silver Fox because of his cunning ways with
contracts and players, told me bluntly: 'Son, you are not
good enough and if I have anything to do with the selection
of the teams you would not get a game for our juniors.'
Feeling totally dejected I left Durban and went to Johannesburg to watch the test match between South Africa and
Rhodesia. As I sat in the stands with some friends, Graham
Boyle, who had also been left out in favour of an all-black
line-up, whispered to me that I might be in some trouble
as Major Taylor had been asking my whereabouts in view
of the fact that I was neither in the nominated team nor
among the subs. To make matters worse I watched as the

Boks hammered seven goals past the former car-wash boy Sibanda without reply. It was a massacre and when the team were four down, Jack Meagher told Graham to warm up. Graham told the manager to get lost, saying that he was not going to be made to look a fool. As for Sibanda, he should have stuck to washing cars. In any event I made sure that I was back in barracks in good time but as I walked through the gates I was immediately put under arrest and quick marched to the cells to await Major Taylor and another court martial in his office at 09.30. The charge this time was going absent without leave. What a charge to face on the day I was due to leave the army!

It transpired that the other lads had been demobbed and Major Taylor had only wanted to know where I was so that I could leave as well. After all this time I was faced with another extension, only this time in a prison cell. I began to have my doubts, however, when I was told to knock on the Major's door and politely enter when he called instead of being doubled-in by the sergeant-major. Baffled, I walked in to find the Major clearing away his desk. He had been promoted and was leaving that day himself. He was not at all impressed when I told him that I thought I was within my rights to travel to South Africa and replied that my first duty had been to return to my company and that, as far as the army was concerned, I was guilty of going absent without leave. Visions of 56 days' sparring with the heavy-handed Sergeant Pretorious passed before my eyes, only for Major Taylor to bring me back to the moment of truth when he told me to collect my kit, return it to the quartermaster and then report to the paymaster and have three days' money deducted from my pay. With that he shook hands and I walked away a free man. Major Taylor was a good officer.

I headed back for Salisbury determined to pick up the

threads of my life and my football career. There were no
problems in finding a new club as I was automatically freed
when Chibuku disbanded. I looked up some of my old
friends and we all went back to the Callies, determined to
show the white man's footballing supremacy in the last few
weeks of the season. Boy did we show them! We played
ten matches — and lost ten. We could not field the same
side for two weeks running because of call-ups and other
problems and, even though we were only playing for
pleasure and ten dollars' pocket money, we were not happy.
The side collapsed, just like the country.

One thing it did do was to give me plenty of practice
in which to make up for those lost years and, to my
surprise, I found myself called up to rejoin the Rhodesian
National squad for the return game against South Africa in
our own Rufaro Stadium in Salisbury. After having watched
those seven goals being hammered past my old club-mate,
Sibanda, in the first game, it was a somewhat dubious
honour to be told by Jack that I would definitely be in the
side now that I was once again playing regular football.
No sooner had it been announced than Norman Elliott
telephoned from Durban to offer his congratulations and to
say that if I was still interested they would be delighted to
have me at Durban City now that I was out of the army.
This was the Silver Fox at his smoothest for I had already
heard that their regular goalkeeper Gerald McCann had
suffered a back injury which was threatening his career. The
Silver Fox did not want me when I was just Bruce
Grobbelaar up for a trial but now I was to be an international he was only too keen. I checked the offer out with
Weir who confirmed that it was genuine and that I could
stay with him at a negotiable rent.

That game against South Africa was probably the most
important of my young life and it was one of those days

when nothing went wrong. I dived this way and that, raced in and out of my penalty area and generally put myself about. I was beaten once in the first half by a Rodney Bush header but we came back to equalise through Shaw Handriade two minutes after the interval and held on for a draw in front of a record, wildly-cheering, 45,000 crowd. Coming only three months after our huge defeat it was a remarkable and unexpected score. It was the country's best football result since taking Australia to two replays in the World Cup qualifying competition and we were all proclaimed national heroes.

It also meant decision time. My mother was all for me trying my luck back in South Africa as there were so few opportunities in war-ravaged Rhodesia. The only problem was that my girlfriend Theresa Wyley had informed me that she was expecting our baby and, not surprisingly, wanted to get married and settle down. Under normal circumstances I would have done the 'decent thing', but these were anything but normal times. Still only 19 I had just spent two traumatic years avoiding becoming another war statistic and I now wanted to live a little, and earn some money. I could offer Theresa and the baby virtually nothing in terms of prospects or money by staying in Bulawayo but I felt that I could possibly make my fortune playing football in South Africa. Nothing ventured, nothing gained. I was off to South Africa, baby or not.

It was made easy by the fact that Graham Boyle had also been invited for a trial while Billy Sharman was already with the club. I had my début for Durban City against Maritzburg and did well enough to be selected for the big game against Wits University, on Sunday, 31 July 1977 at the New Kingsmead Stadium. In the opposite goal was another young South African of great promise, a certain Gary Bailey, son of the former Ipswich goalkeeper Roy who had been one of the coaches for the South Africa test match a week or so earlier. Our billing captured the public's imagination and the game was hailed as the test of the two young goalkeepers. Durban City lost 2-1 and the headline in the newspaper screamed out: 'Bang goes that winning record' and, underneath, the sub-heading rubbed it in by adding, 'Bruce boobs and Schoeman shoots home the winner.' The text went on to read, 'Bruce Grobbelaar, City's Rhodesian International keeper, made a terrible blunder when he sent a clearance straight to Schoeman who gratefully accepted the gift by driving the ball into an empty net.' What can I say? If that sounds only too familiar, I have to hold up my hands and admit that a leopard does not change its spots!

Gary Bailey's father, Roy, was not at all impressed by what he saw and not even my acrobatics for my country could alter his opinion. Roy was travelling around South Africa at the time giving goalkeeping clinics and when he came to Durban I attended it, completed the course and was told that I would never make a first-class goalkeeper so long as there was life in my limbs. I thought it unfair of him to judge me on so little knowledge and after watching me only twice. I was very upset and I don't think I would ever tell a kid that he had no chance in such a blunt fashion. Maybe he did it to spur me on. If he did he was successful for I decided then that I would prove him wrong. I was certainly gaining plenty of experience for I was playing for Durban City in the Datsun League and was also guesting for a black team called AmaZulu in the Mainstay League Cup. The connection was made through Harry Weir who had, by now, left Durban and was coaching one of the cane spirits company sponsored black sides who played out of the Kwamashu Township. The Mainstay Cup was a multi-racial competition which actively encouraged white players to guest for the black teams but, like so many of these events in South African sport, it was done to help the image and was largely cosmetic. If it was designed to reduce racial tension it was not always successful as was evident when we played a white side called Lusitano who, having beaten my Durban City side earlier in the season by six goals to two, needed only to win to reach the semi-finals. We held them to a draw which prompted this newspaper report:

AmaZulu, the black Durban soccer team, not only held the glamour NFL side Lusitano to a shock 1-1 draw at the Rand Stadium yesterday. In so doing they denied the Portuguese-orientated NFL side a semi-final berth in the remunerative Mainstay League in favour of Cape Town City. To add insult to injury, Lusitano's goal, which came first, was netted by AmaZulu's Eric Ngidi with Moffat Zulu hitting a remarkable equaliser midway in the second half. At the final whistle, pandemonium broke loose as supporters of both sides tried to get to grips with the players. But the police were on the spot and after two warning shots were fired the crowd began to disperse.

This exciting game was soured when linesman Mr Glyn Williams of Johannesburg, was put out of the game when a large-size rock struck him just above the temple. Blood gushed forth as he lay on the turf before a stretcher carried him off in a concussed state. A substitute linesman, Mr Alan Knott of Johannesburg, was drawn from the crowd and he completed the game in mufti.

The other linesman, Mr Simon Salepe, sought protection from referee Mr Dave Trinder after he had been pelted with beer cans and other missiles. Salepe was shifted to the more peaceful northern half of the field. A

minute before full-time the AmaZulu forward Chippa
Khoza flattened the Lusitano goalkeeper, Peter B'alac,
with a punch. Surprisingly Khoza received only a caution.
A send-off was fully justified. Lusitano's goal came just
before half-time when Ngidi, receiving from Mdlela,
tried to pass back to his goalkeeper [me!]. Instead it
trickled over the line and linesman Salepe correctly
flagged for a goal — only to receive a barrage of orange
peels.

The equaliser came in the 72nd minute when Zuma
cleverly latched onto a long ball and dribbled smartly
past Lusitano goalkeeper B'alac. Lusitano now needed
another goal to draw level with City or plus two to
make the semi-final — but it was not to be.

Hero of the match was the AmaZulu goalkeeper, the
former Rhodesian player, Bruce Grobbelaar, now with
Durban City, who saved shots from all angles. This man
inspired a very ordinary side to great heights. AmaZulu
did what no other black side seemed capable of doing —
hard, really hard tackling. This completely upset Lusitano's
rhythm and led to the surprise result. A 7,000 crowd
saw a game full of tension and unfortunately mixed with
an uncalled-for assault on linesman Williams. At the end
of the game B'alac, not happy with the punch he had
received, tried to square up with his tormentor. Mike
Collins also did some shadow boxing but officials and
police were on hand to keep the peace.

I think that will give you a good idea of the sort of
football that was played in South Africa, and also the sort
of journalism that accompanied it! At least the reporter did
my reputation no harm while the crowd provided me with
enough cans of beer to start a party.

Durban City Chairman Norman Elliott did not like me

playing for the black side, especially as Harry was their coach. The two were constantly rowing over who should pay my rent and, in the end, I used to pay Harry myself and then argue it out with the Silver Fox. I wasn't complaining, though, for I was earning a good deal more than I could have done in Rhodesia as I picked up 300 rand a month for playing football and the club had also found me a regular job to supplement my income. I started off as a salesman in Markham's menswear shop in West Street, working for former Blackpool player, Brian Peterson, who looked after me by paying good bonuses on top of my salary. I stayed there for two months before moving on to a much better-paid job as a salesman with the Olympic Toyota Motor Company on Smith Street. I passed the necessary exams and was jack-the-lad with a car provided by the firm. Many of Durban City FC's supporters are Indian and they all came to me for their cars because I quickly earned a reputation for giving the biggest discount in town, offering $12\frac{1}{2}$ per cent instead of the normal 10 per cent. They were always so pleased that they were only too happy to buy the 'extras', like radios, for another $2\frac{1}{2}$ percent!

I managed to save enough from my two jobs to be able to go back and see my family and friends in Bulawayo, and also be at home in time to see Theresa give birth to 'our' baby. The infant had been conceived when Theresa had come to meet me while I was on leave from the army and staying with my sister Jackie and her husband in Salisbury. It was only later that my mother recalled overhearing a snatch of conversation between Theresa and her mother at Bulawayo railway station. It had meant nothing to her at the time when she heard my girlfriend's mother saying, 'Don't worry. It will be all right from now on.' Judge for yourself. I am a fairly swarthy, dark-haired man of a predominantly Afrikaans background, while Theresa was a brown-eyed, raven-haired beauty of Spanish-Rhodesian stock. On the eve of 1978, immediately after watching a film called *Squirm*, Theresa gave birth to a blond-haired, blue-eyed bouncing little boy named Hayden Carl Wyley. His mother explained to me that children are often born with blue eyes and that they change colour when they grow older. I wondered about it at the time but, being fairly naive, I signed as the legal father when the boy's birth was registered.

No one forced me to do so but I couldn't let the child go through life without a father. Even so there was no way I was going to marry Theresa and settle in Rhodesia and I am sure that if I had, I would be there still and probably divorced. As it was I provided for Hayden, paying maintenance until Theresa married and then using the money to set up a trust for the little chap. I have seen him a couple of times since and those eyes are still blue and the hair still fair. More recently I was in Swaziland and bumped into an old friend, Alan Boonzaire, a blond-haired, handsome, blue-eyed man who had kindly looked after Theresa for me while I was in the army. I asked him if he had seen Hayden recently and he looked me in the eyes and laughingly replied: 'He still looks like you.' Only a blood test would tell for sure but even if it was not mine, it could easily have been, and if Theresa was unfaithful who could have blamed her? The government were as responsible for that baby as anyone. Maybe they should have paid the maintenance.

Even though there were serious doubts over the baby's parentage, the combination of the new born and the new year proved to be irresistible and the Grobbelaar family set about celebrating with a vengeance. Brother-in-law Joe was there as well and after a few pints of Shumba beer we began to look around for the stronger stuff. Joe sniffed out a case of best Scotch whisky but as he reached for a bottle he was told by Uncle Dan: 'Leave that alone! That's for uncles and adults only. You kids wouldn't know what to do with it.' In typical family fashion the row developed from there, meandering over several fronts before the topic turned, inevitably, to soccer. Joe and I were now on firmer ground and we ripped into Uncle Dan with a will, telling him he knew less about football than our pet dog. Unfortunately Mum walked in right in the middle of the row and promptly told Joe that if he didn't like what he heard he could go. With a twinkle in his eye Joe packed his grip, walked out of the front door and hid behind the bougainvillaea bush. I quickly warmed to the idea and told Mum I thought Joe was right.

Mum didn't realise that we were deliberately winding her up and she immediately launched an attack on my already weakened nose. I was told to go as well and I packed a rucksack and joined Joe in the road awaiting developments. We did not have long to wait for my sister came downstairs, having put Shane to bed, and asked where her husband and brother had gone. She was told in no uncertain manner that if she did not like it she could join us. She did and there we were in the early hours of New Year's Day sitting in the rain, hugging each other with tears of laughter running down our cheeks. We stayed the night with Joe's brother, returning home next morning to apologise to Mum for teasing her. She still thought that the row had been serious and only understood what had happened when she turned to see our stepfather laughing in the background.

It was all good fun and, in a way, I was sorry to be heading back to South Africa for the new soccer season, which was in even more disarray than our New Year's Eve party, for the white league had disbanded leaving the club with the choice of going into the black league or throwing in their lot with the Indian Federation. Durban elected to join the Indians, not because of any racial prejudice, but because they believed that the standard was lower and that they had a better chance of winning something and bringing back a few of the missing supporters – the main reason why the white league had disbanded. They were not far wrong. When I last checked, I still held the record for the most successive clean sheets for I did not concede a goal for the first ten games and, in fact, let in only two in the first fifteen games. Although the standard was not good I must have impressed someone for it was during this spell that Harry Weir and Colin Addison asked me if I fancied going to play in the English League. Do lions like raw meat? It had been my dream from the moment I had begun to take football seriously, for, after all, wasn't that where the game was born? If I could play in England I could measure myself against the best goalkeepers anywhere in the world and discover whether I could really play the game.

The one problem was Norman, the 'Silver Fox', who would see this as a way of making a fast buck on the transfer market. An escape route opened, however, through my other love, baseball. I was pitching for the Oriels and earned myself rave reviews for Natal Province in a tournament against Rhodesia and the other provinces. The scouts began to take an interest and I was approached by one from North Adams State College in the United States and offered a baseball scholarship. The local newspapers were full of it and it came as no surprise to the Silver Fox when I told him that I was off to the land of opportunity to pursue my career in baseball. All he could do was to grit his teeth and wish me well and, on April Fool's Day, 1978, knowing that in July I would begin pre-season training with West Bromwich Albion at the Hawthorns. It suited me for though I had never heard of the manager, Ron Atkinson, I knew his assistant Colin Addison very well indeed.

4

Making My Mark

I was looking forward to visiting England, that green and pleasant land, and the birthplace of football. However, my first impressions of it were somewhat tainted in that they were gained from the inside of a prison cell in the company of four suspected black terrorists. It all came about because of the devious way in which I had left Africa in search of my new football career. As far as everyone at home was concerned I was on my way to the United States to take up a baseball scholarship. If I had been seen leaving the country with Harry Weir the game would have been well and truly up. So, cloak and dagger style, we departed at different times on separate aircraft and by alternative routes.

By a stroke of good fortune I did not have to make my first trip out of Africa on my own for, on the same flight to London, was another Durban City footballer, Craig Saunders. I carefully avoided Craig in the departure lounge in case someone saw us and became suspicious but once aboard we met up and I learned that he was heading for Britain in the hope of trials with one of the lower division clubs. He was most impressed that my trials were already fixed up with First Division West Bromwich Albion.

I had arranged to meet up with Harry at Heathrow as our flights were scheduled to land within a short while of each other, but, as luck would have it, he was delayed and I was forced to wait. I aroused the suspicions of the customs and immigration officers. The trouble was that I couldn't answer many of their questions, not even where I was due to stay in England because Harry had all the details – and he was not there.

It might have been easier for me had I had more money but £50 and $100 in travellers cheques hardly made me a rich man, and certainly not in the eyes of those Heathrow officials. It was all I had left after forking out for my air ticket, which Ron Atkinson had promised to refund on my arrival, and having left a hefty sum for the upkeep of young Hayden back in Rhodesia. Mum would have been mortified had she known how little cash I had with me. But in the end it was decided that I was to stay in a cell until my unlikely story could be verified. I spent two and a half hours desperately trying to disguise my South African accent from my fellow cell-mates who were keen to discover what I had done to warrant such extravagant treatment from the authorities. Harry's flight eventually arrived and he was duly summoned to confirm my story and give my destination as Torquay, where his sister lived. I have never been so glad to leave an airport in my life and what makes the episode even more painful to recall is that Ron Atkinson never refunded the money for my air ticket!

It was hardly a case of 'Hail, The Conquering Hero Comes,' but my rather incongruous arrival was soon forgotten as I enjoyed a glorious English spring day. Instead of the cold and rain I had been warned to expect, it was a warm, sunny May day and the drive south to Devon put me in good spirits. Harry installed me in bed and breakfast 'digs' with one of his relatives and I was soon training and keeping fit on the local beach. It proved to be a good move for I was asked if I would like to help with the pedaloes for the tourists. As I had no work permit and so little money with me, the £5 I received in hand, tax free, seemed like a fortune.

It seemed to be a good way to spend the close season and to prepare myself for my trials in the Midlands but before long Craig Saunders turned up for a work-out with Torquay United. There was not room for both of us at the 'digs' and as Craig's need was greater than mine, I packed a bag and bought a coach ticket from Torquay to Inverness. Everyone thought I was mad but, with the wide expanses of Africa, we have a different concept of distances and the length of the journey did not daunt me in the least. It gave me an excellent chance to view the countryside and, even more important, the lovely Jean MacDougall would be at the other end of it! There was definitely method in my madness. Jean had written to me saying that she and her family had returned to their native Scotland and were buying a hotel in a place called Kirkcaldy. I not only made new friends on the coach but also linked up with an old pal, former Salisbury Callies player John Rutherford, in Edinburgh where he was working for the distillers, Bell's. He introduced me to his product while I waited for the midnight departure to Inverness. On arrival I booked into a bed and breakfast place and promptly telephoned Jean at her family hotel. To my dismay, I found that Jean was away studying at Middlesbrough College of Art, but her father immediately jumped into his car, picked me up and paid off the B & B insisting that I stayed as his guest at the hotel. But as soon as Jean heard that I was in Inverness she dropped everything, including her current boyfriend, and headed home. We were, I admit, infatuated with each other.

Being a country boy at heart I loved the slow, easy pace of Inverness and as the days passed by we became even more deeply involved and, when the time came for me to go for my trials in the Midlands, we made a solemn pledge to keep in touch. She went back to the college in Teesside while I made use of my return bus ticket to Torquay. This time I arrived in Edinburgh to discover that the coach did not leave until the morning and I had to slip the doorman at the YMCA a gentle bribe to push two chairs together and let me doss down until the manager was due to arrive at 6 a.m. Once inside I found that the night porter was running a thriving business, as there were several of us in the same position. But at least he gave us all a cup of tea before he kicked us out.

The summer came and went far too quickly but it hastened on my long-awaited trials with West Bromwich Albion and my hopes for a future in the English game rose when Harry drove me to Birmingham to meet our contact Colin Addison and Albion manager Ron Atkinson. My standard of living also rose with a room in a hotel on the Edgbaston Road and £50 in my hand every week to pay for my expenses. The only cloud on the horizon was that I had outstayed my two months' permit and had to return to the Home Office in London for an extension. My 'Police Book' also had to be stamped every Friday night wherever I was. It was a terrible bind, particularly when I had to play football the next day, but it had to be done because if you missed three stamps, you were out on your ear. I did not realise it at the time but that cloud was to develop into a thunderstorm and even the 'Police Book' was to become the cause of a disagreement. The vital work permit was to prove the undoing of my early hopes of a football career in England and when I gave up for the first time and turned in my Police Book, I was charged with defacing government property for I had used this handy sheaf of papers to make a note of all the new telephone numbers I was rapidly collecting. So I not only lost the argument over staying in England but also my book with all my telephone numbers.

However, I wasn't thinking that far ahead at the time for training was good and I was impressed by the standard of football at the Hawthorns. It was better than anything I had seen in Africa. I was also becoming fitter than I had ever been, but not all of that was down to Ron Atkinson's training routines. Unfortunately the Norfolk Hotel, where I had a back room next to some other trialists, was not licensed for the sale of alcohol which meant going out with the older apprentices to such establishments as the Duck Inn, the Rainbow Club and Romulus's where my weekly allowance did not last long, especially when I took one of the hotel staff or the pub barmaid along to show me the sights of my new country. It was all very pleasant but it meant that sometimes I did not have enough left to pay my bus fare and I would jog the six miles or so to and from the training ground.

It stood me in good stead when Ron Atkinson took us all over the Oxfordshire countryside, which he knew well because of his long association with Oxford United Football Club before they had become a full League side, to put us through our paces in the hills. I did not mind and neither did the other fit young fellows like Laurie Cunningham and Bryan Robson but some of the older hands were not at all happy about taking us on and veteran central defender John Wile used to threaten to hit me if I went racing past him and showed him up. Oxfordshire may seem far removed from my training in the bush but when you missed the fairways on the golf course as often as I did, I needed to live up to my 'Jungle Man' reputation just to find where my wayward drives had deposited the ball. My tracking stood me in very good stead and, despite myself, I didn't lose too many balls, indeed Bryan Robson and I had the temerity to beat our bosses Ron Atkinson and Colin Addison over 18 holes for a £10 per corner bet. Come to think of it, Ron Atkinson never paid me for that either! Bryan Robson was looked after when Ron Atkinson paid him nearly £2 million to follow him to Manchester United. But what about me? If ever Ron fancies a return game for double or quits, I hope his game has got better. I have improved to around a ten handicap these days whereas I used to take ten on each of the first two holes.

I enjoyed my time at Albion even though I was still battling with the Home Office for the crucial work permit. As it was the season loomed with no sign of me being able to play League football. The closest I came was when we went on a pre-season trip to Scotland, to take part in a testimonial for Motherwell manager Ally MacLeod and then on to a tournament at Ibrox Park. The chance was too good to miss and I asked the manager if it was all right for my girlfriend Jean to come and visit me. Ron said that it would be no problem as both he and I assumed it would be after the game against Motherwell. But, Jean, misunderstanding the message and keen to see me, arrived at the same time as we did. Fortunately for me, there was an odd number of players on the trip and, as luck would have it, I was the player who had a room to himself. I sneaked Jean in and there she stayed for three days though I pretended she had left after the first day. It was all a bit embarrassing especially when John Wile later mentioned it in his regular article in a local Birmingham paper. The whole episode turned into a bit of a pantomime, though I refuse to share any of the subsequent blame. Before the game they arranged a special sprint challenge between two of the local Motherwell players and our two explosive wingers Laurie Cunningham and that unpredictable Scot Willie Johnston. It was to be over 70 yards but after 30, Willie just decided to quit and left Laurie to win the race.

We won the game 8–1 and I came on for the second half to keep a clean sheet. It was a great experience but, sadly, it was the only game I ever played in the West Bromwich Albion first team and hardly one to get me a mention in the *Rothmans' Football Year Book*. I stayed with them for a full five months while they tried to obtain the necessary papers to clear me to play as a professional. I was restricted to sharing reserve games with Mark Grew. We played alternately for a few weeks and I did not really have a bad match, indeed we won all four. We also played a touring Arab side when we shared half each and the goal I conceded in the 1–1 draw was my one disappointment.

In the end West Brom suggested that I go to Bournemouth to train and see if it made any difference applying from a club from a lower division. I moved out of my comfortable hotel and into digs down on the south coast. They, and the club, were nice but it was an eye opener to see the difference between clubs in the First and Fourth Divisions. The only similarity was that I was still unable to obtain my work permit. I was frustrated and annoyed and felt, quite wrongly, that the two clubs were not doing enough to help me. It all came to a head on the notable occasion of my twenty-first birthday on 6 October. It was a terrific party and when I woke up on a Bournemouth beach on the morning of 7 October I decided that enough was enough and that, having failed, I was going to return to South Africa.

I said goodbye to my new friends in Bournemouth and then decided that I should do the same at the Hawthorns. I went back to Birmingham, got my old room back at the

Norfolk and went to book my ticket home the very next night, a Monday. On Monday morning I packed my gear and went off to the West Brom ground to say my farewells. It was one of those inexplicable coincidences that, the same morning, Colin Addison was trying to get hold of me to tell me that the former England goalkeeper Tony Waiters was passing through England on a European tour scouting for talent for Vancouver Whitecaps in Canada and was holding trials in Derby that very day. I did not even know where Derby was. Colin told me it was up to me and that there was nothing more he or anyone else could do for me.

I dashed back to the hotel, changed my flight and borrowed a car to drive to Derby, arriving 15 minutes late to be met by Waiters and a man named John Craven. They put me through 40 minutes of shooting, crossing and agility work. Afterwards Tony told me to get the tea ready while he went off on a run. Fitness fanatic that he was, he was away longer than I thought and the tea was cold when I poured it. It was not the most promising of starts and when he asked me how I thought I had performed I blustered and stammered about how my mind had not been right, explaining about the situation and assuring him I could do a lot better. He either believed me or I had played better than I thought for in the next breath he invited me to go to Vancouver, adding that he was considering me as a back-up for Englishman Phil Parkes and saying that I could learn a lot if I was offered a contract with a guarantee that I would not suffer the same difficulties that had frustrated me in England. There was no rush and no objection to me returning home to Rhodesia to see my family before starting a possible new life in Canada. We exchanged numbers and he told me he would call me in Bulawayo three days later.

I was a happy man on that flight home. At last something positive was happening and not even meeting Theresa's mother at the airport to tell me that now was an ideal moment to set a wedding date could take away my joy. Mum and the family were happy to see me after a five-month absence but were obviously dubious about the prospects of my latest venture and when there was no telephone call on Thursday they openly said that the whole thing was garbage and it was time I looked for a proper job. I felt such an idiot I could hardly refuse and in November 1978 I began work on the Rhodesian Railways as an apprentice refrigerator mechanic for what was then a high salary. I had been working for four days when, exactly seven days late, I received Tony Waiters' call telling me to pack my boots and a heavy top coat and to pick up my ticket to Vancouver that day. I couldn't wait. I told Rhodesia Railways what they could do with their job and their refrigerators only to be told at the Air Canada offices that as I held a South African passport I would need a visa — and the only way I could get that was from South Africa!

It was the start of another chapter of events which should have convinced me that I was not destined to be a footballer. It took 24 hours to set the wheels in motion as I got in touch with my Aunt Yvonne in Pretoria who contacted the Canadian Embassy telling them I needed a visa because I was going to Canada on holiday. They refused because I had only two months' stamps from Britain and it was not until I personally showed them the ticket bought by Vancouver Whitecaps that they relented. By now I was already two days' late and it was Wednesday night by the time I boarded a plane for Heathrow where I caught my connecting flight to Toronto.

Tony Waiters hadn't been joking when he told me to bring a heavy coat for there I was in a lightweight sweater with the temperature outside reading minus 48°F. My own temperature, however, rose several degrees when the customs official told me that my visa was not in order and that I would not be allowed into the country. I pleaded with him to telephone the Whitecaps, which he eventually did, and I was permitted to continue the last leg of my long journey to Vancouver. It had taken me four days from leaving home in Rhodesia to be throwing my bag into my hotel room in Davies Street, Vancouver and heading for the ground. As I walked in I was greeted by Tony Waiters who told me to go back and fetch my gear as I was playing that night for the reserves. There wasn't even time for a nap and here I was trying to launch a new career after four days' journeying across three continents.

We played a team called Pegasus in the Empire Stadium and drew 1–1. I was just glad to get it over with and looked forward to a couple of days and nights in a nice warm bed. No such luck. As I came off I was told that we would be playing the same side again the very next night. I stifled a groan and this time kept a clean sheet in a goalless draw. The games were specially-arranged trials and at the end of them I signed a one-year contract without even reading the large type. I was so determined to make something of myself as a footballer that I did not look at it because there was no way I was going to argue over a few dollars and, until I married and had a family, my attitude remained largely the same. The contract was to begin on 2 January 1981, the only problem being that it was not even the end of November. I was in a strange country with Christmas approaching and further away than ever from my family. The club appreciated my difficulties and offered me a return air ticket which I immediately accepted and used to spend Christmas with Jean MacDougall and her family in Scotland. It was a great Christmas and an

New Year in Inverness-shire as the turn of the year means a lot more in Scotland than in England and I was amazed that people you did not know could be so friendly. On the night of 31 December we were walking down a street when I heard what I thought was abuse being shouted at us from a house. It turned out that we were just being invited in for a drink and so it went on.

It was a good job I had 24 hours to recover as, allowing for the time change, I was due to fly out on 2 January via Amsterdam. Although I arrived at Schipol Airport in plenty of time for my connection, the problem was that they were not ready for me. Our flight from London was the only one to land that day and not a single one took off as the snow swept in and closed one of the world's busiest airports. There we stayed for three days with me having visions of being turned away from football again, this time for breach of contract. Fortunately I could also see the funny side of it and when we landed in Vancouver at 3 p.m. I went straight to the Whitecaps' offices, pausing only to slip on a latex mask of a very old, wrinkled, grey-haired man. I walked in saying: 'I'm back—even if it has taken me a long while.' Everyone had a laugh but they still checked out my story.

So I was starting pre-season training for the second time in the space of six months. This time, however, it was different for there were no problems with my 'Green Card' which gave me the right to work and within days we were off on tour to Santa Barbara, California. It was a new world, the sort I had dreamed about back home in Africa, with the biggest problem being which girl to take out for a drink each night. Although I was only the reserve and, as such, designated the number 22 shirt, I was made to feel part of the set-up and before every game all of the players would be introduced to the crowd. I sat warming my backside on the substitutes' bench and playing for the reserves until I eventually made my début against the visiting Bristol City side from England in the second half of a friendly. It was memorable in that England striker Joe Royle played against us and then persuaded me to lend him my club car in return for a Bristol City sweater.

I had to wait until almost halfway through that season before I made my proper début and then it was against one of the world's great players, Johann Cruyff of Holland, who was playing for the Los Angeles Aztecs. We played in the Rose Bowl Stadium in Pasadena and, as in most of my first appearances, I finished up on the losing side with Cruyff scoring one of the two goals that flew past me as I stood in for the injured Phil Parkes. Vancouver was a great place to play football and also a wonderful place to live for a young sportsman. The problem of not knowing too many people was soon resolved as I began to get out and about to explore this cosmopolitan city. I was living in a two-bedroom apartment and, after a while, I was called into the Whitecaps' offices and told that I would be sharing it with an Englishman. I said that was fine but why had they called me into the office just to tell me that? The reason was because my new room-mate was, they revealed with some hesitation, black. Obviously they had heard the stories of my fighting the black men in the bush and were concerned how I would accept a coloured flat-mate. I was amused at their needless concern but played along in case I didn't like the fellow.

His name was Carl Valentine, a half-caste or 'goffle' with a Jamaican father and a white Mancunian mother, and we became friends from the moment we met and have remained so ever since with Carl following me over to England later to play for, of all teams, West Bromwich Albion. It was a real 'Salt and Pepper' relationship which embraced not only football but also our social life. It was a good day for me when Carl moved in but I am not sure that the club were of the same opinion. They were quite strict about the hours kept, even by the reserves. Our coach was an upright man named Les Wilson who was not above lurking in the apartment garages to see what sort of time Carl and I went out. It became quite a game, with Phil Parkes and his wife, who lived next door, keeping watch for us. Les would check to see whether our cars were in the garage and if not he would come and knock on the door. It meant a lot of lifts and taxi rides to avoid detection, but even that did not stop us getting caught as on the night I slipped off to our favourite disco, leaving Carl watching television. He suddenly became bored and decided to join me, putting on his best dancing gear only to be met in the car park by the ever-watchful Les. I am not sure that Les believed Carl's tale that he was just nipping out for a take-away supper dressed up as he was but as I was not with him, he readily swallowed the story that I was tucked up in bed, having left explicit instructions not to be disturbed under any circumstances as I was preparing for our big reserve game against local rivals Seattle.

Professional footballers in Canada and the United States are far more aware of their community responsibilities than some of their British counterparts and Carl and I regularly went round to the local schools to talk to and coach the youngsters. We were always particularly eager to volunteer for that particular duty as the kids were often taught by attractive young teachers. We both took a shine to one in particular and so were always ready to visit the kids at the New Westminster School. The problem was that, at the time, I had Jean MacDougall staying with me on holiday while Carl had his girlfriend Gill over from England. But the moment they left Wendy came round to see Carl and the moment they left Wendy came round to see Carl and when he was away, I would take over.

All the other lads knew what we were up to and found it a great laugh, especially as Carl, living up to his surname, was also dating a girl from the club offices who was the regular girlfriend of another player called Sammy Lenarduzzi, one of three brothers at the club. It was not for nothing that they were nicknamed 'The Mafia' and the first time Carl took the girl home in his car he was followed all the way, not finding out who it was until Sammy tried to kick him in training. Without becoming romantically involved, I also became friendly with the same girl and, in fact, drove her to hospital when she caught pneumonia. Sammy ignored her cries for help, as did her parents. I had to tell her mother that she was close to death and, fortunately, that persuaded them but when I told Sammy what I thought of him I had all three brothers trying to kick me in training. Fortunately, Sammy soon went to Toronto Blizzards, Danny was released and the remaining brother, Bobby, was not much of a kicker anyway!

However, in spite of this, it was a great club with a great atmosphere. There were some good professionals there who could play as hard as they lived, players like: England's World Cup hero Alan Ball, now a successful manager himself; the unpredictable Scottish international winger Willie Johnston; Jon Sammels, an important member of Arsenal's double-winning side; the popular Derek Possee; and Ipswich striker Trevor Whymark to name just a few. They all responded well to our manager Tony Waiters who would not stand any cheating in games or training. He made training hard with plenty of running and we poor goalkeepers had to do the lot, including a 12-minute run at the end of each session. I thought I was a fit man until I joined Vancouver.

I owe Tony Waiters a great deal personally. I was extremely lucky to go to a club managed by such an outstanding goalkeeper who was also a good coach. Even though Phil Parkes was the number-one choice, and quite rightly so, Tony always had time for me, passing on little tips and correcting my mistakes. Some coaches and managers can tell you when you are making errors but this man could also show you why you were going wrong. He was always positive with me, encouraging me, working on my agility and never trying to curb my individuality. He would spend hours simply hitting through passes for me to come out at players' feet. In latter years it has almost become my trademark at Liverpool. We were enjoying plenty of success under his guidance, with our reserves gaining promotion, while the first team went to Jersey and won the Super Bowl by beating Tampa Bay Rowdies. That was a fantastic trip with all the reserves included as part of the game. After winning, we were given the Freedom of the City and each of us was presented with a miniature gold soccer ball encrusted with diamonds. Mum still wears mine around her neck.

While in Jersey, Tony Waiters turned to me and said: 'We have not seen a lot of you this season. When we get back to Vancouver I want to talk to you about your future. I want to send you to England to gain some experience with the strongest team in the League.' He was not wrong about my contribution to the club's success for, after the début, I played only once more when we beat California Surfs 2–1 in overtime at the Anaheim Stadium. But, despite that, I was not at all frustrated as I felt that I was learning my trade and, for once in my life, I was prepared to be patient and work at improving my game.

After my problems with West Bromwich Albion, the English League had lost some of its attraction and I had myself that only if Liverpool, Arsenal or my childhood favourites, Derby County, wanted me, would I consider moving back to England. But this was something entirely different. It was September and the English season was already under way. I scanned the First Division tables and hoped that it would be Liverpool and not Manchester United that Tony Waiters would lend me to. When we returned to Vancouver he carefully explained that I was at a vital stage of my career and only I could decide my future and that was why he was going to send me to, of all places, Crewe Alexandra! 'Who?' I asked. 'Crewe Alexandra,' replied Tony with a grin. 'But I thought you said that I was going to the strongest club in England,' I retorted. 'I am,' came back Tony. 'They are ninety-second in the League, bottom of the Fourth Division and are holding everyone else up. They've got to be the strongest club to do that and, if you get bored, you can always go to the railway station and watch the trains.'

Joker Grobbelaar had fallen for the oldest joke in the English Football League and I was so surprised that I did not even try to find out what he meant by his remark about the trains, not realising that Crewe is most famous for being one of Britain's busiest train junctions. I was still in a daze when I set off for the airport. One minute I was on the bench at the American Super Bowl final and the next I was heading for a town I had never even heard of. I was not sure whether they would let me in the country, lock me up in Heathrow prison cells or even why I could be going on loan to an English club when I had already been turned down for a work permit with West Bromwich Albion and Bournemouth. Remembering all my past problems, I was delighted when my Canadian visa saw me safely through the formalities at the airport and in no time at all I was on the underground heading for Euston Station.

I immediately saw what Tony Waiters had meant about
the trains for every other one seemed to be stopping at
Crewe and I began to imagine with increasing relish that I
was heading for a busy, bustling city.

Crewe Station at four o'clock in the afternoon rapidly
proved otherwise, especially when I arrived to discover
that neither manager Tony Waddington nor his coach were
there to meet me as promised. Not only that but the Crewe
Arms Hotel over the road had never heard of me and
neither had the Royal. What is more there were no rooms
available and I was forced to jump in a cab and ask the
driver to take me to a cheap hotel. The man who checked
me in at a little place in Nantwich looked at me with great
suspicion and, when I told him I was a South-African born
Rhodesian who had come from Canada to play for Crewe
Alexandra, he clearly thought I was either a liar or an
escaped lunatic. He was as pleased as I that I left early the
next morning, taking a taxi to the Crewe ground to meet
Tony Waddington. Inevitably, his first question was whether
my room at the Royal had been suitable. It had been
booked in the club's name and not mine. That was quickly
sorted out but, once again, my South African passport
proved to be the major stumbling block and no sooner had
I arrived than I found myself shunted into Crewe's sidings
as the Home Office turned down the Football Association's
request for a work permit.

The whole situation was unbelievable. Here I was back
in England with the bottom club in the Fourth Division
and still I could not get a game of football for a first team.
Autumn turned to winter as I trained with the first team
and played for the reserves as the row rumbled on. Even
though I was officially playing without being paid and had
been given permission by the Football Association and the
United States' authorities, the immigration people dug their

toes in and said 'No!'. Tony Waddington was furious for it meant that he had to take David Felgate on loan from Bolton Wanderers, which cost the hard-up little club wages that they could ill afford. The manager said: 'To me it seems rather inconsistent to say a player is being employed when he is not being paid. He is here for experience only and it seems a little unfair that they will not allow him to play.' I was eventually told that my only chance of staying was if I could find some strong English connections in my family. I telephoned my mother and she told me about her grandparents. We submitted a new application to the Home Office and, incredibly, they gave in and produced a work permit that would allow me to play English football for the remainder of the season. I was baffled. Why all the problems last time when I wanted to play for West Bromwich Albion? What was the difference?

But it was no use fretting over the past. Crewe might well have been the last club in the Fourth Division with only three wins all season and just one point away from home. I had my first inkling that I was about to make my English début when our manager Tony Waddington pulled me out of a reserve game against Liverpool at Melwood and I travelled to Wigan with the first team for a Friday night game four days before Christmas, 1979. Sure enough, Dave Felgate was asked to stand down at the last minute. It was a very cold night and it was the first time I had ever been asked to play on a frozen surface. I frantically searched through all the studs in the trainers' box trying to find something that would give me a grip before deciding to wear a pair of flat rubbers. To be honest the game went well for me, if not for the team. Wigan threw everything at us bar their stand. I managed to get parts of my anatomy in the way of most of it until the seventy-second minute when a young man named Jeff Wright struck a 6-yard volley past me for a well-taken, well-deserved goal, which was the first of many to be scored against me in English football. I did not have to wait long for the second either as Tommy Gore put a penalty past me late in the second half. But I knew I had played well and I was delighted to hear the opposition asking the Wigan players who the new goalkeeper was. I didn't even mind when our big defender Bob Scott replied that it was only some foreigner.

That night I didn't go home on the coach, and went back instead with Scott and his oil-rig worker mate Billy Griffiths in a Jaguar. Anyone with any knowledge of the geography of the North of England will be staggered to hear that we made the trip from Wigan to Crewe in just 25 minutes. We flew over the humpback bridges and arrived back in time for a few celebratory jars of beer. When the coach turned up Tony Waddington went white on hearing by how long we had beaten the team bus back. Tony did not mince words when he told us how stupid we were but the dressing down he gave me was somewhat softened when I read his comments in the local paper. He described my début as 'phenomenal' and went on to add: 'The lad did not know he was playing until just before the kick-off, yet he gave one of the best goalkeeping displays I have ever seen and I have seen some great keepers in my time, including Banks and Shilton. Grobbelaar's form in practice suggested he might be a bit special, but his saves kept us in the game right to the end. I went to great lengths to sign him on the basis of reports I had been given and the transfer seemed to be on and off for a long time, but now it seems to be all worth while.'

Crewe began something of a revival after that, winning eight and drawing nine of our twenty-three games and I managed to keep eight clean sheets. We even managed to climb up to 22 in the table, eventually finishing twenty-third with Crewe's usual application for re-election carrying more weight than usual. It was a great experience and I learned a lot from those few months in that little soccer outpost. It was very different from anything I had experienced before, and particularly from Vancouver's smart facilities and high-pitched image. As for the football it was the fastest I had ever experienced.

I was living in the Royal Hotel, sharing a room with two former Manchester United apprentices, Geoff Hunter and Ian Ashworth. The hotel was only across the road from the ground and on my first morning I had wandered over, put my bag on a hook in the dressing room and strolled out to look at the Gresty Road pitch. No one had told me that there was a very strict pecking order concerning changing places. 'What's this doing on my peg?' boomed Father Bear in the shape of the six feet two and a half inch tall, Liverpool-born Bob Scott. I was out on my ear and in the visitors' dressing room until I had proved myself, which I set out to do that very morning as our coach Colin Prophett had me diving about in the mud with Bob Scott getting angrier by the minute as he tried to put one past me. It was the first of many confrontations I had with Bob Scott, which in the end led to a lasting friendship. Not that many people would have guessed it had they seen us arguing on the pitch and in one game we actually had each other by the throats. His complaint, which was quite justified, was that when I came for crosses I did not call and he was fed up finishing games with lumps on his head. However, a few pints after the game, it was soon forgotten and Bob would often doss down in my hotel room rather than drive all the way back to Wrexham.

The whole team enjoyed drinking from the manager down. Tony Waddington was nicknamed 'Mr Gin'. I discovered why one night in the Crewe Arms Hotel when discovered why one night in the Crewe Arms Hotel when I saw him from the other bar with what was clearly his own bottle. It had a cardboard cut-out of his face on the neck, a little red and white scarf underneath and two cotton reels on the bottom painted to look like red and white football socks. Not surprisingly he had gathered a team of right characters around him. Defender Kevin Lewis, yet another former Manchester United youngster, was probably the worst, always leg pulling and playing practical jokes. Can you imagine sliding on your boots on a cold winter's morning and finding that they had been filled with icy water? Both Kevin and Neil Wilkinson had played in South Africa, Neil for Helenic and Kevin for Cape Town where he had broken a leg and made his reputation by making love to a nurse in the hospital while still in plaster. Others included: graduate Mark Palios; Peter Coyne, a brilliant former England Schoolboy international who had lost his way at Manchester United (where else?); Wayne Goldthorpe who could drink 5 pints of bitter in a session — and play the same night; and Dai Davies, born in the Rhondda Valley, who always refused a lift home after a boozing session because he reckoned he could run it off on the two-mile trip.

I suppose I was one of the dafter ones and more than contributed towards a few of Tony Waddington's grey hairs. One such incident was the return game against Wigan when I warmed up wearing an old man's mask with long white hair hanging down my back. I was marking the pitch in the goalmouth when the referee ran up and booked me. He said it was for ungentlemanly conduct for marking the pitch but he added that if he saw me in the mask again he would send me off. It was only to amuse the supporters and when playing or watching in the Fourth Division you need a few giggles. I wanted to try it again but Tony

Leeds United and Sheffield Wednesday were represented at the game and were thought to be watching me. I also trotted out with an umbrella one particularly wet afternoon and on another occasion I stood talking to the supporters behind the goal at the Railway End and had to scramble back over the wall a bit sharpish when the opposition suddenly broke away. It might have worried Waddington and Prophett but the fans loved it all. They were fantastic people and living near the ground I came to know a lot of them.

The results going our way also helped and when we earned a good away draw at Doncaster Rovers, Tony Waddington was only too happy to give me a few days off down on the south coast to visit Harry Weir's wife and children who were in Torquay for a holiday. I met up with the team for our last away game of the season on the Friday night in Bournemouth. At dinner that night, as Bob and I experimented with frogs' legs, Tony Waddington stood up and said: 'You are all grown-up lads and I know that you will be slipping off for a drink before bed. All I ask is that you are discreet and careful not to let the club down.' We took Tony at his word and had a few pints and would have headed back for the hotel and bed but for those frogs' legs. They were not enough for two healthy chaps and by closing time we were both starving and went off in search of a kebab. We found what we wanted but the only trouble was that the chilli sauce was a fraction on the hot side and by the time we reached the hotel we both had raging thirsts. Now, as luck would have it, the hotel had a disco and it was quite obviously the place to be in Bournemouth as there was a large queue building up outside. Bob and I looked at each other and he joined the line while I went inside to see whether there was simpler access for residents.

There was and by the time Bob reached the door I was waiting for him with a big, foaming pint of beer. The disco closed at four in the morning and, by the time our guests had left our rooms, the birds were chirping and the sun was beginning to rise. Now if honesty and virtue have their just rewards, middle-of-the-table Bournemouth would have punished us for our sins but life does not always work that way and little Crewe went on to record their very first away win of the season with a goal from Palios. But the real heroes were, you've guessed it, Bruce Grobbelaar and Bob Scott. When I didn't save them, Bob was throwing himself head first or sticking out a boot to clear them off the line.

No one found out about our evening exploits in Bournemouth but manager Tony Waddington turned a blind eye to another incident. It began when a few of us were invited to a working men's club in Crewe and I was rather taken with the attractive barmaid. She proved to be a very game lady indeed and over some private discussions after the bar had shut she expressed a desire to look around our football ground in return for showing me the nooks and crannies at her club. Sure enough she arrived on the appointed day and entered into the spirit of things when she joined some of the lads in the big bath after training. There was lots of steam, and not all of it from the hot water taps, but Tony Waddington could not have helped but spot the difference when he walked into the bathroom area. He stopped whatever it was he was going to say, turned on his heel and muttered that he would see us the next day. Not a word was said.

It was all great fun. South Africa may have had the wonderful weather and Canada the most marvellous facilities, but Crewe will always hold a special place in my heart. Goodness knows I needed something to cheer me up in

Goodness knows I needed something to cheer me up in those last few weeks of the season as I suffered a double blow, firstly when my mother called me from the newly-named Zimbabwe to tell me that Robert Mugabe had won the first elections and then, only a matter of hours later, Tony Waiters telephoned me from Canada to inform me that he had just clinched the signing of Scottish international goalkeeper David Harvey and that there was no need to hurry back.

Needless to say I was devastated for, with Phil Parkes joining Chicago Stings, I had honestly thought I would be Vancouver Whitecaps' first choice for the North American Soccer League in the coming season, especially after my experiences in the English League. What made it even worse was the fact that I discovered that they had already started the League programme in the States with Harvey first choice and me nowhere. But Whitecaps had a terrible start, for after winning the Super Bowl the previous season, they slumped to two successive defeats and I suddenly received another Transatlantic call from Tony Waiters wanting to know when I was coming back. There was one Crewe match left, at home to York, and I had planned to go to Wembley the following Saturday to watch West Ham United play Arsenal. 'You play against York on the 3rd,' replied Waiters, 'and I'll expect you back in Canada on the 4th — ready to play.'

I was genuinely sorry to be leaving Crewe. They were a tremendous bunch of lads with a lot of spirit and character. Being seven points behind the second-lowest club in the Fourth Division halfway through the season is about as low as you can go but they did not let their heads drop and battled as though they were chasing a place in Europe. They seemed to like me as well because I was made skipper for that last game with everyone's approval. I took full were awarded a penalty I would take it myself. Waddington admonished: 'Only if you are at least two up at the time.' As it happened we were a goal up when, with 58 minutes of my last game for Crewe gone, Dai Davies was brought down by the York goalkeeper Taylor. I was off, racing up the pitch, only stopping to hand my cap to a surprised Bob Scott on the way, and crashed the ball high into the net giving Taylor no chance but my team-mates and me heart failure for had it been an inch or two higher it would have hit the crossbar and York would have been on the break with no goalkeeper to beat.

I don't know what the watching scouts made of that or my other antics but, despite the excellent press I was receiving, no one ever actually spoke to me. All I knew of other clubs' interest was from newspaper gossip and from Tony Waddington telling me before a game who had applied for tickets. He made a policy of this whether they were watching me, Geoff Hunter, Kevin Lewis or whoever and, rather than putting pressure on us, it always used to key us up for a good game. If everything he and the papers said were true then both Manchester City and Manchester United, along with Liverpool, Everton, Leeds, Sheffield Wednesday, Chelsea and Derby County ran the rule over me at some stage or the other but when I returned to Vancouver no actual offers had been made.

When I got back it was confirmed that Phil Parkes, looking for a little security after being named the best goalkeeper in the League, had priced himself out of the Whitecaps and into Stings. That came as no great surprise for the last time we had played in the 'Windy City' he had enjoyed a tremendous game and when we jumped in a taxi to visit the local English pub, the German manager of the Stings had followed us, shouting out of the window that he wanted Phil to sign for him. They must have wanted him very badly to pay the figure Phil had been demanding from Tony Waiters. But, despite Waiters' insistence that I hurry back, I found myself warming my backside on the substitutes' bench yet again as David Harvey played his fourth successive game against New England Teamen. Having been told I was playing, I was naturally upset and remarked to the boss that if I were to have another season on the bench I would need a cushion. Waiters responded by designating me '00' for my number in case I needed an extra pair of eyes to see the ball in the back of the net. I promptly went home and sewed in two eyeballs but Waiters is one of the old school and he refused to allow me to wear it.

Harvey's indifferent start cost him dearly and I began the next game as number-one choice and stayed there for the rest of the season apart from a couple of games when I had a bursitis problem with a knee. However, some of the pressure was taken off when my rival drove his car into another causing him to spend a long time in a high collar. While I had been away our quarters had also been changed and we had been moved into an even smarter apartment block. Carl Valentine had his girlfriend Gill over to stay so I settled down on the couch in the lounge for a month before moving into the apartment next door, which I shared with a lad named Paul Nelson. It was every bit as chaotic as before as we succeeded to flood the kitchen in suds from floor to ceiling when Paul insisted on using Persil in the dish-washing machine. Seeing this wall of bubbles rolling out towards us was like something out of a James Herbert horror story. Although Carl had Gill out from England he still saw his old friend Wendy now and again, but there were problems when she arrived one day after a ladies' football match asking for Carl and wanting to borrow the shower. Carl was in a panic with Gill sitting in his lounge, so he enlisted the help of Paul and me in steering her unknowingly into room 102 instead of 101, saying that he was out.

As Paul leant against the number I distracted Wendy's attention and pushed her into our flat and towards the shower. She suddenly twigged that all was not quite as it should be and came bursting out of the bathroom demanding an explanation. Under the circumstances I thought it best to come clean and told her that Carl was next door with his girlfriend. With that Wendy wrapped a towel around her and walked in next door to tell him she didn't mind and that he should have explained that Gill was over from England. Wendy was an understanding lady and so, I suppose, was Gill for she and Carl eventually settled down together. Not that it stopped Wendy. She even came to one or two of our away games and more than once I found myself locked out of the hotel room. Gill may sound long suffering but when Jean MacDougall came over to see me, the two used to dress up and go out together. I had not seen as much of Jean as I had expected in England. She had moved from Middlesbrough to Maidstone College of Art in Kent. When I did see her again she was not the carefree, happy girl I had known in Rhodesia and Scotland, she had begun to change into a woman becoming a lot more aware and no longer the girl I expected her to be. I should have realised that the affair was fading then but nevertheless invited Jean to come over to Canada with my mother and step-father. It was an unmitigated disaster. Mum, who had never been out of Africa, did not get on with her and they frequently had words which made the apartment uncomfortable and hardly helped my relationship with Jean. Had I been able to offer her some sort of security maybe we would have married but, as it transpired, it was a blessing in disguise that we went our separate ways. I married Debbie and Jean married too and now lives in Switzerland. Happily, I am still friendly with both her and her lovely family.

Although we lost our Championship I enjoyed a good season playing for a strong team which included many experienced players such as: Alan Ball; Trevor Whymark; John Craven; Roger Kenyon; and the Dutchman Rudi Krol. Maybe, in the final reckoning, we had a little too much experience and not enough youthful enthusiasm but no such charges could be levelled at the former Ajax great Rudi Krol. He was a great player and a terrific person. A classy dresser and a classy man who carried his professionalism off the field and out of the dressing room. He could put the ball on a spot either running or standing still. I shared a room with him and he helped me to brush up my Dutch.

Unbeknown to me, Liverpool had emerged as the club in England who wanted to sign me and they were surprised when they went back to Crewe to discover that I had returned to Canada. They were looking for cover for England's Ray Clemence and seemed to have decided on me. Tony Waiters told English journalists: 'My phone had been red hot recently with English clubs chasing Grobbelaar and, if I were to make him available, a deal would be on immediately.' Whitecaps appeared as though they were going to squeeze every penny out of any possible move and as the stories grew I heard that they had offered to swap me for Ray Clemence and Kenny Dalglish. I can imagine how Bob Paisley and the Liverpool board responded to that one! It was pure fantasy stuff and I knew enough about both players to realise that Vancouver would have had to throw in their main stand as well.

After all my disappointments in English football, I was not going to believe anything until I signed on the dotted

line of a genuine contract and it was not until we were
approaching the run-in to the season that everything began
to come together. We needed to win all four of our
remaining games to qualify once again for the Super Bowl.
We won three and lost just the one in San Diego, the very
game for which Liverpool manager Bob Paisley and Youth
Development Officer Tom Saunders had made the trip to
watch me. At least Tony Waiters had the courtesy to
inform me and arranged for the two to meet me after the
game. I did not know at the time that down-to-earth Bob
Paisley was a man of few words but I was soon to find
out. 'Do you want to play for Liverpool?' he asked me after
the game. 'Yes,' I answered immediately. 'That will do for
me,' he replied and the meeting was over.

What was I supposed to do? Sit on my hands and wait
for something to happen? Go to England and wait on
Anfield's doorstep? None of those prospects particularly
thrilled me especially as the season was well under way at
Liverpool and the winter was settling in. Fortunately the
solution was right on my doorstep for my old playing
mate and fellow Rhodesian international Graham Boyle had
been staying with me and he suggested that I return with
him to Zimbabwe to play for the country now that we
were officially recognised by FIFA and scheduled to play
Cameroon in the World Cup qualifying competition with a
place in Spain beckoning. Graham assured me that the
Zimbabwe Federation would welcome me back with open
arms and I even paid for my own ticket happy in the
knowledge it would be fully refunded on the hero's return
home. You would have thought by then I would have
learned my lesson about aeroplane tickets!

5

In Reserve

I have often been asked why I committed myself to playing for Zimbabwe when I could have stayed on in Canada and qualified to play for them or even for England. As much as I would have loved to have gone to Mexico with Canada or, even better, with England, the simple answer is that Zimbabwe, for all my travels, is my home and always will be even though I am now the proud owner of a British passport. I have no real regrets despite the fact that I am never likely to be able to play international football again unless Zimbabwe changes its rules.

I have always suspected that when Graham Boyle came over to visit me in Canada, he did so with the full knowledge of the Zimbabwe Football Association and had been given a brief to get back for the crucial World Cup qualifying games against Cameroon. My suspicions were confirmed by the welcome I received when our plane touched down in Salisbury early in September. There to greet me was the National team's acting manager John Rugg along with his Rio Tinto international players, Sunday Marimo the Zimbabwe captain, my Rhodesian army friends and my old team-mates from the Callies. There were also lots of ordinary supporters who had followed my progress in Canada and England through the many newspaper reports. As far as they were concerned I was one of them who had gone abroad and made it as a professional footballer.

It was made pretty clear that I would be selected without question to play against the powerful West African side even though I would have no match practice as I did not have international clearance from Vancouver to play for anyone other than my country. I kept fit by training with Graham's team Arcadia United before we set off for the port of Douala, but the predictions were that we would be lucky to keep the score down to single figures while the local hero, goalkeeper Thomas N'Kono, was going to show Bruce Grobbelaar just why he had been voted 'African Player of the Year'. European players would have found this setting for a World Cup-tie somewhat incongruous. The pitch looked like a beach, and this impression was enhanced by the fact that the tree-lined port was in the midst of a tropical rainstorm when we arrived. It was the worst I have ever seen, yet when the rains stopped and we were able to train it was so sandy and dusty that our striker George Rollo built a sandcastle on the sidelines. If that wasn't enough, it was also discovered that the crossbars were too low to comply with FIFA regulations and that they needed raising before the arrival of the Nigerian officials and the FIFA observer from Ghana.

As well as the awful condition of the pitch we looked to be the poor relations for while our opponents had imported top Yugoslav coach Branko Zutic, we could not even afford suits or blazers having spent our budget on flying the squad to Douala. Our prospects of springing a surprise were considerably reduced by the fact that Graham confided in our other room-mate Byron Manuel (called 'the last Apache' because of his long, straight hair and high cheekbones) and me that he had no chance of being fit. The odds were stacked high against us and were not helped when the Nigerian referee gave advance warning of where his sympathies lay when, just half an hour before the kick-off, he demanded to see our passports as proof of identity and we all had to return to our hotel to collect them. When he booked Shacky Tauro for running offside we knew we were in for real problems.

Incredibly we held out for 80 minutes and might even have taken the lead but for a brilliant save from N'Kono who was to go on and earn himself an international reputation over the next two years. I had one of my best ever games in the thick, humid atmosphere and it was not until Zutic sent on two substitutes that our defence finally caved in as one of them, Manga Onguene, scored from close range. That goal produced one of the strangest experiences of my often bizarre football career. The 40,000-capacity crowd greeted it with a noise that sounded like a swarm of angry bees. It went on and on, ringing in my ears until I thought it was going to drive me completely crazy. It seemed to affect our entire defence and whereas we had been tight and disciplined for 80 minutes, our concentration went and we were no longer able to contain them. It led to a second goal from the other substitute, Gregoire Mbida, five minutes later when the linesman raised his flag and then changed his mind as the referee pointed to the centre spot.

However, our performance earned us a great deal of respect from the fans and the media. Suddenly we were being taken seriously. We had been described as a bunch of schoolboys after our first training session but we had performed like men and given ourselves an outside chance in the second leg in our own Rufaro Stadium a month later. You would certainly have sensed our optimism if you had seen our party after the game with Graham Boyle and me helping ourselves to a couple of bottles of French wine from the hotel bar, which is an expensive luxury in Africa, while the rest of the team distracted the attention of the poor barmen.

I had no time to drink it for no sooner had we arrived back in Salisbury than I took a telephone call from Tony Waiters telling me that he had agreed terms with Liverpool and asking me to meet him the next day at the Holiday Inn, Heathrow to drive to Birmingham where I was to sign for the club. By then the penny was beginning to drop and I said I would come as soon as I had an air ticket. It was arranged immediately and on Thursday, 21 October I met Bob Paisley again, along with the Liverpool Chairman John Smith and the General Secretary Peter Robinson. Vancouver, through Waiters and their General Manager Peter Bridge-water, were still making incredible demands on Liverpool but Bob Paisley told me not to worry and that it would all be sorted out. But I was not at all sure that I was being well represented and I told Liverpool that, though I was very keen to sign for them, I felt out of my depth in the negotiations and needed to consult my friend and lawyer from Canada, Ron Perrick whom, I knew, had experienced deals of a similar nature with professional ice hockey players and American footballers. They wanted to agree terms then and there, but with Ron on holiday in Hawaii and me due to play for Zimbabwe against Malawi in Blantyre on Sunday I did not feel that it was the right time to take such a big step.

I stopped in England long enough to watch Arsenal draw 2–2 with Sunderland at Highbury and then caught a plane back to Africa to walk straight into a strike by my fellow Zimbabwe players. It transpired that they had not been paid, as promised, for the game against Cameroon, that they would not be paid for playing in Malawi and that they were not properly insured against injury while with the National squad. Consequently they had pulled out of training and were refusing to travel to Blantyre for the African Nations Cup-tie. I joined them, wondering to myself what chance I had of recovering my airfares if they were not being paid their $50 for sweating blood in a world cup-tie. It needed an hour and a half meeting with the Minister of Sport, Dr Tichaona Jokonya, to sort out the matter and persuade the players to play on. Talks by then had been going on for eleven hours altogether and I had the misfortune of arriving right in the middle of it. The atmosphere was hardly bubbling especially as it had been discovered that the 'knot' in Graham Boyle's calf was a hairline fracture. He had been walking around on it, training and had even, with the help of an excessive number of Valium tablets, been playing before the trouble was finally diagnosed. No wonder they called him 'Ironman' in Africa!

The last time Zimbabwe had played in Malawi it had been Graham who had scored the winning goal which ended an incredible undefeated run of 16 years in their Kamuzu Stadium. When we turned up for the African Unity Cup-tie not only was I the only white man in the side but I had also grown a beard like Graham's and they were convinced that I was him and even called me 'Ironman', laughing when I told them I was playing in goal. They were open mouthed when I actually did appear in goal and were convinced that it was witchcraft when we scored the only goal of the match in exactly the same minute that Graham Boyle had scored in the previous game. Their supporters clapped us off with something akin to awe but the Malawi players had to run for their lives.

We drew the return match 1–1 in Rufaro to clinch our place in the next round against Zambia but, before that, we had the return with Cameroon back at the Rufaro in the now renamed capital of Zimbabwe, Harare. It seemed a good time to collect the money they owed me for my airfares and other expenses. I had been living off the charity of friends and relatives for long enough. But, despite their previous assurances, they refused to repay me the $2,000 and I promptly withdrew from the World Cup squad. The news came as a bombshell to the rest of the squad and within 24 hours they had threatened to pull out as well unless I was paid. There was a hasty meeting with the ZIFA President John Madzima and treasurer Michael Mboma when they gave me $200 for the Malawi game and a few more promises. I hadn't got what I wanted and I knew that my chances of getting my money back after the game against Cameroon were negligible but I admired the players and coaches so much that I did not want to let them or our supporters down. I decided to let it rest, say nothing and play the match.

Every footballer's ambition must be to play in a World Cup final and we came desperately close that day in Harare to going to Spain. The game was played in a storm with the thunder rolling overhead and the lightning illuminating the frenzied, capacity crowd. John Rugg had told the team before the kick-off to throw caution to the wind and to attack with everything we had. It meant we were dreadfully stretched at the back but, somehow, we stopped their continual breaks and when I did not stop them, captain Sunday Marimo or defender Oliver Kateya would kick the ball off the line. With the ball skidding about in the mud and us going forward at every opportunity we should have massacred them, especially after scoring in the first half, but their goal bore a charmed life as we hit every inch of the woodwork and every part of the goalkeeper's body. There were a few tears mingling with the raindrops as we came off the pitch but they would have been more plentiful had we known just how far Cameroon would go. In African terms Cameroon is a rich country, which can afford a top foreign coach and to bring back their players from the French and Spanish Leagues for their games. They went on to beat Zaire 6–2 on aggregate and in the final round won 2–0 against the favourites Morocco in Kenitra and then 2–1 at home in Yaoundé in front of 120,000 fans.

It was galling to hear them say that their toughest hurdle in reaching Spain was beating Zimbabwe and it did not help when, in Group One, they drew 0–0 with both Peru and Poland in La Coruña before holding the eventual World Champions Italy to a 1–1 draw in Vigo. Poland won the group with the Italians edging out the African qualifiers only on the slenderest of goal differentials, Italy 2 for and 2 against to Cameroon's 1–1. The world is full of ifs, and instead of dreaming of castles in Spain I set off for Vancouver on my open return ticket to play in the first season of the American Indoor League. It was fun enough renewing friendships around the States but too much of that football would have left me crippled. Liverpool, still pursuing me, would have been horrified to see the damage diving around on those surfaces inflicts. It cost me the points of both elbows as I rounded them off by chipping away bits of bone. It was so bad that they had to draw off the fluid before each game.

Thankfully we resumed training for the normal games in January under the new managership of the former Eire international and West Bromwich Albion manager Johnny Giles. He took us to Southern Ireland for a pre-season warm-up and it was while we were staying at the Montrose Hotel that he told me that he was more than happy with the presence of his former Leeds United colleague David Harvey and that if any club wanted me he would let me go. The hint was barely necessary and when we returned to Vancouver it was to start packing and to reopen negotiations with Liverpool. With Ron Perrick in attendance and Giles ready to sell there were no hitches this time as Bob Paisley explained that he wanted me as cover for England goalkeeper Ray Clemence and they agreed to pay £250,000 for me. The signing formalities were to be completed in Liverpool and I flew to Heathrow on 16 March, certain that I could avoid the cells this time but still wondering what I was to do about a work permit. I shouldn't have worried for Liverpool had already had some experience in this department after gaining permission from the Home Office for the Israeli star Avi Cohen, or at least they should have done.

Officially I was supposed to have entered the country with my work permit and to overcome this it had been arranged for me to fly straight out to Paris, stay for 24 hours and to re-enter with all my documents properly stamped. Naturally enough Liverpool did not want to publicise the event and they told me that if, when I arrived at Anfield to pick up my tickets, there were reporters and photographers around, I should ask the taxi to turn round and head back to the Adelphi Hotel without being seen. It was real cloak and dagger stuff and, sure enough, when we arrived in the Liverpool car park the place was alive with reporters, photographers and television crews as the club were about to sign another player with strong South African connections, Craig Johnston. He had come to the club by way of Australia and Middlesbrough, which was almost as complicated a route as my own. The taxi driver must have thought me raving mad when I told him to turn around and take me back to the hotel where, as per instructions, I waited for the club to deliver the tickets before going to Manchester's Ringway Airport with orders to meet Dr Peter Heuith at the other end. But not even Liverpool could cover every eventuality where Bruce Grobbelaar and airports are concerned and, sure enough, when I landed at Charles de Gaulle the immigration officer demanded my visa for entry into France. Of course, I didn't have one. I tried to explain that I was to meet Paris's most eminent dentist and that I was staying for just one night before returning to England. He would not budge and I was eventually rescued by an English businessman who told me to ask for a 24-hour shopper's visa which was issued on the spot.

It took two hours to extricate myself from the red tape but Dr Heuith was still patiently waiting for me. He was so well known in the French capital that he was known as the 'Dentist of Paris' and both his wife and his son were in the same business. They were a tremendous family but it was disconcerting every time you opened your mouth to wonder whether they were peering in and finding things wrong. Unfortunately they had arranged to go to a private party at the Café de Paris that night but the doctor told his Italian chauffeur to take me to the Crazy Horse for the evening where we had a great time. My papers in order, I returned to Liverpool for the final few weeks of the season ready to share the reserve goalkeeping duties with Steve Ogrizovic who eventually went on to prove his ability by helping to keep Coventry City in the First Division when all appeared lost.

I was staying at a local hotel and was booked in there for three months. It was more like Colditz Castle and I was worried that if I died of a heart attack I would lie there for months undiscovered. If the chambermaids saw you asleep in bed, they would tiptoe out and not bother to return until the next day. I lasted for exactly three weeks before my old mate from Crewe, Bob Scott, invited me to stay with him in Wrexham until I found a place of my own. I think Bob was worried I would turn into another George Best as I would go anywhere and do anything to avoid staying in that hotel for longer than was absolutely necessary. It was good advice for out of sight was out of mind. I had only to be seen in a pub having a half of beer for someone to ring up and tell the club what an old drunk they had signed.

The Scotts invited me to stay for two weeks. I was there for two months, making the hour-long trip into Merseyside every day. I liked it so much that I bought a little cottage of my own just down the road in a place called Gwynfrwn, near Coedpoeth four miles out of Wrexham. I was lucky with my house because the owner wanted to sell her possessions as well and make as much money as she could to travel around the United States. All I had to bring was my clothes, the rest was there from carpets, curtains and bed linen to television, washing machine and even cutlery. It was perfect and with some of the money I had saved in Canada I bought a lovely white Granada.

I was 'Jack the Lad', opening the doors of my little cottage with its sensational view of the Welsh hills to all and sundry — and how they turned up! Every flight from Africa seemed to bring a house guest and more often than not it was an airline stewardess named Charmaine and each time she stayed, she would leave behind more and more of her personal belongings. It was only when I telephoned my mother that I realised just how much this young lady was sticking her foot in my cottage door for every time she returned to Zimbabwe she would visit Mum and take her a box of chocolates. Enough was enough and I told her that her clothes must go because they were cramping my style, and people were beginning to think I had a wife tucked away. But you can't win. Mum moaned that her supply of chocolates had dried up while Charmaine switched her attentions to my mate Bob Scott.

My appearances for Liverpool at the time were limited because of the brilliant Ray Clemence in the first team and the giant Steve Ogrizovic sharing the reserve duties. I eventually made my début in the mini-derby against Everton. Even that is an occasion on Merseyside for though it often clashes with the real thing there are certain dyed-in-the-wool supporters who would not go on the other team's ground and prefer to watch the second teams play on familiar territory. It was certainly a good atmosphere and we won with two goals from Colin Russell while I was pleased to keep a clean sheet. The only problem was that I now faced two weeks of inactivity and I had itchy fingers. Zimbabwe had been in touch with me to ask if there was any chance of me being available for an African Nations Cup game against Zambia. The club officials were not at all happy about the idea and told ZIFA as much but when I asked our manager Bob Paisley he saw no reason why not as I was faced with a free fortnight from competitive football and he gave permission as long as I was fully insured.

I should have said no as ZIFA still owed me a lot of money but playing for my country was still far more important than a few hundred dollars and, once again, I was airborne and heading back for Africa, this time as a Liverpool player. I missed the Friday flight and arrived late on the Saturday for the game next day which was considered of such importance to the country's footballing future that both President Canaan Banana and Prime Minister Robert Mugabe were going to be in attendance. The only problem was that the Kenyan officials for the big game were even later than me and, in desperation, ZIFA chartered an aircraft to collect a Malawi referee and his two linesmen to stand in. In the event they must have wished they hadn't bothered as our forwards spurned every chance while I, at the back, made an error in the only goal of the game. The only consolation was that Zimbabwe had an opportunity to put matters right a week later when they were to meet the Mozambique 'B' team in the semi-finals of a competition called Zone Six. I suddenly became interested when I heard that it was going to be played in my old stadium, Barbourfields in Bulawayo, giving me the opportunity to see a lot of old friends and, of course, my family. To my amazement Bob Paisley, in a marvellous gesture, overruled all objections to give me permission to extend my stay another two weeks.

We won the semi-final 6-1 in Bulawayo on the Sunday and then returned straight to the Rufaro Stadium for the final against Malawi the very next day. I can just imagine the dressing-room comments back in England if they ever had to play the FA Cup semi-final and final on successive days but it certainly did not seem to worry Zimbabwe as we clinched the Independence Cup Competition with another four goals, without conceding one ourselves. It put us in good heart for the second leg of the game against Zambia in Lusaka's Independence Stadium, particularly when we read newspaper reports that their team had held a protest meeting claiming they were starving because there was not enough money available to buy decent food. Hungry or not they still managed to beat us 2–0 with Egyptian referee Hussein Fahmy refusing us two penalties. Although I had now conceded three goals with two defeats in four games, I returned to Liverpool for the final two reserve games of the season full of confidence after the African media had heaped superlatives on me.

My final two reserve games for Liverpool comprised a 1–1 draw with Leeds reserves and a one-goal win over Bolton Wanderers at Burnden Park. That, as it transpired, was one of the most important games I have played, though I did not know it at the time. Bolton had former England striker Brian Kidd playing up front and I was giving him plenty of lip, telling him that he was getting too old for the game and should hand in his boots for a pension book. It was beginning to get to him when he drove a ball hard for the top corner. I not only saved it but held on as well and, as I picked myself up, I grinned and told him he would have to do better if he was going to beat me. He responded with another fierce drive for the other corner and I saved it again and I knew I had won the battle when he began to rant and rave, shouting 'Get that gorilla out of goal.' I know that the reserve team coach was impressed by my performance and went back to Anfield saying so. It put me on such a high that I went rather over the top. I had already fooled about with Ray Clemence in training sessions, telling him that he was too old and to make way for a younger man but I then went too far and was quoted in the newspapers as telling him to move over and that I was going to take his place next season.

Some nerve! He was not only one of the best goalkeepers in the world at the time but had just helped Liverpool to win both the European and League Cups and to finish runners-up in the League Championship. My three games for the reserves did not even qualify me for a part in the Central League Championship. God knows what Ray must have thought of me at the time but I do know that another Liverpool player, Howard Gayle, was none too keen on me. There is always a lot of chat and winding up in the Liverpool dressing room and the first-team players, quick to pick up my 'Jungle Man' nickname and my military

service background, warned the coloured Howard Gayle
that I would be after him. Instead of laughing about it
Howie became edgy and it did not help when the Olympic
Decathlon Champion Daley Thompson came to train with
us. Daley is not only the world's best all-round athlete but
is also a useful footballer. Howie, however, was not
impressed and reckoned that he could outsprint the
Londoner.

We set up the race and Terry McDermott was asked to
stand on the halfway line to act as judge in case it was a
close finish while I was appointed the starter. It was all
very serious until I said: 'Ready, steady, pick up your lips,
GO!' Daley promptly collapsed in fits of laughter but
Howard was not at all amused and found nothing to smile
at. The story must have done the rounds for even Graham
Boyle telephoned me from Africa to say that he had not
realised what a racist I had become. Howie tried to get his
own back in training but I could look after myself and with
my next tackle I slid 20 yards in the mud to take him and
the ball. He cursed me and I joked that if he were in the
bush I would shoot him. The funny thing is that I rather
liked Howard Gayle and if he hadn't carried around a great
big chip on his shoulder he could have become an English
international. He showed his true qualities when he came
on in a European Cup semi-final away to Bayern Munich
and won the game for Liverpool. If he were to allow that
ability to take over and express himself in football terms
he could still be a truly outstanding player.

I was hardly around long enough to make too many
friends at Anfield that season though I liked my fellow
reserve goalkeeper 'Oggi' who was somewhat of a gentle
giant and also a good cricketer. There was also David
Johnson who was a tremendous encouragement to me in
those days, telling me to be my own man whatever anyone

else said to the contrary, and the Israeli international Avi Cohen. I suppose my affinity with Avi was due to us both being foreigners and when I asked him what advice he could give from his experiences at Anfield, he replied in all seriousness: 'Don't trust those Jocks. They are all cheats.' Avi was having a dig at our Scottish players, skipper Graeme Souness, Alan Hansen, Kenny Dalglish and Frank McGarvey, for the way they played in the club five-a-side games. These were always taken very seriously at Liverpool particularly when the Scots took on the English. They would give it all they had and any dubious decisions were always claimed by the Jocks. Kenny Dalglish was easily the worst; urged on by the fierce competitive nature of his permanent room-mate Graeme Souness. It was sound advice from Avi and I have always passed it on, 'Watch out for those Jocks!'

But there was scarcely time to consider the niceties of race relations in Liverpool for the season was over and those who were not off to Spain for the World Cup Finals were heading for various sunspots around the world to make the most of their close seasons. My own problems in that area were resolved when I received an invitation from my lawyer friend Ron Perrick to stay in one of his apartments in Hawaii. I didn't need to be asked twice and caught a flight to the island of Maui. It was paradise. I had my own apartment next to Ron's and his family's which overlooked the 14th tee and had a view of the Pacific Ocean. A pack of six beers on the beach for breakfast followed by a run with fitness fanatic Ron before lunch and a game of golf after it. I settled into this idyllic routine contemplating the changes in my life and looking forward to learning quickly about the English game in the Liverpool reserves with the knowledge that as good as Ray Clemence was he could not carry on forever and I, nine years his junior, wanted to be ready to replace him.

It was on one of our daily rounds of golf that our game was suddenly interrupted as we passed our apartments on the 14th tee with Ron's eldest son running down to tell us that there was a long-distance call. Ron took it as I carried on, practising a few swings. I was just on my downswing when Ron, with perfect timing, shouted: 'Liverpool have just sold Ray Clemence to Spurs.' My ball went careering out of bounds and people making their way across the course to the beach looked on in total amazement as the golfer who had just lost his ball began to leap up and down screaming with delight. Ron, always sharp where money is concerned, made me take three off the tee.

I did not care, and was totally elated. My heart was pounding and I could hardly wait to get back to Liverpool to start the season, play for the Champions and help them win the European Cup. I was not at all daunted by my lack of experience in that class of football. I did not doubt my own ability for a minute nor did I consider the prospect that Liverpool would not believe me ready and buy a replacement. After all hadn't they just invested £250,000 in me. Beers for breakfast were now out as I resumed training with a run in the morning, weights at the Sheraton in the afternoon and another run along the beach as the sun set in the evening. I was going to go back bursting with health and fitness for my First Division début. I even managed to stay celibate but that was probably only because the island attracted honeymooners rather than single girls though I lived in hope and visited various nightspots regularly. If I had known what lay in store for me I would have been a little more anxious, nowhere near as cocky and far less arrogant. I was about to be plunged in at the deep end.

6

In at the
Deep End

It is said that I cost Liverpool £250,000 when they signed me from Vancouver Whitecaps in Canada – and a further £500,000 when my errors caused unexpected defeats in two successive European Cups to unfancied European sides. The euphoria I had felt in Hawaii disappeared within weeks as I discovered that playing First Division football was more difficult than anything I had ever experienced. The pressure was immense and, because I was colourful, unconventional and largely unknown, I was not readily accepted in some quarters and and every mistake I made was pounced on with great relish. I was nicknamed 'The Clown' in some newspaper headlines and was the frequent subject of slow-motion replays on television whenever I dropped a cross or fluffed a clearance. I put on a brave face, joked with the fans and threw away the more obscene of the poison pen letters, but inside I was wondering what on earth was going on.

In truth I became very depressed and sensitive about the publicity I was receiving, even going to the extent of buying every daily newspaper to find out which journalists

liked me and which didn't. I should, of course, have ignored
it and learned from experienced professionals like Phil Neal,
who, in his remarkable career won more than most
footballers dream about and yet took continual criticism in
the media, particularly when he played for England. Phil
told me that if I had to read the newspapers, I wasn't to
bother with the back pages and if I did to leave it until
Thursday when they carried the fixtures for the weekend
and the up-to-date League tables. It was good advice but I
could not resist reading about the team and myself and I
always had to look when we lost to see whether I was to
be blamed again. It may sound a little paranoid but I was
sure that certain of the sporting journalists based in Liverpool disliked me because I was not English. I began to feel
my whole game was being undermined and that my
confidence was being drained away. There was a time I
even contemplated asking Bob Paisley to let me go but,
fortunately, it never quite reached that stage. Instead I
telephoned Harry Gregg, the former Manchester United
and Northern Ireland goalkeeper, whom I had found so
helpful last time I was in England with Crewe.

I had asked Harry if he could meet me and tell me what
I was doing wrong. He said that there was no need for
that and we could sort it out on the telephone. We
discussed games that had troubled me, the positions I had
been in when I had made my mistakes and where Harry
would have been. He also told me to forget that I was the
new boy behind an experienced defence and to be in sole
command of my penalty area, to demand the ball when I
thought it was mine and to be my own man. Harry Gregg
helped me enormously in those first two desperate seasons
when everything could have collapsed around my ears. It
was reassuring to know that such a calm, knowledgeable
man was at the end of the telephone whenever I needed

him. Others helped too. Bob Paisley was a constant source of support. He had faith in me and understood how difficult it was for a young goalkeeper to be plunged in at the deep end in the way I was when Ray Clemence signed for Spurs. Some of the older players rallied round as well, particularly Phil Thompson who told me to take no notice of the criticisms. Just talking to them was a help.

Liverpool have never been noted as particularly good starters. Bob Paisley always used to say that the Championship was for stayers and not sprinters but, even by Liverpool's standards, it was a bad beginning to the 1981 – 82 season as we opened with a defeat away to Wolves and, by Boxing Day, we had also gone down at Ipswich. Worse still, we had lost at Anfield to Manchester United, Manchester City and Southampton and dropped points to Middlesbrough, Aston Villa, and Swansea City at home as well. This is what really upset the supporters and it reached the stage where I was happier playing away from home. The strange thing was that I was not playing particularly badly at the time. Maybe my reputation stemmed from our pre-season matches where I had shown off and fooled around, getting up to antics that the crowds in Canada, North America and even Africa had loved. I would walk on my hands, spin the ball on the end of my finger, run it up my back and over my head before clearing, and generally trying to entertain the crowd. It did, but not, however, my team-mates or the coaching staff, and I was warned in no uncertain terms not to clown around for not only did it jeopardise my concentration but our own defenders' as well.

The Kop, which has long appreciated good goalkeepers whichever team they have played for, gave me a warm welcome and seemed to be on my side even when raised eyebrows and dark scowls from my defenders suggested that not all my own team-mates were completely with me.

I did have a few horrors, of which strangely the worst was at Coventry when we recorded our first away win of the season. We conceded a goal in the first 30 seconds when I dropped a high centre and after that I had an attack of the jitters and couldn't hold anything at all. With two giants like Garry Thompson and Mark Hateley sniffing around I was lucky to get away with it and we recovered to win with goals from Alan Kennedy and a Terry McDermott penalty.

In complete contrast was our away win at Nottingham Forest in early December when I had a great game in a 2 – 0 win and, for once, I even got away with a couple of 'brainstorms' as I raced 20 yards out of my area to clear one ball and headed away another as I took Liverpool at their word that I was to act as a sweeper behind the back four. I also made useful saves from Juergen Rober, Justin Fashanu and Mark Proctor. Bob Paisley, who had supported me all along, seemed to enjoy it as much as I did and this man of few words came out of the dressing room afterwards to praise me to some of those who had been giving me a hard time. 'Grobbelaar,' he said, 'was near perfect, he made four saves that were out of this world. I doubt if even Peter Shilton or Ray Clemence could have made a couple of them.

'His ability is unquestionable. I have never had any major worries about Bruce and I knew that he would be all right with a little experience. I have said all along that if he was the only problem we had defensively I would not be too concerned. He has settled down in six months which is something of a bonus to us as it often takes a goalkeeper two or three years.'

One or two of my critics must have been writhing when Peter Shilton iced the cake for me, saying: 'Liverpool would have been dead and buried by half-time if it had not been

Above left Showing an early aptitude for my lessons aged seven at Rynfeld Primary School!

Above right My father, Hendrik Grobbelaar, at my parents' wedding

Below Apart from football, I represented my country at junior level in both cricket and baseball. In this school group Lawrence de Grandholmme, later a Zimbabwean International, is seated third from the left in the front row; wicketkeeper Grobbelaar is fifth from the left

Above The Salisbury Callies' Under 16 team. I'm in the back row, fourth from the left, and Graham 'Iron Man' Boyle is on my right. The captain, Ian Noble, is in the centre of the front row

Below In the army. A new recruit feeling his way in totally different surroundings. Private Grobbelaar is second from the right in the back row

Above My first honour with Liverpool when we beat Spurs 3–1 in the 1982 Milk Cup final

Below These were the joyous scenes which greeted the victorious treble winners from their return after the European Cup against Roma in 1984. A year later the scenes were very different

Above left Jan Molby, Liverpool's talented Danish midfield player who came through under Dalglish

Above right Ian Rush, one of the world's great strikers

Below right Mark Lawrenson, Britain's top defender who needed a World Cup to display his full potential

Below left Steve Nicol, the young Scot with a great future ahead of him

Above Graeme Souness, who was a major influence on the team at Liverpool and whose loss to Sampdoria it took us a year to recover from

Below left Craig Johnston in his other role as photographer

Below right One of the games that persuaded Liverpool to buy Michael Robinson from our bogey team Brighton and Hove Albion

The various faces of Bruce Grobbelaar

Left After feeling guilty about our early exit in two previous European Cups, I helped redeem myself in Rome in 1984. No one was going to take it away from me even after our all night party to celebrate

Right With my wife Debbie and daughter Tahli

for their goalkeeper. Some of his saves were unbelievable.'
Even I began to think I had sorted it all out by then and I
was ready to show my talents on the world platform when
Liverpool flew off before Christmas to play the South
American club champions Flamengo in the National Stadium
in Tokyo. I had the in-built advantage of being able to step
straight off an aircraft and into a football match without
suffering jet-lag.

The only problem was that I had almost failed to make
it at all. Bob Scott, my old mate at Crewe, had been a pillar
of support. He had been a young player at Liverpool and
knew the ropes. He told me to keep my head down, play
the game and say nothing. We used to disappear after
games, drive into Wales and sit and talk the action through
at the Plough Inn. He knew my frustrations, the difficulty I
had in communicating with the back four of Neal, Thompson,
Lawrenson and Hansen. Bob also gave me some very
practical advice when he warned me that living in my
Welsh village I was in danger of being snowed in and thus
needed suitable transport. I bought a jeep that was instantly
christened 'Tonka Toy' but without it I would not have
gone to Tokyo and I would have been in big trouble with
the club. I enjoyed a good night out in Liverpool on the
Tuesday before the Tokyo game and by the time I returned
to my cottage the first flakes had already begun to fall. It
became heavier and I decided that I had better not risk
going to bed. I had something to eat, packed my things
and decided on a very early start. But, by the time I was
ready to leave, the snow had swept over the field and
drifted up against my front door. I could not even open it
and had to get a shovel to dig my way to my jeep, or at
least to the one corner that was sticking out of the snow.

Fortunately Graham Boyle was staying with me and,
despite his amazement at seeing snow, he helped me clear

a path. Just before we started off Bob Scott telephoned to say that the Wrexham–Chester road that I needed to use to get to Liverpool's Speke Airport was completely blocked. I was seized with panic. My first trip and I was going to miss it. Steve Ogrizovic was going to play, he would be brilliant and I would lose my place. The traffic was tailing back for five miles. There was only one thing for it and that was to drive down the wrong side of the road and hope for the best. Cars hooted, everyone gave us black looks and Graham looked as though he wished that the ground would swallow him up. Sure enough, the next minute there were blue flashing lights, sirens and angry policemen who wanted to know what we were doing. I explained my predicament and their attitude immediately changed. They told us to follow them and away we went with our personal escort. Even so we were an hour late and arrived just as the team were boarding a coach for Manchester Airport because nothing could take off from Liverpool. I was soon on my way to Tokyo and a white-faced Graham Boyle was on his way back to snow-bound Wales with the jeep.

We didn't stay long in Tokyo but we made the most of it. Our guide showed us round the Japanese capital and introduced us to the geisha girls, something I would recommend to any young man who was having trouble relaxing. I was excited at the prospect of facing the likes of Leandro, Junior, Marinho, Nunes and Zico but it seemed that my enthusiasm was not totally shared by everyone else in the squad. It was my first 'final' for Liverpool and, naturally, I wanted to put my problems behind me on such a big occasion, but I dropped a shot from Zico, Nunes scored twice and Adilio added another and we went in at half-time three down and already beaten. Bob Paisley laid into the team for their casual attitude and, with the prospect

of a really humiliating defeat, we pulled ourselves together
and though we did not score, neither did they. Even so I
was a disappointed young man for I had had visions of
helping Liverpool become the first British side to win the
World Club Championship.

Worse was to follow for when I came off the pitch Bob
Paisley took me to one side to tell me that my father had
died a few days earlier. My mother had informed the club
but asked them not to tell me until after the game. It was
thoughtful and she had done what she considered best for
me. I do not know how I would have reacted if I had
known before the game. The club told me not to worry
and that they had already made all the travel arrangements
for me to return to Africa for the funeral. It was typical of
the club's thoughtfulness and organisational ability – though
I must admit that I did not realise that they were going to
take the air fare out of my wages.

I travelled with the team as far as Paris. On the flight I
thought the best bet was to get my head down on the
longest leg of the journey and found three vacant seats
right in front of the film screen. I took a couple of sleeping
pills to make sure and made myself comfortable on the
floor in front of the seats. I suppose I had been asleep for
about half an hour when an Indian gentleman sitting across
the aisle shook me and asked me to move. I awoke from
my drug-induced sleep and demanded to know if I was
blocking his view of the screen or was in his way in any
manner at all. He admitted I was not and I told him to go
away, though not quite in those words, and went back to
sleep. An hour late I was shaken awake again. This time it
was the senior Japanese steward who apologised profusely
but said that someone had complained and would I please
move. By this time I was wide awake and very, very angry,
giving the Indian gentleman a withering look as I went

past to the back of the plane to join Terry McDermott, Doc Johnson and a couple of journalists, who were having a drink, telling them the strange tale of my new acquaintance and my lack of sleep. Terry Mac was all for going back and sorting him out. He needn't have bothered for suddenly the gentleman himself arrived to say he was sorry for the trouble he had caused and to explain that he was upset because the way I was lying, my feet were pointing at the taped-up locker above his seat which contained a figure of Buddha. Far from being placated, Terry wanted to throw him and his statue off the plane over Alaska and the little chap wisely hurried back to his seat, glancing fearfully over his shoulder.

I left the team in Paris where I picked up the tickets and telephoned my relatives to say I was on my way. The funeral was to be on Thursday and the club arranged for me to meet them at the Holiday Inn, Marble Arch before the game against Spurs at White Hart Lane on the Saturday. Flying first class helped a lot particularly as, at last, I was able to sleep on the way to Johannesburg.

My father had known that he was dying. I realised now why he had telephoned me a few weeks earlier to ask if he could borrow 1,000 rand to help pay some debts. I asked him how much he really needed and wired him the necessary £3,500. That was not much more than a month before he died.

Funerals are never the best of times but this was particularly difficult. Dad's family were Dutch Reformists and he had become a Mormon in later life. Thus there were two priests presiding and three wives, though the second was turned away because she had put their two daughters up for adoption. The whole family was present as Dad was buried in the family plot and it was strange thinking that that was where I would probably finish up. I was very sad but also pleased that my father had turned to me at the end and I knew that not only had my cash helped pay off what he owed but that it had also helped to take care of my half-sisters' schooling and that there was even some left to put towards a decent headstone. It would have been nice to have spent some time with my family but my professional duties called and I left straight after the funeral, promising to return in the summer. I was not in the best frame of mind when I headed from Heathrow to the centre of London and it was not helped when I checked in at the Holiday Inn to discover that the game had been called off and that no one was there. I could have had an extra couple of days with my family after all.

One of the biggest problems I faced at Liverpool was that the defence, the foundation on which their past success had been built, was not working together. Whether it was because of me I do not know but, while we were struggling to find our form in the League, we were making rather good progress in the Cup competitions. At home we were doing exceptionally well in the defence of our League Cup, having seen off: Exeter City by an 11-goal aggregate; Middlesbrough 4–1; Arsenal and Barnsley after replays; and then Ipswich in a two-legged semi-final which we clinched with a two-goal victory at Portman Road.

Our confidence was sky high as we went into February already assured of a place at Wembley in the League Cup Final and with five successive League victories behind us. We were also in the fifth round of the FA Cup having crushed Swansea by four goals and Sunderland by three, both away from home. Europe was also looking good, for we had been given a nice easy start in the north of Finland where we had won a scrappy game against Oulu with a Kenny Dalglish goal and then the second leg at home with a runaway seven-goal victory. AZ 67 Alkmaar, the Dutch

Champions, were next with the away leg first. My Dutch, which had been brushed up with Rudi Krol in Vancouver, came in useful. We drew the first leg 2–2 after leading 2–0 and were heading for a 2–1 victory at Anfield when I punched a cross clear. Everyone had come off the line except Phil Thompson and the ball hit the crossbar, rebounded off his back and went in. I was roundly blamed for that one, somewhat unjustly I thought, but Alan Hansen got me off the hook by scoring a late, solo winner. We had reached the quarter-finals.

However, just when we all thought we had it right, things began to go badly again. We went out of the FA Cup against Chelsea at Stamford Bridge with a display which lacked our usual character and then three days later we lost a League game at Swansea where we had won a cup-tie by four goals just a month earlier. We managed to only scramble past CSKA Sofia of Bulgaria with a Ronnie Whelan goal and the imminent League Cup final against Tottenham looked distinctly dodgy as we lost at home to Brighton. The bad feeling against me was building up again while my room-mate Craig Johnston was in much the same boat having had only a handful of games and more often than not being substitute. We were hardly able to console each other. But we had the boost of a 5-1 win over Stoke four days before Wembley. I needed something like that because the media were putting me under pressure by the inevitable comparisons with Ray Clemence as our former goalkeeper who would be in the opposite goal for Spurs. Losing in those circumstances was unthinkable and this was the first time Clem had faced Liverpool. I suppose the strain on him was almost as great, but this was a time to be selfish.

At the time I was going steady with a pretty young girl named Janet whose parents had a pub near Goodison Park

called the 'Strawberry Tavern'. They were all Everton fans
and constantly used to wind me up and it was there that I
made the bet that if we won I would walk the length of
Wembley pitch on my hands. If someone could have
guaranteed that victory I would have done it naked. I
feared the worst when Steve Archibald put Tottenham in
front but we fought our way back into the game with Ian
Rush scoring one and Ronnie Whelan becoming the hero
with two, the winning goal coming in extra time. It was a
wonderful feeling and I didn't mind making a fool of myself
with that long walk on my hands. That was my first medal
for Liverpool and I will always have happy memories of it.
I loved Wembley Stadium at first sight. It is an inspiring
venue and, for no reason I can put my finger on, it is
especially so for goalkeepers. This is confirmed by the
number of tremendous performances from foreign goalkeepers who play above their form against England.
Certainly the atmosphere is great but then so it is for
everyone else on the pitch. The only simple explanation I
can think of for it helping goalkeepers is that the markings
of the pitch are so good that you always know exactly
where you are in relationship to your goal and, consequently, you tend to get your angles right and can be in
the correct place at the correct time.

I thought that win would lay all the ghosts. My hope
lasted exactly four days when we lost 2–0 after extra time
to the Bulgarians of CSKA Sofia in the Levski Stadium. In
the end it was all put down to my one error but though I
accept the responsibility I still maintain that it was partly
due to an Austrian referee named Frans Woehrer. The
problems at my end would never have arisen had he kept
up with play early on when Ian Rush scored a perfectly
good goal which their goalkeeper Georgi Velinov pulled
back from a long way over his line. Incredibly the Austrian

waved play on and we were once again clinging to Ronnie Whelan's first-leg goal instead of having the added security of an away strike which would have left them needing three to beat us.

Even so we looked like winning until I came hurtling off my line for a cross I could have stood and watched. I missed it and Bulgarian international Mladenov was left unchecked to nod the ball into the empty net. That goal changed the direction of the game. The referee sent off Mark Lawrenson for defending himself against a serious assault and we were left to face extra time with ten men against an increasingly violent team. Terry McDermott went off with an injury and we hit the woodwork three times before sloppy defending let in Mladenov for their winner. I was distraught and it was of little consolation when Bob Paisley was sympathetic, telling me that it was my first year in Europe and I had to learn that it was not necessary to come for everything. He then told the gentlemen of the Press that it was the worst example of officiating he had seen in Europe since the infamous game against Inter Milan back in 1965.

All my good work had been undone. People in football can be very unforgiving. However, with hindsight, I would say that my first season in Division One at the age of 23 was fairly successful. We went on from our League Cup success at Wembley to win the League Championship. After being ninth in January and losing to Brighton in March we stormed off to clinch the Championship with a 3–1 victory over Tottenham at Anfield. From that defeat by Brighton we did not lose a single League match and I kept 12 clean sheets out of 16 games to finish with only 32 goals against me, which was the second-best record in the First Division behind Gary Bailey at Manchester United who had finished third in the League with 29 goals. If a

Cup and League double is failure then I hate to think what is demanded for success!

I went off on the usual close season tour and then back to Africa to see my relatives. I returned to Wales and astonished Bob Scott when I telephoned him in the early hours of the morning to tell him that I had just become engaged to Janet. He couldn't believe it and asked when the wedding was going to be. 'Oh,' I said, 'I only asked her if she would like to get engaged, I never mentioned marriage. We will have to see how it goes.' It was another of my spur-of-the-moment decisions and, while I enjoyed Janet's company, it led to one of the worst moves of my life. The club had been trying to persuade me to live nearer the city ever since I had been snowed in before Tokyo, while Janet didn't like Wales and wanted us to live in Liverpool. I bought a show house on an estate in Liverpool and spent the next few years trying to sell it so that I could move out of the city again. Janet and I eventually split up after a visit to Zimbabwe. Having complained about Wales, she then expressed her dislike of Africa and from that moment on I somehow knew we would never be married and our affair gradually tailed off to end in some sadness and more than a little bitterness. I accept my full share of the responsibility for I must have been hard to live with while I was going through my difficult time.

I was more concerned at the time with establishing myself as Liverpool's number-one goalkeeper and proving the critics wrong. I resolved to keep a cheerful face but also to try and maintain my concentration. I still believed that entertaining the crowd was important but I decided to do my bits and pieces either when we were a couple of goals up or when the pressure was off. It was particularly important during this season because, four days before our opening game against West Bromwich Albion, our manager

Bob Paisley announced that he was to retire from the management at the end of the season. Bob was the most successful manager of all time yet despite winning European crowns, League titles and Milk Cups he had never won the FA Cup and everyone naturally assumed that the Cup would be our farewell present. Our skipper Graeme Souness was quick to announce that we would play as we had always done and take it a game at a time. But in truth we all fancied giving Bob the FA Cup, while my secret longing was to make up for the previous year by returning the European Cup to Anfield. We blew both! And once again I was blamed.

In the FA Cup we began with a 2–1 win at Blackburn and followed it up with a comfortable two-goal win over Stoke in the fourth round but then we came up against our bogey team Brighton and Hove Albion and, on a Sunday afternoon, we went out in front of the disbelieving majority of the 44,868 crowd. No one had fancied playing on Sunday but the game had been switched to avoid the big tie at Goodison Park on Saturday when Everton ended Tottenham's great run in the competition. Obviously our name was never meant to be on that trophy for though we came back to equalise Gerry Ryan's goal from our substitute Craig Johnston, Phil Neal missed a penalty after former Liverpool player Jimmy Case had restored Brighton's lead.

If that was a disaster it was nothing compared with our elimination from the European Cup. We began our campaign well enough with a 4–1 win against the Irishmen of Dundalk with, suitably, their countryman Ronnie Whelan scoring twice. He also scored the only goal of the second leg at Anfield to give us a safe passage into the next round to face JK Helsinki. The standard of European Cup football, as at international level, rises with every passing season and we were firmly put in our place when we lost by a single goal in Finland before regaining our form to beat them by five clear goals in the second leg with Kennedy scoring two and Neal, Johnston and Dalglish adding the others. With the European Cup and the Cup Winner's Cup having one round fewer than the UEFA Cup it meant that we were able to concentrate on winning our third successive League title for four months and resume our challenge in March against the Polish side Widzew Lodz. It should have been a doddle. The Solidarity movement was at its peak and Poland was in a state of emergency, with a shortage of essential foods. The Polish champions had just returned to action after their mid-season break and had suffered a flu epidemic that affected nine of their players just a week before we met them. We played some good football, weathered the expected early storm and looked to be on our way to a useful result to take back to Anfield. Enter Bruce Grobbelaar. The clown was back in all his glory when, three minutes after the interval, he came for a cross just as he had done a year earlier and missed it! What happened, in fact, was that as I started to leave my line I slipped. I recovered in ample time but misjudged the pace of the centre and, instead of taking it in two hands, I tried to scoop it up one handed like Pat Jennings — and dropped it. Tlokinski tapped home the gift. I was a bundle of nerves after that and have to take my share of the blame for the second goal from Wraga. It left us with an uphill task for the second leg.

I would have held my head in my hands but I was afraid of dropping that as well. The rest of the team were entitled to feel angry with me but Souness who, by this time, had developed into an outstanding leader, tried his best to make it easier for me when he told the gathered vultures: 'Bruce admits his mistakes but he has kept us in so many games recently that he is entitled to the odd error. He will be back.' I had two weeks to prove him right and my confidence began to return as we hammered Stoke 5—1 and West Ham 3—0. We were in good spirits as we began the game and when we went in front from a Phil Neal penalty we all believed we could do it and even the Poles looked as though they only needed a small push to send them tumbling. Instead we gifted them another goal and, of all people, it was Souness who was the culprit when he won the ball in typical fashion, only to slip and lose it. He might well have had a foul before that but he himself chose to play on, leaving our entire defence at sea. The man in possession remained as cool as ice as I charged out of my goal to try and recover the situation. He slipped me and I was left with no alternative but to bring him down and concede the penalty which Tlokinski converted for an all-important away goal. All our planning went to pieces after this set-back and we were forced to over commit ourselves to all-out attack. Rush and Hodgson scored but so did the Polish international Smolarek. We were out again and it was Bruce who was blamed.

It all began once more. The headlines, the letters and the abuse shouted outside our house. One old man wrote to me regularly. He said that he had been watching top-class football for 32 years and if Tommy Smith had still been captain he would have already broken my legs three times. That was one of the more pleasant letters. I also began to hear the obscenities yelled from certain sections of the crowd and I took them to heart. It hurt that they were from our own supporters and I found that hard to take for I had deliberately worked hard to win their support and I honestly thought they liked me.

When I had first arrived at Anfield I had heard all sorts of stories about the Scouse wit and the Kop humour. I heard tale of the foggy nights when one end would ask the other who had scored the goals and the other would tell them and receive a thank you in perfect unison. The Kop supporters used to ask me the score and I would hold up the required fingers or prance around my goal for their entertainment and to our manager's annoyance. It is in my nature to be outgoing but to build up that rapport with the crowd I put on a bit of an act and I admit that it was partly to create my own image and help overcome the huge shadow cast on my goalmouth by the outstanding Ray Clemence. I felt I could do it by being different because I realised I still had plenty to learn before I became as good a goalkeeper as he was. I thought after helping Liverpool win the League and League Cup in that first season they would forgive the odd indiscretion but it seems that they were so used to the team's success by then that nothing less than perfection would do.

The only individual games which took precedence over the winning of pots and trophies for the Boardroom were the two local derby games against Everton. It was the event of Merseyside, looked forward to for months by supporters of both sides. Tickets were as hard to come by as those for the Cup Final and, by the time the game came round, the players would be affected by the tense atmosphere and it was just as important to us to win the games. Lose them and you stayed indoors for a couple of weeks, win them and you could eat free in certain Liverpool restaurants. In my first year we took the 'double' as Howard Kendall tried to rebuild the Everton side. Our first tilt at them in my second season was on 6 November at Goodison and we went there a little unsure of our form. We had begun the season as though we were going to sweep the board as a farewell present for our departing manager. We went through our first seven games undefeated with three clean sheets followed by two games in which I conceded three. We came back from 1–3 to beat Forest 4–3 and then drew 3–3 with a Luton side which sported three different goalkeepers after Jake Findlay had got himself injured.

Successive defeats against Ipswich and West Ham were followed by two draws against Manchester United and Stoke and a win over Brighton, which left us wondering what was in store for us against Everton especially when Ian Rush declared himself doubtful. He limped out of his fitness test but decided to play anyway, which was a boost to all of us. Shortly before the kick-off two Everton supporters dressed as court jesters ran onto the pitch and presented me with a cardboard cut-out of a clown before running back into the Gladys Road End. I laughed and made a joke of it but inside I was furious even though I have to concede that the costumes were good. Also I do believe that the two kids were beaten up when they went back into the crowd. Why I do not know. Fortunately the only clowns that day were Everton as we quietened their crowd with a five-goal thrashing—four of them coming from the injured Ian Rush. God knows what he would have done to them had he been fit. They were all first-class goals from a first-class striker and to prove the point he knocked in another three at Coventry City in a four-goal win seven days later.

We may have spoiled our chances in the two main cup competitions but elsewhere we were lethal. Kenny Dalglish and Ian Rush were playing out of their skins up front while Graeme Souness strutted through midfield, holding it together and dictating the pace. We had an amazing run in the First Division and had turned the title challenge into a one-horse race as we went ten points clear on 3 January when we hammered Arsenal 3–1. After losing at West Ham on 9 October we lost only one League game, by a single goal at Norwich, until we had wrapped up our hat-trick of Championships. After that we played disgracefully. Liverpool, I had learned, play to win, but once the challenge is over interest wanes and Bob Paisley's farewell went a bit sour as we failed to win any of our last seven League games. Even so we finished 11 points in front of second-placed Watford and a dozen ahead of Manchester United, the team who had been tipped to take our crown. Had we finished the season properly we would have amassed nearly 100 points. As it was we went top in October and stayed there for the rest of the season and I achieved a personal ambition by finishing with the fewest goals against me in the entire top division, 37 compared with Gary Bailey's 38. I had kept 19 clean sheets in the League and of those 37 goals, I had lost 11 of them in those last half-dozen games when the whole team went on walk-about.

Not only did we retain our League title but we also won two cups in one match. We made the old League Cup our own while becoming the first winners of the new Milk Cup when we defeated Manchester United 2–1 after extra time at Wembley. Explain if you can why we were virtually unbeatable in the Milk Cup and yet against exactly the same teams in the FA Cup we were non-starters? In the newly-named Milk Cup we felt invincible. We saw off Ipswich home and away in the second round; beat Emlyn Hughes and Rotherham with a Craig Johnston goal in the next, Norwich 2–0 in the fourth round and West Ham in the quarter-finals with a late Souness goal in a 2–1 win. The semi-final paired us with giant killers Burnley who had put out Spurs in the previous round and, though we won the first leg 3–0 at Anfield, it was never quite as easy as the scoreline suggests. We were all impressed with a thin young midfield player named Trevor Steven who was soon to move to our neighbours Everton with such success that he went almost straight into the England team. Burnley won the second leg at Turf Moor by a Derek Scott goal but it hardly mattered for we were far more concerned whether Arsenal could pull back a 2–4 deficit from their first leg at Highbury against Manchester United. We had to wait for a week to find out they couldn't as United clinched their place with a 2–1 success. It was to be a battle of the giants.

The final, for once, lived up to its pre-match publicity with United deservedly taking the lead through Norman Whiteside but we forced them further and further back, which left me little more than a spectator. No one could argue when Alan Kennedy scored our equaliser to take the final into extra time for the third year in succession. United battled bravely but eventually had to give in to pressure, which had been intensified by injuries which saw Moran limp off to be replaced by Lou Macari and McQueen, scarcely able to walk after my impetuous challenge, hobbling up and down the wing. For once the spotlight was on the other goalkeeper with Gary Bailey beaten by the bounce on the first goal and then left for dead by Ronnie Whelan's brilliant, swerving shot from our extra-time winner. The afternoon had the perfect finale when Graeme Souness, with the backing of every player in the team, called on our retiring manager Bob Paisley to collect the trophy. For the first time at Wembley, a manager led the team up the stairs to a marvellous ovation from the 100,000 crowd.

The team's spirit was unbelievable and after the uncertainties over my abilities in the first season, everyone was with me in the second, even to the extent of encouraging my fooling about, albeit off the pitch rather than on it. One of my favourite tricks was to open bottles of beer or other drink with my eyebrow. That really used to get them at it, particularly Ian Rush. I would struggle, heave and strain, scratching my eyelid before the bottle would give up its cap. Sadly it was all a trick for I would loosen the stopper with my teeth on the way up and after that simply pretend. The cut chin, however, was a different matter. I did that at a stag party when we went on a little tour of the Liverpool wine bars before eventually bumping into an ex-con who had become a fitness fanatic. He was scathing about footballer's levels of fitness and set us various tests including one where we had to put our hands behind our backs and fall face forward, using our hands in the last split second only. That suited my reflexes and I showed our friend that it could be done, only to be accused of being chicken. With a few drinks inside me I rose, or rather fell, to the challenge and did not bother moving my hands at all. It was only when little Sammy Lee told me he thought I would need stitches in the cut on my chin that I realised anything was amiss. The hole was so big I could put my finger into it and Bob Bolder took me off to hospital for four stitches before we rejoined the party.

I felt I had turned the corner, especially with the lads. That was confirmed on a superb close season tour to Hong Kong and Bangkok or, as Sammy Lee persisted, Hong Cock and Bangkong. I had finally split up with Janet and the timing proved just right for it was while we were on tour that I met and fell in love with an air hostess named Debbie. I fancied her immediately, not just because of her undoubted good looks but because I struck up an immediate rapport with her. I was not sure that I had made the same impression on her until she went to great lengths to see me in the departure lounge in Hong Kong before we went our separate ways. I was free for the summer and had even cancelled my trip home to Africa, but she was flying here, there and everywhere. We met whenever she came back to London, before she announced that she was off to the South of France on holiday with a girlfriend. Midway through a game of tennis I suddenly decided that I wanted to be with her. My convertible was with my insurance broker Gordon Dearden and I arranged to pick that up and a visa before setting off for the South of France. It took me exactly 19 hours and 30 minutes from leaving Liverpool, before I was walking up the beach and saying: 'Fancy seeing you here.'

We enjoyed a great holiday, though I am not so sure that Debbie's friend thought a lot of it. We were so wrapped up in each other that I completely ignored a stream of messages to telephone Gordon Dearden back in England, for after all, who wanted to be bothered with insurance and pensions at a time like this? In the end it was Debbie who insisted that I telephoned him from a call box on the beach. Gordon was frantic. He explained that when he had borrowed my car he had left a gold bar in a cloth bag under the passenger seat. He had been asked to get it valued and feared that if it was not returned soon he might have difficulty in walking. I was dubious about the story and even if it were true I doubted whether the gold bar would still be there. I had taken the sun roof down as soon as I had arrived in France and it had stayed down with the car open to anyone for the three days I had been with Debbie. To my absolute amazement it was still there. I had driven through customs carrying a gold bar without knowing it. For that I made Gordon wait, pretending I could not find it, before relenting and putting him out of his misery. Even so it meant taking the bullion back through customs. Imagine the headlines if I had been stopped with that little item under my seat. I could hardly have claimed it was a bonus for winning the First Division Championship!

But I would have happily handed it over in return for a promise of winning the European Cup the next season and making amends for my mistakes in the previous two seasons.

7

The Treble

Four major honours in my first two seasons with Liverpool were more than any player could have reasonably demanded but my errors in the European Cup still dominated my professional career. Not only did I lay that ghost completely to my own satisfaction in my third season, but I also took part in the biggest silver raid in the history of English football when we won the League Championship for the third successive season and the League Cup for the fourth time on the trot. The best prize of all, however, was provided when I became a married man.

All my carefully-laid plans for the summer went right out of the window as I followed my air hostess Debbie back from the South of France and into a smarter society than the one I was used to in Liverpool. This one demanded stylish clothes, champagne cocktails and good manners. Hardly the sort of scene for Jungle Man and the ideal setting for me to make a gaffe and have me crossed off all the best party lists. Wrong! It was not me who had problems but the blushing Debbie when her backless evening gown suddenly became frontless as well in the middle of the dance floor. Overwhelmed with embarrassment and little else, she dashed off home to change leaving me to fend off the pretty young things who poured out their problems to me. Debbie returned in time to save me but no sooner had we started dancing again than the strap on her new dress broke, putting her in danger of displaying her tan for the second time that night.

I had already put off my return to Africa once but could not do so again because I had promised to take my mate Martin Prothero from Canada with me and show him the sights and, apart from that, my family, Graham Boyle and various other friends were expecting me. The problem was solved when I met up with Debbie at a Heathrow hotel. She had come back from a trip to New York with bronchitis and her doctor recommended sunshine. We flew to Zimbabwe together. It certainly took 'Boysie' Boyle by surprise when I turned up with Debbie instead of Martin, who arrived two hours later. Enough couches and beds were found, the introductions completed and it was down to the Wise Donkey for a quick breakfast in the French-style pavement café, where Debbie sadly had her purse taken. That little experience was quickly forgotten when we moved up from the city to a cottage in Inyanga, nestling in the hills with delightful views. One of the sights was my old barracks but these were now occupied by Robert Mugabe's private army, the Fifth Brigade, and many of the scenic routes had been blocked off for security purposes.

However, the old Troutbeck Inn was still there along with the Montclare Casino, so when Debbie became tired of sightseeing we were able to play tennis at the hotel while the casino offered an evening's entertainment. It was while we were playing tennis that I bumped into an old junior schoolfriend of mine who, by coincidence, was also named Debbie and it turned out that she and her husband were on their honeymoon. This called for celebrations and we arranged to meet them that night in the casino where our luck at blackjack kept the champagne flowing nicely. It was a delightful evening and, on the five-mile drive back to the cottage, we caught a rare sight of a kudu bull antelope in the headlights.

It meant that we arrived home in a contented mood with Martin going straight up to bed as soon as we got back while Debbie and I took advantage of the log fire laid by the old retainer David and of what was left of the last bottle of champagne. It was a frosty night outside, but we were warm and cosy and the conversation was as good as ever as I contemplated the four weeks I had known Debbie. I know it was not long but how long does a man of impulse need to make up his mind? 'Would you marry me?' I asked conversationally. 'You wouldn't marry me,' answered Debbie somewhat obscurely. 'I would,' I answered as seriously as I could, 'right now.' The only problem, it seemed, was that Debbie had promised to go home for her father's sixtieth birthday and retirement party but that could be solved with a telephone call from the Troutbeck next day. We wanted to tell someone of our momentous decision but Martin was the only person for miles around and fast asleep, we had no telephone, so it had to wait until morning.

The next morning I could hardly wait to tell Martin. 'You'll never guess,' I said, 'Debbie and I are going to get married.' 'What's for breakfast?' he said rubbing the sleep from his eyes. 'Did you hear me?' I said, raising my voice, 'We are getting married, now, here in Zimbabwe.' 'That's nice,' he answered. 'What's for breakfast?' 'Will you be best man?' I persisted. 'As there is no one else around I suppose I'll have to be,' he said, 'and give the bride away, and take the photographs and be witness and drive the car.'

The next task was Debbie's parents who had never met me. Were they going to take it as coolly as Martin? The answer was a definite no. 'Hello Mummy,' said Debbie sweetly, 'I am afraid I won't be home for Daddy's birthday.' Pause. 'Because I am getting married tomorrow.' Longer pause. 'You don't know him.' Even longer pause. 'He is a South African-born Zimbabwean named Bruce. He lives in Liverpool in England.' Short silence. 'No, Mummy he's not black. He's white.' Pause. 'If you think it best, you tell Daddy . . . are you there . . . Mummy . . . Mummy . . . Oh hell she's hung up on me.'

We then telephoned the District Commissioners' Office in Umtali, more than a hundred miles away over the hills, which was the nearest place that could make our marriage legal. The Commissioner told us that if we went over there the next day, signed the papers, waited two hours for the formalities to be completed, we would be man and wife, no problem, as long as we brought the right money. The three of us piled into the car, carefully hanging our best clothes in the back and travelling in our tracksuits so that we would look smart for our wedding. We arrived without mishap, which was a miracle in itself, and were called into the office and asked to present our passports. There was an instant difficulty in that though my documents, for once, were in order, Debbie was a foreign citizen and he shook his head on seeing her entry stamp and said we both needed to have been living in Zimbabwe for at least two weeks. Then he glanced at my passport again, saw the name and exclaimed: 'Jungle Man! How are you? Good to see you. What are you doing in Zimbabwe?'

Suddenly his whole attitude altered and he could not do enough for us. He was absolutely delighted that he was going to be the one to marry Jungle Man and when I asked him about the two-week rule, he simply shrugged his shoulders and said: 'Rules are there to be broken—sign here.' He married us then and there. We did not even have to wait the expected two hours and that meant we were married in our tracksuits because we didn't have time to change. It was a far cry from the big white wedding Debbie's parents must have dreamed about for their only child. Still, I thought, look how much money I am saving them.

The reception was a relaxed affair to say the least as we repaired to the local Manica Hotel for a glass or two of Bucks' Fizz and more phone calls home. This time it was my turn and, when I broke the news to my mother, she was not in the least surprised, for after all she had done exactly the same to me when she got married for the second time. But my sister was a different kettle of fish and she gave me a piece of her mind for not letting everyone know and said that I had absolutely no right to do this sort of thing behind everyone's back. She would have gone on at me all day, so, a little cruelly, I pointed out that it was a spur-of-the-moment decision and that I didn't have to get married. She hung up on me. Debbie's parents were beginning to get used to the idea and were naturally full of questions as to who this man was, what was her married name, where were we going to live, when would they meet me and so on. Debbie asked me to speak to her mother but when I did, she was tongue tied, probably trying to get used to the fact that her daughter had married a Liverpool footballer called Grobbelaar. She was probably still trying to pronounce the name.

We then returned to Harare to tell Ironman and his fiancée, and to Martin's delight, booked in at the nearby Miekles Hotel so he no longer had to sleep on a couch. We then flew off to see my parents who were now living in Ballitoville on the North Coast outside Durban. They killed the fatted calf and any doubts they held about my rapid choice of bride were quickly dispelled by Debbie who won the whole family over during the course of that celebration meal. The only problem with getting married out of the blue like that was that nothing had been pre-arranged and within two days Debbie was off home to England to pick up her next assignment, a flight to Barbados. It is a nice place to spend your honeymoon except that she did so without her husband. She worked while I spent my honeymoon with the best man.

I had promised to show Martin the sights and had then left him kicking his heels while I tied the knot. Our time was now limited and we flew straight to Victoria Falls, picking up a car from 'Mira the Hirer' and doing the sights. We took our pictures at a jog, discovering as we did so that we had somehow lost the flash from the camera in the aeroplane on our way over. We just had time to take one of the little five-seater aeroplanes for what they called the 'flight of angels' through the chasms and canyons around the falls. We did not even have time to wait for the aircraft to fill up with passengers and bought all five seats between the two of us, telling the pilot we were in a hurry for a quick look around. He took us at our word and flew like a Second World War fighter ace. We then raced back to the airport to catch our Air Zimbabwe flight to Wankie National Park. We had already telephoned to ask if they had found the flash and been told no, but when we boarded and went to our same seats, there it was tucked down the side by the window. When we showed the stewardess she accused us of planting it there to make them look stupid! Working on the basis that we may as well be hanged for sheep as lambs, we quietly hid her little red book containing the pre-take-off safety talk in Shona, Ndebele and English. She was stumped without it and when we landed we returned it saying: 'This is your life.' She screamed after us that we would be banned from flying Air Zimbabwe for life. I suppose as I had just married an air hostess I should have been a little more considerate.

The magnificent Wankie National Park was more of a honeymoon for Martin than it was for me for he met an attractive lady with two children on the flight who turned out to be staying at the same hotel. We asked her to join us that night in the Bush Camp and even provided her with babysitters in the form of two young African students whom we had bribed by promising them a slap-up meal the next night. We had a wonderful night, which was spoiled for me only by the fact that Debbie was not there. It did not go unnoticed that I was alone for on the same trip was a Qantas crew and one of the slender-hipped stewards made it obvious that he was interested if I was bored. I made it equally clear that I was not that way inclined and attached myself instead to an elderly New Zealand couple to allow Martin to chat up his lady. The warden, Garth Thompson, soon had the boys at it with a chase for spring hares through the bush, with Martin winning for England against the Aussies because I tipped him off that the long-legged rodents would run only so far before they would freeze in the jeep's headlights. While his opponents scrambled he waited and picked up the statuesque animal by its ears and its long, powerful legs.

It helped to impress the object of his desire and, after the steaks from the Braai-Vleis had disappeared and most of the guests gone off to their beds in the tree houses, we were left sitting by the dying fire and were allocated three mud huts, Garth in one, Martin and I in another and the lady in the third one. Each was equipped with two beds and blankets to keep out the cold of the night. Martin went off to try his luck and when I awoke at dawn and made the tea they were snuggled up together in bed. She was quick to explain that there were not enough blankets, that she had heard Martin's teeth chattering and invited him to her bed only to keep warm. Martin's wink told a different story.

Martin's love life was brought to a halt when we left Wankie to fly on to Lake Kariba. He had broken his neck when he was younger and thought that he had done it again when he tried to head a ball while diving into the swimming pool. In great pain, he rushed off to see the local doctor and cursed and swore when he was told he would have to wait his turn. His tirade was brought to a stop when the black doctor told him off in a broad Yorkshire accent. He had studied his medicine in Bradford. Martin's neck wasn't broken, just ricked and, in any case, it was time for me to go back for pre-season training and to sort out my affairs which had changed so dramatically since I had left. We had arranged that Debbie should, for the time being, live in the south because of her job while I carried on living in Liverpool. It didn't work. We missed each other and she moved up to join me. Her parents were also becoming used to the idea of their daughter being a Grobbelaar and they had the church wedding they had hoped for when, on 18 September 1983, our marriage was blessed in a delightful church in Ubley near Bristol. It was a day to remember for the players chartered the team bus and came down for the ceremony making little Ubley famous for a day or two at least with a ten-second clip of the ceremony being shown on Welsh television.

It was a lovely ceremony and we liked the church so much that when our daughter was born 11 months later we took her there for the christening. We thought long and hard about the name and we wanted something different. In the end we chose the name of the place where we were married, Umtali, and changed it to Tahli, adding the name Mellisa in case she did not like her first name when she grew up. In retrospect it was a good job it was not a boy because we had more or less decided to call him Bumi after the Bumi Hills' resort we stayed at just before the baby was born. I am sure the English pronunciation would have changed it from the African 'Boomy' to something that would have bothered the little chap at school.

Our pre-season games had gone badly enough to suggest that we might have a good season. It is strange the way that happens at Liverpool, it may be because when things go wrong so early they are quickly spotted and put right. I certainly hoped that that was going to be the case this season, and particularly in the European Cup. After our previous disasters I was taking nothing for granted even when we drew Odense the Danish Champions in the first round. I did not entirely agree with the pundits that it would be merely a question of how many. After all the Danes were currently in the process of ousting England from the European Championships and even if most of their top footballers played abroad, they had to start their careers in Denmark. In the event we were delighted to ease the pressure by winning the first leg in the lovely Hans Christian Andersen town of Odense with a Kenny Dalglish goal. Before the game each of us was presented with a beautiful volume of the *Fairy Tales* and I wondered then whether or not it would be an omen for the season. There were certainly no bedtime stories for the Danish part-timers in the return leg, which we won by five clear goals with Dalglish and Michael Robinson scoring two apiece. We were on our way and I had managed to keep two clean sheets.

However, it was soon made clear to us that if we were going to go all the way it was not going to be easy, as we drew the Spanish Champions of Bilbao in the next round and they came to Anfield for the first leg, put up the shutters, gave us no room to play and earned themselves a more than creditable goalless draw. We were impressed by their performance but, while the vultures gathered to pick our bones in Northern Spain in two weeks' time, we could see the possibilities of doing to them what they had done to us. After the game at Anfield the Basque manager of Bilbao had singled out Craig Johnston as Liverpool's best player, lifting him above Souness, Dalglish, Rush and everyone else. Craig was described as world class and my room-mate was ecstatic, for at last someone had recognised his true talent. It cut no ice at all with Joe Fagan and after the final training session at Bilbao, he told us that he had specially picked a team to win the match and that meant he preferred young Steve Nicol's defensive qualities to Craig's. The reasoning was hard to argue with though, naturally, Craig was shattered. The praise had gone to his head and when we returned to our hotel he told me that he was going to fly to Malaga, arrange for his wife Jenny to join him and then go back to Australia. He packed his bags and chattered away until I had to tell him to shut up and let me sleep. He may not have been playing the next day but I was.

We felt uneasy when we ran out against Bilbao; there were almost 50,000 crammed into their magnificent new stadium which had hosted England's first-round World Cup matches the summer before. We expected them to be rough and were wary of their tough captain Goicoechea, known as the 'Beast of Bilbao' and the man who had recently put the great Maradona out of the game for three months with a crippling tackle. Their behaviour was immaculate even though we went on to beat them with a headed goal from Ian Rush, one of many headers he was to score that season. It was a memorable night for the weather was superb, the pitch ideal and our performance of the highest possible standard. Souness dominated the game from the start while I was more than a little satisfied with myself for having performed well in both games with two more clean sheets. We had wondered before the match how we would escape from those fearsome, proud Basques if we won. We need not have worried. They applauded us off the pitch and as we sat outside the ground in our coach they came up to wish us well and pass round their little leather flasks of wine. Our victory was mocked in some quarters but Bilbao did go on to win the League and Cup double in Spain that season.

Craig, meanwhile, had swallowed his pride and hadn't carried out his threat. But he hadn't stopped complaining and it was beginning to get me down so much that, in the end, I asked Ronnie Moran if I could be assigned a new room-mate. I felt a bit mean when Craig went to reception for his room key only to be told that he was not in the one he thought he was. He said there was obviously a mistake but Moran, in his diplomatic way, turned to him and told him it was quite correct and that I had asked for the change. Craig had the last laugh, however, for I found myself sharing with Steve Nicol and had even less sleep. When he wasn't eating those interminable crisps and opening Coke cans, he would be drumming his fingers on his chest or making tea at 4 a.m. because he couldn't sleep. If Steve had to stay awake, so did everyone else.

I was back in with Craig by the time the competition resumed after the mid-winter break against Benfica and, once more, we were drawn at home in the first leg. English teams had always enjoyed good results against the former

European Champions from Portugal but they came to Anfield full of hope, beating Braga 7–0 the weekend before our game to extend an unbeaten run in which they had dropped only 2 points out of a possible 40, scoring 52 goals and conceding a mere 4. We were not playing so well. We had lost the influential Kenny Dalglish with a shattered cheek bone and our performances were inconsistent. The unpredictable and now ageing Portuguese goalkeeper Bento had a stormer and kept us out, apart from a 66th-minute goal from Ian Rush. Once again we had left ourselves with it all to do but our skipper Souness was quick to point out that we had kept a clean sheet and that he doubted Benfica's ability to keep us out while they were trying to go forward and score.

He was spot on as ever for when we returned to the unusually hostile Stadium of Light in Lisbon, we thrashed Benfica and, while the Spaniards had appreciated our skills, the Portuguese hated us for them. Our supporters were attacked and we were threatened in the coach after the game. By then we did not care. This time it was Ronnie Whelan who had scored the all-important first away goal after just nine minutes. It meant that Benfica would have to beat me three times to win and they never looked likely to do that. Craig Johnston, back in the side, scored a spectacular second and though I conceded my first goal of the competition shortly before the interval when Nene scored, we were never in danger of losing and, sure enough, Ronnie Whelan and Ian Rush made it 4–1. More often than not we return home immediately after European matches but because kick-off times are always so late in Portugal, we always stay there overnight. We celebrated well into the night and I surprised a few of my team-mates by creeping up on their rooms in the Estoril Palace – from the outside. The club were none too happy but the ledges were wide enough to sleep on. I have been on narrower paths in the mountains and, in any case, there was far more danger waiting for us round the corner, namely a Romanian team called Dinamo Bucharest, the toughest team I have ever played against.

I couldn't help noticing that, once again, we were playing a side from Eastern Europe and the fact wasn't lost on my 'friends' either as I was soon reminded that Liverpool, and Bruce Grobbelaar in particular, had stumbled against sides from Bulgaria and Poland in the two previous years. Incredibly the draw in Switzerland had given us the home leg first and, once again, we struggled in front of our own fans. Dinamo were not to be underestimated for not only had they earned the reputation of being tough but they had reached the semi-final of the best competition in the world by beating reigning Champions Hamburg and the difficult Soviet team Dynamo Minsk. The Romanians were quick to realise that the Swiss referee Daina was something of a soft touch and we suffered the sort of indignities that are usually reserved for away matches only. We were body checked, spat at, kicked and punched. I needed treatment from Ronnie Moran after being stood on by a thug named Movila and I still bear the scar below my kneecap. Movila eventually had his comeuppance when he picked on the wrong man, in Graeme Souness. Dinamo could not have done their homework well or they would have warned their hatchet man to pick on someone else. Movila left the field with his jaw broken in two places, claiming that our skipper had punched him. It must have been some punch.

As we came off the pitch we were warned by the Romanians of what we would face in the return leg at Bucharest, and this was underlined by the fact that we only had a one-goal advantage to take there – and that a rare header from Sammy Lee. They weren't joking for the atmosphere was distinctly chilly when we flew into Romania two weeks later. Going through customs and again as we sat on the coach, first uniformed officials and then men in leather coats made extremely threatening gestures, many of which were directed at Souness. I wasn't going to take it passively and started to return some of those gestures until one of the lads asked me how I fancied spending the next three days in a cell. I might just as well have been in prison for it rained so heavily that, other than training, we scarcely set foot outside the hotel and it was still pouring when we ran out to try and take that last step to the European Cup Final in Rome.

As we ran out we were pelted with fruit and vegetables. The supporters must have been really keyed up by their local media for tomatoes and apples and the such are not just expensive over there but almost unobtainable to the ordinary person. They booed continually, and especially at Souness, and that was before the kick-off. Souness revelled in it. He juggled the ball, dummied passes and generally stirred up the fans. His attitude lifted us as did his contempt when they set Andone, who had been their best player in the first leg, to kick him. His response to that was a volleyed pass to Ian Rush who chipped the sweetest goal you have ever seen. We had done it again. After struggling in the home leg we had scored a critical away goal. Dinamo were even tougher in this leg than they had been in Liverpool and though that came as no surprise, the fact that West German referee Pauly gave us about as much protection as we had had in the first leg did.

The Romanians threw the lot at us and raised the hopes of the rain-soaked crowd when Orac equalised just before the interval. But we held firm. As I was so close to realising a dream, I was going to give them nothing and neither was anyone else. Eventually they ran out of steam and Ian

Rush put it completely out of their grasp when he took advantage of a defensive error, lost his marker and scored a second goal. We had done it, not only had we reached the European Cup Final we had already won our fourth Milk Cup and were well on our way to our third successive Championship. The only problem was that we were to play the Italian Champions Roma on their own ground, the Olympic Stadium where Liverpool had won their very first European Crown against Borussia Moenchengladbach in 1977.

We knew it was going to be hot in Italy on 29 May and the club decided that the best preparation would be to acclimatise ourselves in suitable surroundings. So, while Roma headed for the top of one of the seven hills for a training camp, coming down to the Olympic Stadium every day at the scheduled kick-off time to train, we were in Tel Aviv ostensibly to play the Israeli National side but, more importantly, to relax after a very tough season. After all, everyone said that winning three trophies in a season was impossible and the chances of beating Roma on their own ground remote in the extreme.

The Italian journalists who followed us everywhere must have agreed as they watched us relax on the beach with our chilled beers. When their presence became too much by the sea we would repair to the privacy of the pool at the nearby Sheraton Hotel for a few civilised vodka and tonics. The locals took no notice of our antics for we were regular visitors and they clearly remembered our previous visit when we had renamed the main square in Tel Aviv, 'Maddison Square' because of a drunken brawl involving half-a-dozen players who had been playing a drinking game called 'buzz'. Alan Hansen, Alan Kennedy and I were only innocent bystanders or at least we were until we stood up and Alan was punched in the mouth while David Hodgson jumped on my back. For an instant I was back in the jungle and Hodgy went flying over my shoulder to end with my knee in his chest and a fist raised ready to smash into his face.

The moment passed and the fight was forgotten almost immediately as Hodgson, Ian Rush, Ronnie Whelan and John McGregor, holding one another up, lurched back to the hotel to confront one of our directors who had come to the scene because he had been told by one of the journalists that we were involved in a riot. Mr S. T. Moss, also a Justice of the Peace, was confronted with a tangled mass of arms, legs and bodies as the players fell down some steps. In his most authoritative voice Mr Moss demanded to know what was going on. Hodgy replied in his best Geordie: 'Whay aye Mossy yer old bugger you, you and me are just the same you know.' They were sent back to the hotel and the whole event ended in laughter.

We were not quite as boisterous as that before the European Cup Final but we still enjoyed ourselves. We watched Everton beat Watford 2–0 for the FA Cup at Wembley while sitting in a place called the Glasgow bar. I stayed on for a game of cribbage after the others had left. I did not fancy the walk back and a young lad lent me his bike. I wasn't sure what arrangement we had made for me to return it so I found a youngster, gave him some money and told him to take it back to the bar. It was the last time it was ever seen and it cost me £150 to replace. When we returned to Liverpool we heard that if the score in the final was level after extra-time there would be a penalty shoot-out. This may be an inescapable part of the modern game and Tottenham may have shown the importance of it a couple of weeks earlier when they had beaten Anderlecht to win the UEFA Cup from the penalty spot, but we had been involved in one or two of these contrived finishes and had never won. We decided that a little practice would not go amiss and thought it safe to take on the apprentices after a training session at Melwood. The shame of it! They beat us 5–1 and I didn't save a single shot. At the other end our young keeper Chris Pile did enough either to save or make Graeme Souness, Phil Neal, Kenny Dalglish and Steve Nicol all miss. Only Alan Kennedy scored. We kept our fingers crossed that there would be no shoot-out!

When we arrived in Rome we expected to be whipped through customs when army buses met us off the aeroplane, but we waited around on the tarmac for ages becoming hot and bothered and immediately the dangers of staging a big final in the home city of one of the clubs struck me. There was no danger, however, of any disturbance at our hotel for the local Holiday Inn boss from Liverpool, Jack Ferguson, had assumed control, even to the extent of bringing martial arts' expert Tony Chinn with him to look after the team's interests. No one, but no one, gained admittance to the players' floor. One aspect of playing at an opponents' ground did not trouble us and that was the atmosphere. We had shown throughout the season that the bigger and more hostile the environment, the better we played. All our best performances had been away from home and we revelled in it when we ran out to streamers, flares, red smoke bombs and hooters. How the supporters smuggled them in, I don't know, for security was so tight that even our wives and girlfriends had horns and rattles taken from them. I can only imagine that our girls looked a villainous lot.

It was important for me to get an early touch of the ball to settle my nerves and I engaged in a little side-play, wandering out of my goal, pretending I wasn't looking to lure the Brazilian Falcao into attempting a chip which I caught easily. That made me feel good and Phil Neal's thirteenth minute goal made us all feel even better. It was our first real attack of the game and it produced the first goal that Roma had conceded on their own ground in the competition that year. Their cloak of invincibility was slipping, but they gradually began to put their game together and the pressure began to build up. I became busier and busier, taking crosses and making saves, including one good one from Graziani. Then my world fell in. All we needed to do was hold on until half-time when, with three minutes remaining, Conti received a lucky rebound and crossed to the near post for Pruzzo to send a looping header over my hand and into the net. I have often been criticised for supposed mistakes but no one took me to task for this one. Perhaps I am being overly self-critical but I know in my own mind that I jumped a fraction of a second too soon and the ball went on past me at its apex. Had I gone a little later I would have met it on its downward curve.

In the second half we reached stalemate with the Italians' goalkeeper Tancredi and me stopping whatever came our way without too much difficulty. The prospect of a penalty shoot-out loomed large as we went into extra time but I put it out of my mind as I took the ball off Falcao's toes and blocked a shot from the dangerous Conti. The hard game was taking its toll on everyone with Craig Johnston and Kenny Dalglish being replaced by Steve Nicol and Michael Robinson while Roma took off goalscorer Pruzzo and the cramp-ridden Brazilian Cerezo. But suddenly it was over, 1–1 after extra time, and I was faced with the likelihood that, given our record at penalties, we were going to be beaten in the cruellest way possible. As if Roma had not had enough of an advantage in playing in their own stadium, the otherwise admirable Swedish referee Erik Fredriksson gave them another boost by selecting the end for the sudden death shoot-out where their supporters were massed. The net looked like an animal cage as I prepared myself for the ordeal, trying to tell myself that I had faced worse in the jungle when it was my life at stake and not just my reputation. It was then that kindly Joe Fagan pulled me gently to one side and said: 'Look, son, there is nothing a goalkeeper can do in these circumstances. If we lose there will be no blame attached to you. You had a great game.' As I walked away he called after me: 'But make sure you try to put them off.'

I thought about that as young Steve Nicol, who had demanded that he take the first kick, hoisted his penalty high over the bar as the photographers clicked away at him. The flashes disappeared as Di Bartolomei strode up to take Roma's first penalty. I went the right way just managing to fingertip to the ball, but not enough to deflect it. Phil Neal then beat Tancredi and we were level. It was then that Joe Fagan's words came back and as Conti strolled forward to take the kick, I put my hands on my knees and crossed them over like the old 'Black Bottom' dance routine. The Italian World Cup hero shot over the bar and his team-mates were furious. They complained about my antics to the referee but, having already turned down a complaint from Souness on the flashlight trick, he could hardly do anything about me, particularly as I had kept within the rules by keeping my feet firmly planted on the ground. There is nothing to say you can't move your body.

Well it worked once, so why not again. After all, wasn't I supposed to be the clown? I might as well live up to my reputation—especially if it was going to help us win the European Cup. The drama continued when Souness, as cool as he had been throughout the game even though he knew that his future rested on his performance with a queue of foreign clubs watching him, put us in front for the first time before Righetti levelled. Rush, also being watched by Italian clubs, put his away and now it was the Italians who were sweating. Top Italian striker Graziani was next on the spot. Before he took it, I was caught by the television cameras biting the netting in the back of the goal. It was my angry lion bit, partly joke and partly to key myself up because I knew that if he scored with this, success would be hanging on a thread once more. As I walked to my line we looked each other in the eyes and he crossed himself. I felt in that moment that I had the edge and I was not going to let go. I put on my 'Ali Shuffle' act, wobbling my knees and letting my head and arms loll as if I were desperately tired and about to drop to the ground. I knew from the moment he struck the ball that I did not even need to dive, he was under it and it was either going over or going to hit the bar. In the event his shot grazed the top and went over and I set off in a victory dance as though I had saved it.

I was ready to take the decisive penalty kick to clinch it for us, for after all I had a 100 per cent record having taken one and scored one, but it was Alan Kennedy who strolled forward. There was more than one Liverpool player who didn't fancy 'Barney Rubble's' chances. The 29-year-old Geordie looked the calmest man in the stadium as he sent Tancredi the wrong way, and we had won 4–2. Alan said afterwards that he did not even look at their goalkeeper. He had decided to hit it exactly the same way as he did against our kids at Melwood. We went crazy. Even Graeme Souness cried, and I never thought I would live to see that day.

There has never been a party like the one we had that night organised by our sponsors, Crown Paints. It was held in the Villa Miani on top of one of Rome's hills and it carried on long after the sun had reappeared. But even so there were still hundreds of fans waiting to greet us when we returned to our hotel. The Rome police were full of praise for the way the 10,000 supporters had behaved, particularly in view of some severe provocation they had received from the unhappy Roma fans who attacked them as they left the stadium. That should have provided the authorities with ample warning 12 months later when Liverpool faced Juventus in Brussels. They need only to have looked at the newspaper cutting from 12 months earlier to know that there would be repercussions. It was the climax to a season I will never forget and that night I looked at my heavily-pregnant wife and felt great happiness. Even my critics had gone to ground, albeit temporarily. At that moment I would not have changed places with anyone.

At the start of the season everyone had predicted a two-horse race between Manchester United and us and when we lost to them by a single goal at Old Trafford from Frank Stapleton, they went second and we went fourth. When we played them at home we had a great chance of putting them out of contention as we had gone into the New Year top with them in second place. We led from a Craig Johnston goal but were shaken when we lost Kenny Dalglish with a badly-shattered cheekbone after a clash with Kevin Moran. It was an injury which was to keep him out of the side for three months and to make matters worse, Norman Whiteside scored a last-minute goal to give them an undeserved share of the points.

Considering we were so successful that season there were an awful lot of hiccups on the way. I remember having a dreadful game, perhaps my worst ever, just a couple of days before we played United for the second time. It was on New Year's Eve at Nottingham Forest. Over the previous couple of years Brian Clough had been one of my staunchest supporters in times of stress when the critics were sniping at me. He must have been embarrassed at what he saw that day as the ball slipped through my hands, crosses spilled out, shots hit the post and crossbar while Hansen and Lawrenson kicked so many off the line that they must have wondered whether I was playing. What made it worse was that Mick Poole, the Zimbabwe coach, had come over to watch me, report back on my form and check my availability for the World Cup qualifier against Egypt. Poole would have been justified in ending my international career on the spot, but he was kind to me after the game and promised that no report would go in, just the fact that I was fit and available for selection. The staggering thing was that, despite my inept performance, we won the game with an Ian Rush goal. It just goes to show the resilience of that side. I tried hard to analyse what was wrong with me and, in the end, could put it down to lack of concentration only. With Mick Poole at the game I spent most of my time thinking about Africa. I drift off like that sometimes, thinking of home and the bush. On a scale of one to ten, I would have given myself three that day. One for turning up, one for finding my way back to the dressing room and one for putting my shorts on the right way round. I was having some trouble with my gloves at the time as I was experimenting to find the best sort but that day I must have worn Teflon non-stick ones!

I wasn't the only one who was having a bad season. We all suffered our off-days, particularly against the lower sides in the division. We lost to relegated Wolves, Stoke, Coventry and Sunderland in the League and made our usual red-faced exit from the FA Cup when our old bogey team Brighton and Hove Albion did it to us again, this time beating us by two goals on their own Goldstone ground. But probably the worst defeat of the season for the eventual champions came at Coventry on 10 December. We went down by four goals and little Terry Gibson pinched a hat-trick. We were still top but obviously not for long for, according to the critics, this new Coventry team led by young manager Bobby Gould was going to take the football world by storm. Move over Liverpool, with a goalkeeper like that you don't have a chance.

We bounced back to stick five past poor Notts County while Coventry, who went fourth that day, began a slide down the First Division which saw them finish in nineteenth place and they were lucky not to slip further after we scored five against them at Anfield on 7 May. It was sweet revenge and gently reminded the pundits that they did not know everything. Ian Rush scored four that day, which was not an unusual feat for the remarkable Welshman the year in which he knocked in five against Luton and three against Aston Villa. He scored thirty-two League goals that season; eight in the Milk Cup; two in the FA Cup and five in the European Cup, not to mention the penalty in the shoot-out against Roma. It was small wonder that Napoli tried to sign him before Maradona. We eventually clinched the title with a goalless draw at Notts County and once more the critics were proved wrong for United's challenge dropped off so badly in those final weeks that they fell to fourth place behind runners-up Southampton and third-placed Nottingham Forest. But it still did not explain why we lost such daft matches. All I can put it down to was that it was a long, hard season with a total of 66 fiercely-competitive games as we chased four trophies and sometimes we relaxed a little too much.

It was much the same in the Milk Cup which, having won it three times in a row, we were beginning to believe was our property. We began well enough with a couple of four-goal victories over Brentford in our first-round match but were distinctly fortunate to overcome the next hurdle against Malcolm Macdonald's talented young Fulham side. They drew us twice and were unlucky to go out to a Souness goal in extra time of the third game. No one can know how much we wanted to beat Birmingham City on the first attempt because any replay would have to be played at Anfield three evenings later on the night of our players' Christmas party. We slaughtered them for three-quarters of the game but, after Harford had scored an equaliser, we were hard pushed to survive. The Birmingham players could not understand why we were so mad and they were baffled again on the Thursday night when we hit three past them and rushed off, leaving them on their own in our players' lounge while we changed into our fancy dress on the team bus en route to Tommy Smith's club.

With so much football to play, replays were the last thing we wanted but it was preferable to defeat and we came back from the grave to draw at Sheffield Wednesday with a Phil Neal penalty before scoring three against them without reply at Anfield eight days later. That left us to beat little Third Division club Walsall and Everton to defeat Aston Villa for the first-ever Merseyside derby at Wembley Stadium. What an incentive it was to everyone concerned, but we came desperately close to blowing it when we could only draw 2–2 at Anfield with the plucky Midlanders coming back at us twice to set up what they hoped would be a great night at Fellows Park.

In the event it was almost a disaster when, as Ronnie Whelan knocked in our second goal, a wall collapsed. It could have been very nasty indeed had the terraces been steeper, but as it was there was the poignant sight of Souness carrying an injured boy to safety. It was bad enough for us to have to leave the pitch for a while as they sorted it out but, by then, the two goals were enough and we had clinched our place at Wembley the night before Everton played the first leg of their semi-final. We watched with interest as they won with goals from Sheedy and Richardson at Goodison and then held on grimly at Villa Park after Rideout had reduced the deficit with his 62nd-minute goal. Merseyside went crazy at the prospect of their very own derby match at Wembley with us tipped as favourites after beating Everton 3–0 at home and 1–1 away just before the final.

It was a very special final at Wembley that Sunday, not just because of the unique occasion and two very talented sides, but because of the atmosphere. On and off the pitch it was an example to football. The game was played in excellent spirit and it was watched by 100,000 who had come to enjoy a game of football. After all the sweat and skill, it ended goalless after 90 minutes. There was plenty of action with Everton claiming they should have had a seventh-minute penalty when Alan Hansen was alleged to have handled, while Alan Kennedy had what looked to be a good goal disallowed for offside and Neville Southall made a wonderful save from an Ian Rush volley in extra time. I stood and applauded that and it was used to show what a friendly spirit the game was played in. If people were more observant they would know that I always show my appreciation of good goalkeeping—and that was goalkeeping at its best.

The draw was the perfect result and at the end of the game the two teams ran a lap of honour, had their pictures taken together and listened with joy to the two sets of supporters singing the same song. How sad that a little more than a year later this should have been forgotten and Liverpool supporters branded as the worst in the world. The replay was at Maine Road and the atmosphere was more tense but still played at a high sporting level and in the end only a Souness goal separated the two great rivals. From a personal point of view I was happy with my performances in both games but more so in the second when I made important saves from Peter Reid, Graeme Sharp and Adrian Heath. So I had my bad moments in the season. So what! I also had a few good ones, I must have done so to finish with 20 clean sheets out of 42 in the most competitive league in the world. For the second year running, I conceded fewer goals in the First Division than any other goalkeeper and in three seasons I had not missed a game as Liverpool won three titles, three League Milk Cups and the European Championship. As a result I was growing in confidence and stature and any criticism that came my way was water off a duck's back. If anything it was an added spur to go on proving my detractors wrong. That season gave me almost total satisfaction. It is the sort of record that usually occurs in the weaker leagues but not in the English First Division.

It was on to Swaziland after the season but with Debbie soon to give birth and Graham Boyle due to wed his fiancée, Moira, I asked if I could skip the last match when a mixed Liverpool and Tottenham team were due to play the national side. It was a strange summer for Tahli could have been born in South Africa, Zimbabwe, Spain or England the way we dodged about. It's a wonder she was not born when we went out to Bumi Hills' Safari Park as we were woken up in the middle of the night by the local rogue elephant feasting on the trees and bushes by our front door. What with monkeys helping themselves to food from our breakfast table and the bouncing around of the jeep as we went looking for big game like buffalo, elephant and rhino, the baby could have come at any moment. We even went out onto the river to look at Starvation Island where many animals had been stranded and died when the area was deliberately flooded. We were lucky sightseers that day for, through the clouds of dust, we could see two bull elephants fighting for supremacy. Elephants are good swimmers and they had taken over the island and these two were snapping off trees in their bid for control of the herd.

When we went back to Zimbabwe the aeroplane was full and I was allowed to sit in the co-pilot's seat as an old army friend, Tim Kemp, was pilot. After we had taken off, he calmly handed over the controls and, giving me instructions, he let me fly her for 40 minutes even telling me to drop the wing so that the passengers could see a herd of buffalo. It was a wonderful sensation and I can understand men like Tim wanting to fly for a living. I was delighted that he had finished up doing what he wanted after being turned down by the Air Force because he was too tall. He only regained the controls as we came in to land.

Debbie recovered from that latest shock and we set off for Ironman's wedding. There were a few more guests than for ours a year earlier. There were all sorts of footballers at the ceremony including John Rugg and his Rio Tinto team, top Zimbabwe international Ephert Lingu as well as all the old players. Looking round I was amazed and delighted to see so many black and white faces around the church. It was something you would not have seen in the country five years earlier and which is still not seen in South Africa. I had had to make a speech in the morning and ended up leading the old Callies' team in a sing-song which brought the house down. After being the entertainer I became the peacemaker as I sat between Boysie's sister and his mother-in-law. They were two strong ladies and had very different opinions on whether the marriage was going to work. Graham and his bride left on their honeymoon, oblivious to the discussions over their future and also to the fact that everyone at the wedding was only too aware of where their secret destination was, as did the police patrol car who stopped them for dragging a road traffic sign behind the car declaring, 'Men at Work'. When they discovered it was Ironman they gave him a personal escort.

Our next problem was to try and find a flight out of Zimbabwe. I tried to pull strings and it was only the fact that Debbie was so advanced in her pregnancy that seats were eventually found for us. They searched Debbie first to make sure she wasn't trying to smuggle something out of the country under her dress and then we discovered we were in the jump seats alongside the pilot. It suited us both for the pilot, terrified that my wife would give birth in mid-flight, gave up his crew bunkbed upstairs in the jumbo so that she had her most comfortable flight ever. I sat behind him, more eager than ever to learn to fly.

In the event Tahli arrived on the scheduled day which was somewhat fortunate as, after Africa, we flew to Spain to relax for a couple of weeks. We went with another couple so that I could play golf with John Cook while Debbie relaxed with his wife Tina who was seven months' pregnant. We arrived back in Liverpool the day before pre-season training started. The club takes this very seriously, so seriously in fact that it was decided that if the baby did not arrive on time it would be induced so that I could be around on the big day and go on tour with the club. As it was they went off to Germany while I stayed behind and played for the reserves against Northwich Victoria on the Saturday, with the baby due next day.

I took Debbie into hospital without any problems and she was given a nice room with a television and telephone. I was pleased about that for the anaesthetist was not happy and it was decided that Debbie should have a Caesarian and I was banned from the birth I had looked forward to so much. Instead I watched Messrs Cram, Coe and Ovett perform in the Los Angeles Olympic Games. I heard the first cry and a nurse ask: 'Shall I weigh him?' The 'he' turned out to be a little girl! I didn't mind in the least for, like all parents, all you care about at that moment is that mother and baby are healthy. They both were and I was off to join the team in Switzerland.

We had a good pre-season and even won a tournament in Berne which ironically worried me as we usually always played better after a poor start. There were other bad omens, too. Souness had gone to Sampdoria; Craig Johnston had stayed in Australia while his wife Jenny gave birth to a baby, Chelsea; and Ian Rush discovered he needed surgery. We then lost 1–0 to Everton at Wembley in the Charity Shield and, surprise, surprise, Bruce Grobbelaar was found guilty of being a clown again! The goal was credited as an own goal against me. By any other standards it would have been a successful season but this is Liverpool we are talking about, a club whose supporters had been used to trophies for the past nine years and to three in the previous season. But Liverpool went from the low position of twentieth to finish as runners-up in the First Division, they went out of the Milk Cup at Spurs after winning the trophy four times in succession. They reached the semi-final of the FA Cup for the first time in five years and only went out to Manchester United after a replay and, finally, they reached the final of the European Cup when the result against Juventus cannot really be counted. Our performance was made to look much worse than it was on Merseyside because our great rivals Everton did well at last, following up their FA Cup triumph of the previous season by beating us in the Charity Shield as well as twice in the League, winning the Milk Cup, the Cup Winners' Cup and, best of

all for them, our League Championship. They came close
to taking the lot, before losing in the FA Cup to Manchester
United in the final at Wembley against only ten men.

There is no getting away from it, by our standards we
did not play well and I admit my share of errors in that
first half of the season. But others made them too and the
atmosphere in the dressing room was not good. Obviously
we were missing world-class players such as Souness and
Rush while even Kenny Dalglish's goals had dried up.
Everyone kept harping on about the loss of Souness and,
of course, we also missed his leadership on the pitch and
in the dressing room. Our manager Joe Fagan tried seven
different players in Graeme's spot, including £400,000
Kevin McDonald who had been bought from Leicester in
November. It is easy to judge with hindsight, but the only
way you could have replaced Souness would have been to
have bought a player of the same class and that would
have meant a Platini or a Brady; players who were just not
available. The solution is rather to change style, but Graeme
continued to haunt the dressing room.

Those early weeks were all about losing. Our proud
home record fell when we lost to Sheffield Wednesday and
then even West Bromwich Albion held us to a draw at
Anfield. The defeat by Everton came as a result of a
spectacular Graeme Sharp goal. He had been trying to do
that to me ever since I had arrived and you have to give
the Scottish international striker credit not only for the way
he took it but for the way he persisted. There was no
stigma in conceding that, for not even Dassayev would
have got a hand to it, never mind stopped it. We dropped
down to twentieth place soon after that and even our old
stand-by, the Milk Cup, let us down. After being held to a
goalless draw by Fourth Division Stockport, we went out
to Spurs when Hazard scored a goal which was every bit

as good as Sharp's. I took some of the blame for not
holding a Galvin shot after Phil Neal had given the winger
too much room. I tipped Galvin's shot round the post and
it was from the resultant corner that Galvin scored. Sadly,
we did not deserve to lose and really turned the screws on
Spurs only for Ray Clemence, displaying his great natural
ability, to defy us with two spectacular saves, one of which
was from a deflected shot from Rush.

It was around then we began to put it together and start
the long haul up the League ladder. It was a slow and
painful process and we had many stumbles on the way
including a defeat at home to Tottenham, which was the
first time they had won at Anfield since the Titanic sank,
and from Manchester United — a hint for the FA Cup semi-
final to come later. Even if we had won these two games
we would not have made any impression on our local
rivals, Everton. They had shown us a clean pair of heels.
We also made a return visit to Tokyo where we lost 1–0
to Independiente of Buenos Aires for the World Club
Championship and 2–0 to Juventus on a virtual ice rink in
Turin.

There was renewed determination in the dressing room,
despite such setbacks as injuries to Rush, Lee, Lawrenson,
Kennedy and Walsh, that we were going to fight back and
show, as all Liverpool sides have done in recent years, that
they are never more dangerous than when they have been
written-off. It is my belief that, though we won nothing,
we showed as much quality in the second half of that
season as we ever had before while Joe Fagan proved to
everyone in football that he knew what he was doing. He
may have tried seven players in Souness's position but,
even counting those long-term injuries, he used only
eighteen players as he shuffled his pack to the best of his
and their ability. All that was missing that season was a

little bit of luck and, maybe, we had used up our share in previous seasons.

Take, for example, the FA Cup. We thought that 1984 would be our year for the one trophy which has kept eluding us. We crushed Aston Villa 3–0 at Anfield and then responded to a little motivation from Ronnie Moran to beat Spurs 1–0 on a snowy Anfield pitch, which was the only time we beat the North Londoners in four attempts that season. We had taken a lot of stick before that game, which was shown live on television, and we fancied ourselves as soon as we woke up and saw the snow. 'Spurs won't like this,' we said and sure enough, Glenn Hoddle limped off with a hip injury and Rush showed the character that Tottenham lacked that day with a wonderfully opportunist goal. It was a hard winter and when we went to York we were confronted by a straw-covered pitch and so asked the York players where the sheep were! It brought back my days at Crewe and we soon discovered why Arsenal had gone out as Sbragia equalised an earlier Rush goal and I was kept busy as the game went to a replay. 'Who's sheepish now?' asked the delighted York players as we left the pitch, but there were no sheep at Anfield, just 43,010 spectators who watched us beat them by seven goals. Even so our fans were outshouted by the York contingent who were determined to enjoy their day out.

In the middle of the miners' strike Barnsley was hardly the place to be for a Sunday quarter-final tie to be televised live and we saw the depth of feeling in the area before the kick-off when two young lads briefly hoisted a banner saying, 'Owen strikes faster than Scargill'. It was hauled down in seconds and the two unfortunate kids were given an immediate hiding. Rush scored a hat-trick as we sank the Yorkshire side 4–0. It meant that we were paired in the semi-final with Manchester United at, of all places, Goodison

Park, and if there was ever any doubt about Liverpool's determination that season we dispelled it then. Ronnie Whelan equalised Bryan Robson's goal in the last minute of the game and Paul Walsh then forced a replay in the last minute of extra time after United had looked home and dry through Stapleton. So off we went to Maine Road and were coasting towards Wembley with an own goal from McGrath. The back-room staff told us at half-time that we were doing well but warned us to be aware of players coming through from the middle. Within minutes of the restart Bryan Robson, of all people, was allowed to burst through the no-go area to score and then Mark Hughes did the same to put them ahead with an unstoppable drive. I was not to blame but felt that I should have done better with the Robson shot. Had I stopped it we would have been at Wembley.

Strangely, the one competition where we were not affected by adverse form or anything else was the European Cup. We had begun our defence with a tough draw against the Poles of Lech Poznan. John Wark, who has an even better goalscoring record in Europe than Ian Rush, saw them off with the only goal in Poland and a hat-trick at Anfield which put us through by a five-goal aggregate. It was our friends Benfica next and a Rush hat-trick this time gave us a 3-1 home win. Benfica's crazy goalkeeper, Bento, who some say is even worse than me, had a better game against us than he had done in the previous season, and both stopped us scoring more and put Benfica in with a chance with a quick throw which led directly to Diamantino's goal.

A penalty from the big blond Danish striker Manniche put Benfica within a goal of knocking us out but we contained our anger against the Portuguese crowd again. We celebrated this time with a crowd of us going to a fish restaurant in Cascais where we polished off several cases of beer and vinho verde to wash down a spectacular meal of lobsters, crabs, oysters, prawns and a variety of other shellfish. Mark Lawrenson was not impressed by the rich fare and settled, instead, for a bowl of tomato soup and Dover sole. He was even less impressed when the bill arrived and his equal share was £60. He has never let us forget the most expensive plate of fish and chips he has ever eaten.

It was hardly surprising that Mark was missing when we went out to celebrate after the semi-final when we followed up a four-goal hammering of the Greek Champions Panathinaikos, in which Rush grabbed another two, with a single-goal victory in Athens. A local taverna stayed open late for us as we threw plates, danced the local way and looked forward to the match of the season against the Italian Champions Juventus in Brussels. If only it could have all ended there in that taverna in the Plaka underneath the Acropolis. To all intents and purposes our game in the beautiful Olympic Stadium in Athens was to be Liverpool's last real, competitive game of football in Europe for a long, long time.

8

Good Luck Charms
and Witchdoctors

I thought I had left voodoo and black magic behind me when I left Africa but though I have yet to see Bob Paisley throw the bones in the Anfield dressing rooms, Ron Atkinson light a grass bonfire in the tunnel at Old Trafford or Lawrie McMenemy make his team strip off in the car park at White Hart Lane, it is certainly alive, well and flourishing in England. Responsibility for this must be taken by my old South African rival Gary Bailey who used a bit of African voodoo to help himself to a couple of FA Cup winners' medals!

It all began back in South Africa when an English-born goalkeeper named Peter B'alac arrived to play for Lusitano. He had shrugged off the local rites and superstitions as most European players do when they first arrive, and took no part in it until the local witch doctor took him aside before an important cup-tie. He gave Peter a lock and chain which he said was to be placed carefully in the back of his goal to lock it up against the opponents' shots and not to be lost. Peter's reply was not designed to win friends or please witch doctors and it was only at the insistence of his team-mates that he complied, throwing the chain into the back of the goal and promptly forgetting it as he enjoyed a relatively action-free first half with hardly a shot to save or a cross to catch. At half-time he trotted into the dressing room, confident that his team would build on a one-goal lead and go on to win. As soon as Peter walked into the dressing room the witch doctor pounced. 'Where,' he asked, 'is the lock and chain?'

Peter had not given it another thought since throwing it to the back of the net and he told the irate African that it was still there. The witch doctor fled out of the door as though all the bats in hell were after him but after a fruitless search he returned empty handed, looking very despondent, and convinced that his rival had found the amulet and would use it against his team. This, thought the English goalkeeper, was the ideal time to put these ignorant people right and show them that he could win without hocus pocus against a side clearly inferior to his own. Sure enough, his team threatened to overwhelm the opposition but their goalkeeper was inspired and when he wasn't making world-class saves, the ball would strike the post, crossbar or an unsuspecting backside. Under this constant pounding, the rivals were restricted to half-a-dozen breakaways—and scored off every one with shots going past the bewildered B'alac from all sorts of distances and from every angle.

Needless to say the story spread like wildfire particularly among the Europeans and among us goalkeepers. Like me, Gary Bailey had forgotten all about it until some friends of his arrived from South Africa to watch Gary in an FA Cup replay for Manchester United against underdogs Brighton and Hove Albion. As a gift they presented Gary with a small lock and chain tied with Manchester's red and white ribbon. Gary would have probably dismissed it but for the fact that relegated Brighton had scored twice against him in the first game and also that Gary had never kept a clean sheet at Wembley. He carefully placed it in the back of the net and, of course, United won 4–0! Maybe it was a coincidence but when Gary returned to play his first full game for England against the Republic of Ireland, he blotted his copybook by allowing a soft shot from Liam Brady to creep past him three minutes from the end of the game.

Needless to say when Gary returned to Wembley a few weeks later to play for Manchester United in a Cup Final against favourites Everton, he made sure he had a lock and chain tied round with red and white ribbon. He told only one journalist, whom he was sure would not make fun of his superstition, but it all became common knowledge when he arrived at United's headquarters without his lucky charm. No more fuss could have been made than if the referee had left his whistle behind and the talisman was rushed to Gary who, again, carefully placed it with his spare gloves in the back of the net. Laugh if you will but Everton, who had carried all before them and were heavily tipped to add the Cup to their League title and European Cup Winners' Cup successes, could not find a way past Bailey even when United were reduced to ten men after Kevin Moran was sent off.

Gary kept a clean sheet and United won 1–0. I must ask him someday what happened at the start of the next season when he conceded two against Everton in the Charity Shield!

Constant exposure to these deep-rooted rituals and tales like those sometimes make you wonder a little and though you appreciate that there is little solid evidence to support it, you become reluctant to dismiss it totally. It would have been disruptive to my teams not to have complied with the odd strange request in Rhodesia and South Africa but I also have to admit that I dabbled a bit while at Liverpool.

Like most footballers I have my superstitions, such as putting on my left boot before my right and my goalkeeping top on last of all. Another of my quirks was to kick the ball against the dressing room wall until I had knocked out both light switches. I confess now that it was more of a game than a superstition and I kept it up mainly because it used to annoy our former manager Joe Fagan so much.

Voodoo became more of a reality to the Liverpool players when a black American spiritualist with Nigerian parents started to be a frequent visitor to Anfield. He was studying law in Britain but was well versed in voodoo and when he gave me some substance to rub onto my face before matches it took me back to my African days and, just as then, I went along with it rather than step out of line. The strange thing was that we enjoyed a really good run, losing only to Spurs and Manchester United and conceding just two goals at Anfield. He always had an excuse for me when things did go wrong and though he could hardly blame it on the opposition witch doctor, as they did back home in Africa, we did lose that game to Gary Bailey's team!

In Africa it was the common procedure for the witch doctor to give you a little piece of root to tuck in the roll of your sock, which you returned to him at full-time. Sometimes, if the match was really important, they would give you a little powdered skull to rub on your face. At least it gave the supporters someone other than the players and manager on whom to vent their anger when results weren't good. Once, while I was playing for the Callies in Zimbabwe, we were due to play Chubuku on Sunday and their witch doctor turned up on Friday to try and make his magic work. It was not just bits of root and powdered skull for this guy, he had the full works complete with grass skirt, grass headdress, goats' tails and a bucket full of some strange substance. All that was missing was the bone through his nose.

Our club did everything they could to keep him away, chasing him off the pitch and even putting him on a bus but he was nothing if not persistent and when the big game came he was up and down the touchline more often than the linesman. The only problem was that we won 3–2 in extra time and after the final whistle he was chased down the road by stone-throwing fans and was subsequently fired by the club. We were scarcely in any position to laugh, however, as we were every bit as bad. Before our home games we would regularly travel to the township of Mzilikazi where we would stand around in a circle at the youth centre stripped naked and desperately hoping that none of the locals would see us. We would go into the witch doctor one at a time to have water swished over us with a goat's tail and while we were still wet we would put on our football kit and rejoin the circle where we would chant things like 'eZulu', which meant warrior, and 'Chilamoya Bosso', whose meaning I still don't know.

I was one of two or three regular white players in the team and we would have to go through this mad ritual straight faced and make out we believed in it every bit as much as the rest of our team-mates. If we did not or showed the slightest sign of doubt it would have severely discouraged the others and they would have played well below form. From the room we would go to the ground where we would put on our boots in the dressing room. If we were away from home the team would get changed on the bus because they believed that the opposition witch doctor would have cast a spell on his own dressing room. At this we drew the line, however. It was all very well standing round in the buff in a quiet youth centre but it was a different matter getting undressed on a bus driving through a black township like Gwelo. Three pink bums stand out just a bit too much and Scot Martin Kennedy, Afrikaner Boetie Vanas and I would travel by private car and join the rest of the team at the opponents' ground. We would enter the pitch by threading our way through the crowd and climbing over the fence. It was not quite as dignified as trotting down the tunnel to the welcoming roar of the crowd!

The grass that was burned in the dressing rooms or smoked by the players before games had a marked effect with players running around like crazy and playing on oblivious to often quite serious injuries, such as Zenzo Ndlhovu's double fracture. It also gave rise to some strange excuses for poor play even among the top players. Experienced Arcadia goalkeeper Stuart Gilbert, who performed miracles in the World Cup qualifying play-offs against Australia in 1969, told me himself that when he was playing against Mangula Mines the ball was turned into 'a roaring lion' whenever it was shot at him – and that was why he let in six goals. It was not until I went to Chibuku that Billy Sharman and Nimo Schilacki made a stand against it and told the witch doctor to get the hell out of the dressing room. They were reprimanded by manager John Garatsa but they told him it was a load of rubbish. Some of the blacks were afraid and upset at first but when results were good they soon came round to our way of thinking.

It was little different when I went to play in South Africa, particularly when I played for AmaZulu. We did our training on a rough little pitch outside a seedy bar called the Smugglers' Inn. Before each session we would stand around in a circle and a local fellow would flick a tasseled walking stick at our knees, which was a ritual he would repeat at the end of the session before we nipped off to watch the strip show and pick up the girls in the bar.

They would also burn the leaves in the dressing room, even in the Rand Stadium before a Mainstay Cup match. From experience I knew the smoke had to have some sort of narcotic effect and carefully held my breath while my team-mates inhaled the sweet smelling fumes. There was another occasion when AmaZulu were playing Maritzburg at the Kingsmead Stadium and our witch doctor was refused admission to the dressing room. All hell was let loose and the game was on the point of being postponed when he was allowed in just ten minutes before the kick-off.

Even then the kick-off had to be postponed as we sat round in the dressing room while our medicine man threw his bones, which were actually the bones of a goat or a small buck called duiker. In football terms it was all fairly harmless and not very different from an English manager who has a lucky suit or a favourite tie. It is rather like the sugar pill which if the patient thinks is going to do him good it probably will. Far more serious was the juju practised in the villages of Rhodesia when I served my two years in the army. There the witch doctor was all-powerful with more influence and control than the elders. We were forced to commit some terrible acts ourselves in a bid to overcome the fear the natives had of their juju man and the terrorists. We were in desperate need of information on the whereabouts of the guerrillas but when we went into the villages to find out, we were met with a wall of silence. We would pretend to take off the children to shoot them but after the shots had been fired out of sight the witch doctor would always tell the mothers we were bluffing and not even an elaborate masquerade with goats' blood and masterly acting could convince them otherwise.

All too often it would end with physical abuse but if the terrorists had got to them first they would not have stood a chance. I have seen and heard of some truly awful acts used to buy villagers' silence and none worse than the regular stunt of dragging the main chief's number-one wife to the centre of the kraal, hacking off her top lip and making the chief eat it or be shot dead under the threat that worse would befall the whole village if any secrets were given away. They meant it, too, judging by the burned-out huts and families discovered. It was strong juju, having been practised for centuries and almost impossible to break down whether in a bloody war or in a football dressing room just before kick-off.

9

Goalkeeping:
My Style

Like most boys, my first hero was my father and he was a
goalkeeper. At the age of six I had no doubts at all that he
was the best in the world and, naturally, I decided I wanted
to be like him. The funny thing is that I have not changed.
Dad has gone but he is still my favourite goalkeeper and I
still want to be the best goalkeeper ever to catch a ball.
Even my mother was a goalkeeper. She played hockey and
did the same job as my father, keeping the ball out of the
net. There was no way I was going to play in any other
position in football than goal and, while I enjoyed everything and anything connected with sport, I was never
happier than when I was using my hands and catching. I
loved playing rugby, keeping wicket in cricket and, when I
was not pitching a baseball, I would be a catcher.

We even had our own goalposts in our back garden and
it was my father who taught me not to be afraid to come
from my line to catch the ball. He used to tell me not to
be scared because the opposition would only be heading
the ball and it could not hurt me. Dad used to bang shots
at me, encouraging and helping but never pushing me. It

was not like a teacher-pupil relationship because his attitude was that the most important thing was to enjoy your sport and even after I had played in matches, he always asked if I had enjoyed the game before wanting to know how many goals I had conceded. 'When it stops being fun, stop playing,' he would say. The advent of television increased my interest in the game and in goalkeeping in particular. We used to watch all the top international matches from around the world and most weeks an English League match would be shown. The other kids would have their favourites who would always be strikers but, for me, the only players who mattered were the keepers and I knew every one of them.

For no apparent reason my affections lay with Derby County and thus Reg Matthews was my favourite goalkeeper. But I carefully studied and read about others like: Bob Wilson at Arsenal; Peter Bonetti of Chelsea; Bill Glazier at Coventry; Everton's Gordon West; Gary Sprake at Leeds; Peter Shilton then in goal for his first club Leicester City; his predecessor Gordon Banks at Stoke; Tommy Lawrence of Liverpool; Ron and Peter Springett at QPR and Sheffield Wednesday respectively; Jim Montgomery at Sunderland; Pat Jennings of Spurs and Northern Ireland; Phil Parkes of Wolves and Bobby Ferguson of West Ham. I would watch them on television and then go out into the back garden and throw myself around the way they had done. So when these famous names criticise my style they should beware, I might have learned it from them!

It was my delight in stopping shots anytime and anywhere that earned me my introduction to Salisbury Callies and, after my father, the second greatest influence on me was their first-team goalkeeper Mick Poole who is now assistant coach to the Zimbabwe National side. He took me under his wing and, fortunately, he had the same attitude as my father and allowed me to develop naturally. It was only as I progressed into the seniors that they tried to add to my shot-stopping agility when they told me, in my first game, to patrol the 6-yard box only and leave the rest of the area to my more experienced defenders. I did and the centre-half promptly hammered the ball through my legs for a spectacular own goal and we went down 3–1 with me left wondering what these silly tactical ideas were all about.

I much preferred to come for crosses and, by the time I moved on to Matabeleland Highlanders, I was coming as far as the edge of my penalty area to make catches much to the surprise of opposing forwards. I must admit I find that part as enjoyable as making vital saves. It gives me the same kind of thrill to catch the ball on the edge of my box before a forward can make his strike at goal and, what is more, I still do. I have to be a little more circumspect these days but if the ball is floating towards the goal I cannot see the point in letting someone have a free header at your goal, when it is much easier to catch the ball. A goalkeeper should always be the natural choice to take the ball in his hands before anyone else can head it. Coming from your line when the ball is on the ground or at an opponent's feet is a different matter completely and it was not until I went to Canada and came under the guidance of the former England goalkeeper Tony Waiters that I began to appreciate the importance of this. I have often been accused of coming too far but the theory, which I learned in Vancouver, is that if you stay on your line in those circumstances, the forward with the ball at his feet has a better than even chance of scoring. If you come off your line you not only narrow his view of the goal but also give yourself the chance of stopping the danger before it develops.

Playing in the North American Soccer League was a great breeding ground for the adventurous goalkeeper because of the shoot-out that was developed to decide matches. Because the public like a positive conclusion to games in the States, they devised a system whereby if the game was tied after 90 minutes the teams would take it in turn with the ball placed on a 35-yard line and the forward given five seconds to score. As a goalkeeper the best way of stopping him was to come off the line, like Carl Lewis, in order to try and boot it clear or smother it before he could get in his shot. Thanks to the help and guidance of Tony Waiters and Phil Parkes I came to be regarded as one of the best in shoot-out situations. Tony would make me stay on my feet for as long as possible to make forwards commit themselves and, for hours, he would roll the ball between a forward and me to take 50–50 balls or worse. The biggest fear for a youngster in that situation is that of being injured and goalkeepers' courage over the years has given rise to the saying that you have to be crazy to be a goalkeeper.

Somehow that feeling has been confirmed throughout the years but I would like to know which one the crazy footballer is, the one who stands waiting for the ball to come to him or the one who runs all over the field chasing it? And, as for injuries, I see far more centre-forwards and centre-halves having their teeth knocked out, noses broken or needing stitches in their heads than goalkeepers. Manchester United's Kevin Moran does not think he has been in a game unless he has had a few stitches in his face afterwards.

Of course, you have to be plucky to throw yourself among flying boots to try and pick up the ball and, in my relatively short career, I have broken three fingers and dislocated every one on each hand. I am lucky because the breaks heal quickly and I have always managed to put the dislocations back myself and carried on playing. It is no use crying and no use complaining because if the forwards know you are injured they are sure to take advantage of the situation. They would be stupid not to. I learned my lesson when I was still at Mount Pleasant High School. You had to be tough to survive there for if anyone lost a playground fight, one of the penalties was to throw the loser down a quarry and into the water, which proves the point that there is no one as cruel as a child.

During my life I have twice broken a hand and each time it was through fighting. The first occasion was at Mount Pleasant and I was more worried about losing the fight and getting wet than about the pain from my hand. Having survived to win it, I then decided that the injury would not keep me from playing football for the Callies reserves against Mangula reserves. I knew my Mum would not let me play but I persuaded her to let me watch and, having hid my boots the night before, I made sure she saw me wave goodbye empty handed before picking them up and playing with one hand bandaged and splinted with two fingers sticking in the air like some obscene gesture. I did not receive a great deal of protection as two of our players were sent off and I tried to keep the opposition out with one hand. Not surprisingly we lost 8–1 and I learned a lesson about being too brave.

Peter Shilton is probably one of the most determined goalkeepers in international football and he has the ideal build for the job. When he comes off his line he spreads his body as wide as he can, much more so than his old England rival Ray Clemence who is more likely to come out feet first. However, the boldest I have ever come across is the much-travelled John Burridge who would throw himself under a bus if he thought it would save a goal. But

I would not recommend any aspiring young player to copy him because there is a narrow dividing line between being courageous and being foolhardy.

In any case, goalkeeping is much more of an art than just being brave and gymnastic. I am sure that Tony Waiters' great ambition is to find and develop the best technical goalkeeper in the world. He used to coach me for hours and talk about goalkeeping for just as long and he always maintained that it was more about angles than acrobatic and spectacular saves. He reckoned that the ideal keeper would be more of a mathematician than a contortionist. It was a bad day for all of us in the Tony Waiters' school of goalkeeping when the authorities made marking of the pitch illegal. That line on the 6-yard box in the middle of your goal was a wonderful guideline to find what Tony called the 'A1' position, in other words the ideal point from which to make a save and to give the opposing forward the narrowest of angles.

When I went from Vancouver to Crewe my goalkeeping education was not neglected and, though Tony Waddington could not coach me himself, he made sure I went to people whom he knew could. One of these was former Crewe manager Harry Gregg, who was one of the first to dominate the entire goal area in his golden days with Manchester United and Northern Ireland. I spent a week at Manchester United training with Harry where he was helping another young man with a pronounced South African accent, who was none other than my old adversary Gary Bailey. I learned a great deal from Harry. He was a marvellous tutor, and able to put across his views well. He always said that any free kick from 30 or 40 yards out on a touchline should be a goalkeeper's and one of the first things he did was to make me stand on the edge of my 6-yard box practising for that eventuality, adding a good 2 yards to my normal positioning. He worked me hard on crosses and quick, accurate distribution. I could see the sense in that. A goalkeeper is not only the last line of defence but also the first line of attack and a quick throw in front of a forward can often catch the opponents napping.

After my experience at Manchester United, Tony arranged for me to visit Nottingham Forest to watch how one of his former goalkeepers, Peter Shilton, trained. Permission was obtained from Shilton's manager Brian Clough and Tony Waddington took me over to the City Ground on the first day to introduce me. I had heard varying reports about Brian Clough and I did not know what quite to expect. I need not have worried. He was kind and helpful, not only on that first day but during the training sessions as well. When we were shown into his office, he was dressed in his squash gear, sitting in an easy chair with his feet on his desk and his racquet at the ready. He made us welcome, telling me that Tony was one of his best friends in football and that he was pleased to help him. He looked me up and down and said: 'Boy, I understand you would like to play at this level of football. Well, if you really mean it, I should pack in that Mickey Mouse stuff on the other side of the Atlantic and get over here as quickly as you can. This is where it matters and this is where you should be.'

He was right, of course, and he set me thinking about my future. After working with Peter Shilton, I knew that I should come to England permanently. The England goalkeeper taught me a great deal. I spent two weeks with him and probably learned more in that short time than in the rest of my career. He showed me agility and reflex exercises that I still use to this day and will carry on using until I retire. He must have done a hundred of them every single day and I thought at the time that, perhaps, he was a little obsessive and overdid it. But when you look at his career and his record now, you realise that it was, at the very least, the right preparation for him. Clough used to leave the goalkeeping training to Shilton and I understand that England manager Bobby Robson often does the same, letting Gary Bailey and Chris Woods learn from Shilton when specialist coach Mike Kelly is not around. Shilts kept his young understudy Steve Sutton and me on our toes for the whole two weeks we were with him, doing reflex work, scrambling and never once letting us take our eyes off the ball.

One of Peter Shilton's greatest assets is his peripheral vision. During a 90-minute game he rarely takes his eyes off the ball and yet he is still able to note the all-important positions of both his defenders and the opposing forwards. That is the art of concentration, something in which Ray Clemence also excels. Clem set a First Division record one season when he conceded only 16 goals in 42 games, which is an amazing achievement and one which may never be beaten. Ray had the benefit of a superb defence in front of him but his art and expertise lay in being able to maintain his concentration throughout a game when he had little to do until he was required to make a vital save on the rare occasions he was needed.

I do not think I have ever met a footballer as dedicated to his profession as Peter Shilton while his will to win is matched only by the fiercest of outfielders. He does not come from his line quite as much as he used but that is probably due to caution in view of his advancing years. Even so he is still the best in the First Division. I admit being slightly envious of him for he had a wonderful apprenticeship under Gordon Banks when he must have learned an awful lot from such a highly-skilled keeper. In those years I was fighting for my life in the jungle and, when I went to Liverpool, Ray Clemence left almost immediately. It was great getting straight into the side but professionally it would have been much better for my future if I had worked under the England man for a couple of years. My knowledge has been gained from looking at others from a distance and while Shilts and Clem have been learning their trade for 16 or 17 years I am still the novice with so little First Division experience under my belt.

Outside match days, there is little interest at Liverpool in the goalkeepers and I often used to go back to the training ground at Melwood on my own, when Joe Fagan was not around, to work out. It is a specialist position that needs specialist coaching and as much practice as is physically possible. I have taken a couple of goalkeeping clinics in England and I am only too happy to pass on what I can to youngsters. My opening line is the same as the one from my own first lesson and I tell them that if they don't enjoy goalkeeping they should try something else and if they let in six goals, so what. The time for them to worry about that is when they are playing for a living.

A lot of youngsters, and some older critics who should know better, are impressed by the goalkeeper who turns shots round the post or over the crossbar, catching the ball only when it goes straight to his chest. My aim is to catch the ball away from my body so as not to always put myself and the defence under pressure. If you catch the ball your side immediately has possession, but the flashy fingertip save means that the opponents still have the ball. I know I am guilty of dropping a few but I do catch more than I drop. I tell the kids to do what I did, which is to keep hammering a ball against a wall and try to catch it at whatever angle it comes back. But if I have a son of my own I will tell him to try his hand at every sport before making up his mind which one he likes best. I used to

enjoy racquet games, swimming, hockey and all sorts of
outdoor activities apart from the more established pastimes
that I played well. I only wish I had taken up golf sooner.

Like everyone else I have my favourite players, though
my first favourites do not necessarily figure among my top
few goalkeepers. My Dad, of course, is still my ultimate
hero while engraved in my memory from childhood is a
Malawi international goalkeeper named, if my memory
serves me right, Kapambrere. He let in his share of goals
but what made him special was that he had only one leg.
To attain international standard for whichever country with
that disability is quite incredible and he should stand as an
example to every handicapped person, of whatever age, in
the world. For me the best goalkeeper of all time is the
current Soviet Union captain Renat Dassayev. I thought he
was easily the best goalkeeper in the 1982 Spain World
Cup finals and yet others like Spain's Luis Arconada, West
Germany's Harald Schumacher, Italy's Dino Zoff and my
old friend Thomas N'Kono of Cameroon received greater
publicity. Maybe it is because the Moscow Spartak
goalkeeper is less flamboyant than the others, and content
to do his job in the simplest way possible. His catching
was safe and clean and his distribution superb. I saw him
play on Astro-turf in Seattle and it made not a bit of
difference to him, he was still outstanding. N'Kono was far
more spectacular in Spain, tipping shots around the post
and over the bar. I'm not saying that this style is wrong,
but give me Dassayev every time.

I was surprised at how many international goalkeepers
captain their teams, such as Dino Zoff who led Italy all the
way to the World Championships in 1982, and Peter Shilton
who captained England and made it known he would have
liked to have kept the job. Providing that they command
their areas and are assertive goalkeepers like Shilton and

Dassayev, I see few difficulties but the problem will arise when forwards, who are out of earshot, need motivation. The Real Sociedad goalkeeper, Arconada, was another World Cup captain in Spain, who had the added pressure of carrying the hopes of the host nation on his shoulders. This seemed to weigh heavily on him in Spain for he made some unusual mistakes but, even so, he also made some outstanding stops. He is a natural leader, a penalty-area general who will boss his players round and is well suited to captaincy. I would put him third on my all-time list behind the outstanding Dassayev and Shilton with the acrobatic Ray Clemence, even now a truly great goalkeeper, and Everton's Neville Southall in fifth place.

My heart bleeds for Neville. It has taken him a while to break through into first-team football and once there he performed magnificently and helped Liverpool's old rivals Everton to the treble of League Championship, European Cup Winners' Cup and Milk Cup in 1985. His part in that was inestimable because his talents helped settle down a defence which, a year earlier, was suspect to say the least. He has shovels for hands, knows how to catch the ball and has remarkable reflexes. He is often unorthodox but this does not detract from his effectiveness. If he continues to improve he will become a world beater but, like his fellow countryman Ian Rush, he badly needed the stage of a World Cup Finals. Had he done so I am sure he would have been hailed as one of the greats, but not only did Wales fail to qualify, but the European ban on English clubs has narrowed his field down even more.

Only after these five would I include some of the all-time greats in the following order: Gordon Banks; Pat Jennings; another Russian Lev Yashin; Dino Zoff; and one of my childhood heroes, Felix of Brazil. I can hear the old timers screaming abuse even as I suggest such a heresy but

I firmly believe that football, like every sport, has made dramatic strides over the last ten years or so. In every sport where improvement can be gauged, such as athletics, the statistics are incontrovertible because world records can be measured in times and distances. The same progress must apply to other sports as diets and physical fitness get better. The pressures on top sportsmen are now so great that they are forced to develop their techniques as well as their all-round fitness and agility. The whole game is more sophisticated than it used to be in those terms with smarter players forcing goalkeepers to be more alert. When you look at some old film footage of games, it can be almost embarrassing watching the so-called greats. What I would add, however, is that the truly world-class players like Pelé, Stanley Matthews, Tom Finney, Eusebio, Banks, Yashin and the rest would still be world-class now because their talent was enormous and they would have adapted to modern changes.

I am not belittling their performances or careers at all. I am still thrilled by Banks' wonderful save from Pelé in the first Mexico World Cup Finals while Pat Jennings has probably done more for the image of goalkeeping than any man alive or dead. The Irishman with the bucket hands was the first gentleman of football, the perfect professional on and off the field. You would never hold him up to a youngster as a model for goalkeeping because he was so unconventional, often plucking the ball out of the air with just one of those enormous hands of his. How I envied these goalkeepers when I first set eyes on them. It was like a skinny girl looking at Dolly Parton. Both Pat Jennings and Dino Zoff, the latter of whom played in the World Cup Final against West Germany in Madrid at the age of 40, have more than adequately shown that age is no barrier to a good fit goalkeeper and that is something which is desperately important to me because I missed out on my early years through National Service and then started playing top-class football relatively late in life. I would like to think I could carry on until then. Yashin also played beyond the age of 40 at the top level and it is interesting to note that the average age of the 24 number-one choice goalkeepers in Spain was over 30!

When I was a kid leaping about in goal, it was Reg Matthews or the Brazilian Felix who captured my imagination and when the other kids would ask who I was copying I would say, 'I'm Felix the Cat'. Their response would always be the same, 'Felix the Dead Cat'. But even then my greatest ambition was to be put at the head of someone's top ten of world goalkeepers. Maybe it sounds a little trite but why not? Without ambition you might as well not bother. Maybe I would have stood a better chance had I opted for Scotland as my birthright and not committed myself to Zimbabwe. With all due respect it would be hard to place any Scottish goalkeeper in an all-time list, certainly none that I can remember. They have all been good journeymen but nothing more. By contrast England and even the Welsh and Irish have had great tradition for producing goalkeepers. There are plenty of good Englishmen about now though none to equal Peter Shilton yet, nor even as good as Ray Clemence. Chris Woods and David Seaman might take that extra stride forward if they really work at their game and get the right breaks. Woods now looks to be the outright favourite to replace Shilton eventually now that my old pal from Africa, Gary Bailey, has been forced to quit the game because of a severe knee injury picked up in training with England. He could have been one of the best.

It can often take time to make the grade as a goalkeeper, just ask two Liverpool old boys Steve Ogrizovic and Bob

Bolder. If Oggi continues to work the way he has who knows where it may lead him. When asked who I thought was the most promising some years ago, I picked out Aston Villa goalkeeper Nigel Spink. He had replaced the experienced Jimmy Rimmer just a few minutes into the European Cup Final against Bayern Munich. He followed that emotional experience with a mature first season in Division One but then suffered a cruel injury after making his England début in Australia. He has already shown he has the character to come back again and go all the way. But, all-in-all, the standard of goalkeeping in the Football League remains remarkably high and the future looks to be sound enough.

10

Hooliganism:
Football's Shame

One of the reasons I was hastened on my way to England
was the increasing violence at African football, both on and
off the pitch. It was something I felt I could do without,
especially as the position of goalkeeper is particularly
vulnerable, as you present a close and fairly static target
for the lunatic and his missiles. Little did I realise then that
I was swapping beer cans and rocks for billiard balls, darts
and eventually a riot that ended with the murder of 38
spectators before the European Cup Final between Liverpool
and Juventus in Brussels in May 1985.

However, that was all to come and my foremost thoughts
on that long flight to London were of a game for Durban
City against Lusitano when I had been tossed a full can of
beer for every goal we conceded. Fortunately I had managed
to catch them all and went off with a half pack of six beers
to drink in the dressing room, but the fans were not always
so considerate. It could become quite rough, not just
between blacks and whites but also between the different
tribes who would fight each other if there was no one else
to fight.

At the start of that last season in South Africa I had torn some of my ankle ligaments when our coach Bill Williams came down on my leg as I tripped over a pot hole. It meant a wrap-around cast on my left leg for the next six weeks. But within a couple of weeks I was playing five-a-side for our second team, helping them to reach a final. I used the incapacitated right leg to stand on and kicked with the left. It must have presented an odd sight with none of the opposition caring to come near that lethal-looking cast while the fans showered me with pebbles and stones. It was no better in the full-scale eleven-a-side football. The cast was off within four weeks and I was playing League football against an all-Indian team called Bearea who played in the oddly-named Curry's Fountain Football Stadium! I had been warned by my understudy that there could be trouble if we were winning and I took the precaution of packing a sawn-off baseball bat into my bag and popping it into the back of the net when the game started. Sure enough when we went three goals in front, a large section of the 15,000 crowd came surging through the barriers, climbed a 6-foot high fence and poured onto the pitch. The invaders gave me and my swinging club a wide berth and I escaped unscathed, at least as far as the car park, where I found the fans climbing all over my company car.

The danger was that the heavily-armed police might lose control and react violently as they have done so often during the civilian uprisings but, fortunately, the only time I saw shots fired in South Africa was when the police fired those warning shots over spectators' heads in the Lusitano against AmaZulu cup-tie. The police had gone one stage further, back in Rhodesia, when I was playing for the Callies against Matabeleland Highlanders. A riot had broken out in the second half when we went 2–1 ahead in a tense and exciting game. There looked to be little chance of the game being completed as the inevitable stones rained down and the fans began to clamber over the walls. A Rhodesian policeman surveyed the scene, took out his revolver and deliberately shot one of the Africans in the leg. Everyone held their breath and waited. The stones stopped and, all around the ground, the spectators sat down and we went on to win 3–1.

Leaving the ground and, indeed most grounds, players had to sit with their football bags wedged tightly against the windows so that they were not showered with broken glass as the coach was stoned. But, despite those incidents, the violence was worse in South Africa than in Rhodesia, particularly in the townships where it was a way of life. It was not just the black townships either for one of the most frightening incidents in my experience occurred in the smart Indian suburb of Swaraj. Durban had won 5–0 and were saluted in the traditional way – with a shower of oranges. When the Africans saw this happening they went one better and threw rocks, and big ones!

We did not have too much racial trouble in Durban at the Kingsmeade Stadium. We compromised with a mainly white side with one African, the talented Moffat Zulu, and, to balance this, one Indian, whose playing was so mediocre that I cannot even remember his name. But it was important as the Indian community was so powerful in Durban.

Some of the crowd problems in Africa were caused by the inadequacies of the stadiums, if they even could be called that. There was a ready supply of ammunition—rocks, trees and bottles—which were put to good use when they became upset. In some places there were no stands or terraces and, at one of the grounds in South Africa, there was just a rope separating the players from the supporters. Playing there for AmaZulu in the Mainstay Cup reminded of my rugby days in the army. It was so bad that our wingers were tripped up by the supporters on the touchline just as we had been in our National Service. The police offered no protection and, to make matters worse, we won with a distinctly dodgy penalty. When the final whistle blew I picked up my kit from the back of the net and ran like hell. Two of our players were not quite quick enough and, along with our slower-moving officials, were severely assaulted. We crouched on the floor of our bus, driven by a bloodied and bruised driver who had borne the brunt of the attack. He was almost in tears when we left him to board our aircraft. His bus was a write-off.

When I was a lad growing up in Rhodesia I was encouraged to play the 'British Way'. Win or lose whether it was cricket, tennis, rugby or baseball, it was 'well played' and 'let's have a drink together'. So, though frequently shouting and insulting each other during a game, it would be forgotten in the showers. Even rugby, a hooligan's game played by gentlemen, would pass off largely without incident and be very sociable afterwards. Football was the exception to prove the rule and now, more than ever, I am convinced that it is a gentleman's game not only run by but also watched by hooligans. Only in football were we told not to shake hands with our opponents.

If I had hoped for better in Britain I had hoped in vain. The fans, if anything, were worse and I felt extremely vulnerable in certain places. When playing for Liverpool in the Milk Cup against Burnley at Turf Moor, I suddenly felt a sharp pain in my back. It was a dart. They caught the idiot who threw it and asked me if I wanted to press charges. I said yes because if I hadn't, then he might well have been tempted to do it again and the next time it could have caused even more serious injuries to the unlucky goalkeeper involved. Just as daft was the billiard ball I had thrown at me in a game against Manchester United at Old Trafford. I can't say I have ever seen razor blades stuck in potatoes that were often used at one First Division ground, but a favourite weapon, and one police are powerless to prevent, is coins. I can't understand why people don't keep their money in their pockets, God knows it is hard enough to come by. I once collected almost £2 in loose change at Brighton.

Just down the coast at Southampton great play is made of their hooligan-free family area. They must be kidding. Whenever I try to fetch the ball from behind the goal at that end I get spat at, which is something that never happened in Africa, and, once, I even had second-hand toilet paper thrown at me. What really worries me is when I look round and see maybe three or four hundred fans with their backs to the game, not interested in the slightest in the football but only in what action they can find on the terraces.

Peter Shilton says it is best to keep on the move and I advocate staying on the edge of the penalty area when play is at the other end, not just because that is where a good goalkeeper should be. These precautions are, of course, not necessary at every ground and at some grounds I can build up a good rapport with the fans. London fans have a bad reputation but I have had some great fun at Spurs, Arsenal and West Ham. True they chant things like 'Zulu' and 'Go back to Africa you jungle bunny' but I don't mind that at all and usually respond with a little war dance. Coventry City and Aston Villa are other grounds I enjoy playing at because I can have a laugh and a joke.

On the Continent they tend to make use of their cheap fresh fruit and I have been pelted with apples, oranges and pears from Lisbon to Madrid. I have eaten some and, on one occasion, thrown them back. That was against Benfica in Lisbon and I was severely reprimanded by Liverpool manager Bob Paisley who collared me and demanded: 'What are you trying to do – start a riot?' If they had just stuck to fruit it would not have been so bad but the firecrackers and Roman candles the continentals ignite to celebrate a goal or a victory have now become rockets and flares and, instead of being confined to the terraces, they are aimed at the playing area as well. Again it is the poor goalkeeper who is the easiest target and in Austria I had my hair set alight by a firework. I was glad it was only a firework and not one of those rockets or flares for, soon afterwards, a magnesium stick landed perilously close to my team-mate Gary Gillespie and me. It was unnerving because if one of those hits you it sticks and can cause serious injuries. In this case I was sure it had been deliberately aimed at me.

You would have thought that the recent tragedy at Bradford City, when the stand burned down at the cost of so many lives, would have brought home the dangers of playing with fire but, just a few weeks later in Rotterdam the Rapid Vienna fans were setting flags alight and firing rockets. Fifty-three men, women and children were lost at Valley Parade and a further 38 were crushed to death a few weeks later in Brussels. Another fan died in riots in Birmingham with visiting Leeds United supporters. How long is it before a player joins those gruesome statistics? How long before one of my fellow goalkeepers is maimed or injured?

A player was very nearly badly injured when Rapid Vienna goalkeeper Herbert Feurer was attacked by a spectator during a CWE cup-tie against Celtic and forward Peter Pacult was kneed in the groin by another thug as the players left the pitch. Feurer did the right thing in not fighting back but had any harm come to him, the football authorities would have had to shoulder much of the blame. Those attacks happened in the 'neutral' stadium of Old Trafford, Manchester where Celtic and Rapid Vienna were ordered to replay their cup-tie after one of the Austrian players, Rudi Weinhofer, claimed he had been hit by a missile thrown from the crowd. I watched the television replay and, like most other people, believe that it was a piece of sheer opportunism and that the object thrown from the terraces did not strike the player. Even if it had there was no possible way that UEFA should have ordered a replay to be staged in Manchester. If they had felt that the result had been influenced by the incident in Glasgow so strongly they should have either awarded the tie to the Austrians or ordered a replay to take place behind closed doors.

UEFA set a very dangerous precedent in giving fans of the losing side and unscrupulous players the chance of a way out. In fact, UEFA did not have to wait long for the fox to be released among the chickens as Inter Milan demanded that their UEFA Cup semi-final against Real Madrid be annulled after full-back Giuseppe Bergomi was hit on the head by a marble which was picked up by goalkeeper Walter Zenga. Inter even appealed when their complaint was rejected but Real escaped without punishment.

While not attempting to defend the culprits in Brussels, I feel strongly that the ruling European body should accept some of the blame for initially not checking the standard of the ground they had selected to stage the European Cup Final between Liverpool and Juventus and, later on, for not ensuring that the normal precautions had been taken by the Belgian Football Association. That night in the Heysel Stadium in Brussels I picked up two flick knives from my goalmouth. One was closed while the other had its sharp blade wickedly open. I handed them both to a policeman who dropped them on the running track behind my goal and walked off. His attitude is also symptomatic of the problems that football faces for we live in a violent society where terrorism, murder, rape and violent robbery are everyday events often dramatised through television, films and literature. If football were successful in getting rid of these lunatics from our terraces, what would happen to them? Would they suddenly become normal, law-abiding citizens? Of course not. Banish them from football and they would simply go and make trouble elsewhere.

Football hooliganism is part of a much wider problem which society, not just the football authorities, has failed to deal with. Punishment in Africa was frighteningly violent and swift. Here in Europe and in Britain, in particular, the sentences are too soft and I am not just talking about those handed out to hooligans. How often do you pick up a newspaper and read of a murderer or a rapist being given a prison sentence that bears no relationship to the crime and especially when the years for good behaviour are deducted. For me a 12-year prison sentence should mean just that – 12 years. Identity cards and family enclosures are not going to frighten the criminals away from football but tougher laws and stiffer penalties might deter a few of the fainter hearted. Football must try and help itself as well before all of the genuine supporters are driven away from the game in disgust. One way would be to make the game more exclusive with smaller stadiums and more season tickets. Apart from making the crowds easier to control and the task of picking out the troublemakers simpler, it would give the sport the sort of appeal that American ice hockey commands with waiting lists for vacant season tickets.

When I played for Vancouver in Canada and North America, I saw little or no violence. But there is not much that soccer in Britain can learn from the Americans in this case because the circumstances are so different. Fans do not travel very often over there because of the great distances involved. For example, our nearest away game was against Seattle and to reach that 'local derby' required a three-hour coach trip if you were in the reserves and an hour on a plane in the first team. The only violence I encountered during these games was from the various mascots at away grounds. They usually came in the guise of animals like the New York Cosmos bunny but the worst was the San Diego chicken known to all and sundry as Mad Harry. He, up to now, has been the only person to attack me on a football field, running on and kicking me in the backside as I bent down to place the ball for a goal kick. On another occasion I dived to tip a ball around the post in my best acrobatic fashion only to see this huge feathered fiend performing even more spectacularly to catch the ball and run off with it. He refused to return it until the referee showed him the yellow card.

I can imagine the old fuddy duddies of the Football Association and the Football League going into emergency session if anything like that happened in England. Once, when I ran onto the pitch wearing the mask of an ugly old man while on loan to Crewe Alexandra in the Fourth Division, from Vancouver Whitecaps, the referee threatened to send me off if I did not remove it at once! Maybe that is part of the problem. Perhaps if we could only learn to laugh a little at ourselves and our game, the spectators on the terraces would do the same. It is the hardest thing in the world to make trouble and become involved in fights when there is a relaxed and friendly atmosphere.

11

Brussels

Fighting in a brutal, often dirty war for two years I saw sights which often made me despair but they were nothing compared with the events of the night of 29 May 1985 at the Heysel Stadium in Brussels when 38 football supporters lost their lives, many hundreds more were injured, and the great name of Liverpool Football Club was vilified. Perhaps the atrocities of war are somewhat easier to accept because they are expected. Blood, death, injuries and screams are part and parcel of any military conflict but they should be the last thing on anyone's mind in a sports arena. It should have been a joyous night, a carnival of football between the two acknowledged masters of European soccer, Liverpool and Juventus of Italy, watched by 50,000 committed fans in the Heysel Stadium and by many millions in 37 countries on television.

It instead turned into a nightmare and almost caused me to finish my professional football career. At the end of the game I was ready to quit football altogether and head home for South Africa. I am a man of impulse and, had that not been the last game of the season, I could not possibly have played again. As it was I almost immediately left for a holiday with my family and while sitting in the warm sunshine of Orlando and the Cayman Isles going through the early chapters of this book I thought to myself, 'Why should these animals masquerading as football supporters spoil my life? Why should I run away from a sport I truly love?' Sitting by the poolside I managed to put it all into perspective. Had I been in the game purely to earn a living I would not have considered it worth playing again but, because I feel a commitment to the game and its future, I decided to stay on and, in my own small way, help put the smile back on its face.

Those responsible for beginning the trouble have no place in society; they are sub-human. We have all seen them, their minds warped by drink they cannot handle and their cowardice shielded by the mob that surrounds them. They are not football fans. They are animals who want to fight the world. Equally as bad are the yobs who are too afraid to be violent but confine themselves to verbal abuse, egging on those who will fight anyone's battles. Then, finally, we have the ordinary supporters who turn up simply to watch the football, shout and enjoy themselves. Mums, Dads and children. These are the lifeblood of the professional game and its future and it is up to us to encourage them to come back to the stadiums by offering them good, safe facilities and a sport they can enjoy watching in comfort.

The players can help by giving up a little of their time after games to sign autographs, talk to the kids and try and show them that their heroes are far removed from the lunatic fringe whose only interest in the game is to use it as a vehicle for violence. I just hope and pray that Wednesday, 29 May was the worst tragedy that can befall the game, that the wheel will turn and that football will never have to suffer that kind of degradation again.

The real tragedy, at least for the families of those killed when the wall collapsed behind the goal, was that the whole mess could have been avoided if the right precautions had been taken. We arrived at the Heysel Stadium about 90 minutes before the scheduled kick-off and, while we were waiting for our kit to be laid out, a few of us walked onto the pitch for a look at the ground and a taste of the atmosphere. It was immediately apparent that there were a lot of Juventus supporters at the Liverpool end of the ground, in what we came to know later as 'Z' section, and I remarked on this to Alan Kennedy who was standing next to me, adding: 'It is the same as the final against Roma last year, the Italians have got most of the tickets again.'

It was an explosive mixture and this should have been made more obvious to the authorities when they saw trouble starting outside the ground even before we arrived. Yet there were only a handful of police within the stadium so close to kick-off time. But the mood, at that moment, was not too bad as a few of us wandered over to the main body of Liverpool supporters with Sammy Lee and I kicking a little plastic ball back and forth into the crowd as they laughed and joked while there was a small shower of coins thrown at us from the Juventus supporters at that end.

There was a youth match going on at the time which came to its conclusion while we were out there and, as we walked back across the pitch, I turned to young Steve Nicol and asked him if he wanted to kill a little time by walking round the ground. It was a mistake. The Juventus supporters at the other end were in a wild mood and we were forced well away from their terraces as we were showered with concrete blocks, stones, coins and flash bombs. We had expected to be jeered but this was something far more sinister even if their missiles were landing 20 or 30 yards from where we were walking.

We successfully ducked the missiles, stopping to speak to a couple of the Italian players and to some of the wheelchair-bound fans on the touchline. I decided against returning straight away to the dressing room with the other players, staying instead to have a cup of tea with our reserve goalkeeper Bob Bolder and Alan Kennedy. We stood gazing at the growing unrest in the crowd and Alan Kennedy remarked: 'There is murder going on out there and it is going to get worse. This is going to get a lot worse.' I still thought that it would all quieten down and I eventually slipped into the dressing room and put on shorts, socks and boots, leaving off my top, before hurrying back onto the running track around the pitch out of my concern for my wife and family in the stands. As I emerged from the tunnel I saw a group of no more than 50 supporters in Liverpool colours surging across the terraces behind the goal. That was the beginning of the end.

I watched in horrified fascination as this small minority charged again. It was clear that the group they were running towards did not want to stand and fight. They backed off and backed off until they could go no further, becoming crushed like sardines against a wall. Where the hell were the police? I wanted to shout at them to go and stop it but there were not enough of them inside the stadium and those who were looked as frightened as I felt. Something had to give and it was the crumbling, old wall at the end of the terrace which went with a crack like thunder as the bodies tumbled over in a cascade of arms and legs.

My nightmares of old had suddenly become an horrendous, bloody reality. Those screams that had so often woken me from my sleep were shrieking through my ears again only this time we were not in the bush, it was not a war. This was supposed to be a football match for God's sake! I had just about stomached the brutalities of that war in Africa and I thought I had become used to seeing dead bodies in peacetime too, having tried to pull an old man out of his car after it had crashed, but here were grown men behaving like savages and I found myself thinking that I did not want my family to be a part of this sort of society. My family! Where was my wife Debbie? Her parents? My Mum and stepfather? I saw, with some relief, that all was relatively calm in the stands but, though I could see some of the players' wives, I could not see Debbie. Someone told me that she was round the other side and safe but it was not until later that I knew for sure that everyone in my party was unharmed and that my parents and my in-laws had not arrived until shortly after the devastation when a young, white-faced Scouser had directed them away from the carnage.

By this time those who had escaped the horrific crush were staggering onto the running track surrounding the pitch and the playing surface itself where, incredibly, an impromptu game of football began in one of the goalmouths. The participants could not have realised what had happened, no one did. It was chaos. The Italian fans screamed their anger at the cowardly police, spat at me and the other recognisably British people and screamed abuse at the shocked , onlooking UEFA officials.

It was then that someone told me that there were at least six dead and probably more. I had feared the worst having witnessed the collapse of the wall but I had hoped against hope that my first instincts were wrong. I went back down the tunnel to tell the other players what was happening. At first they couldn't believe it and then as the enormity of it slowly sank in, they were naturally relieved to hear that their own families were untouched by the tragedy.

Our manager Joe Fagan, that kindly man with the fatherly image, was the most visibly shaken. He had made it official only that lunchtime that he was retiring after the European Cup Final. This was to be his last game in charge and he was hoping that he would be given the perfect send-off by our winning the European Cup for the second year in succession. Suddenly football and retirement were the furthest events from his mind as he tried to take in what was happening to his beloved Liverpool Football Club and the game he worshipped. He, like the rest of us, wanted desperately to do something to help. With tears running down his cheeks, he stripped his top off so that his Liverpool shirt was clearly visible and, with our calm security officer Tony Chinn, made his way to the main body of our supporters to plead with them for peace and common sense. That walk across the pitch must have been the longest in his life for he was booed, abused and spat at by the Italians who, along with everyone else, were now learning the full extent of the carnage. People were being pulled free of the pile of bodies, some alive, many injured and some, quite clearly dead. One Belgian policeman told me that the toll was over 40 and rising while another argued that no one really knew how many had died.

Numbers hardly mattered at that stage. The awful truth was that there were many dead and you could see them lined up against the wall of the stand, some covered with sheets and others with the black and white striped flag of Juventus Football Club. I went back to the dressing room, partly because I felt so helpless and also to let my team-mates know exactly what was happening. They, like me, wanted to do something, anything. The Italian team felt the same because gradually they slipped out to try and calm their own rioting supporters behind the goal at the other end. The whole place was in uproar, a powder keg just waiting for another spark to ignite it once more. Some of us went to the boss and said we were sorry if we were speaking out of order but would it help to calm matters down if we went out onto the pitch to warm up? Joe said that only the Swiss referee, Daina, could make that decision. We honestly believed that by going out and kicking a ball around we could distract the fans and the ever-willing Tony Chinn went off to find the officials' dressing room to make the suggestion. He came back saying that they would speak to the managers only and, in any case, it was out of their hands and up to UEFA to make the decisions.

They, we heard, were also in conflict as to what should be done with some saying that it would show a total lack of respect to the dead even to think of playing football on such a night while others, including the police and the town officials of Brussels, were pleading for the game to go ahead to try and prevent any further bloodshed either in the stadium or in the city. For me there was only one solution and that was, grisly as it was, we had to play. If we had not there would have been a total riot, an even greater tragedy. The stadium was in danger of being ripped apart and the city of Brussels after it. I have heard stories of the so-called callous disregard of the footballers who were supposed to have remained ignorant of events in the dressing room and then have gone out and played football as though nothing had happened. The truth could not have been more different. The people in that dressing room in the Heysel Stadium were devastated and the atmosphere indescribable. This was not football we were going to play, it was a charade. There was no warm-up before we left the dressing-room, none of the normal rituals that become more exaggerated the more important the game. I went out there feeling like a second-rate citizen. What would it matter if we beat Juventus and won the cup that night, nothing at all. How could you feel pride over something like that? In football terms it was a non-event.

However, it could not appear to be that way to the fans. We knew that and so, too, did our opponents. We were professionals who had to go out there and play to the best of our abilities. There were tears as we left the dressing room and no major game of football has ever been played against a backdrop like that and, please God, never will it be again. I knew that the Juventus players must have been going through the same emotions. There was not one player on either side who could have felt like playing football that night. I made a point of going up to my opposite number, the Juventus goalkeeper Tacconi, and wishing him all the best in Italian. Once the game began we were all professionals playing as well as we could. But it was cold, without excitement and without any feeling for football.

My goalmouth was surrounded by debris, concrete, metal tubes, spent fireworks and, in the goal itself, those two flick knives. While I stood there, trying to concentrate on the job in hand, I was constantly overcome by flashes of what I had witnessed and the prophetic discussion I had had with Bob Harris the night before the game. I had wanted to take my mind off the final and suggested to Bob that we work on the book. Incredibly the subject was crowd violence throughout the football world, the vulnerability of the goalkeeper and how far it would go before someone would take a gun into a stadium and aim it at a player or another fan. It all became horribly true less than 24 hours later. The more I thought about it the angrier I became. There was nothing I wanted more right then, and now as well, than to see the culprits caught.

The game could not finish quickly enough as far as I was

concerned. For the record, and for all it matters, we lost
Mark Lawrenson with a recurrence of his injured shoulder
two minutes after the start of the game and Paul Walsh a
minute after half-time. The Juventus captain Platini scored
the only goal of the game from the penalty spot for a trip
that was clearly outside the penalty area while the referee
ignored Bonini's obvious foul on Ronnie Whelan about a
quarter of an hour from the end. Under other circumstances
we would have felt bitter, but all we wanted to do was get
changed and find our wives. The night had already been
far too long.

I couldn't bring myself to go over and clap our supporters
as tradition demands in case any of them had been involved
in what had happened. Instead I spoke to Tacconi who, at
any other European Final, would have been the hero of the
night. I congratulated him and told him that he was
'Numero Uno'. He thanked me and went off to pick up his
European Cup Winners' medal before setting off on a rather
pointless lap of honour. There was nothing to celebrate.
Not for anybody.

Danish international Jan Molby and I quickly changed
and went out to find our ladies. We were instantly called
the 'Bastard English' from a sea of contorted and angry
faces. We did not try to run away, instead we tried to
show them how disgusted we were at what had happened
and with those who had caused it. I spat at the ground. It
is a gesture every Italian understands and suddenly we
were treated like human beings again. However, it only
heightened our concern for our wives in case they were in
any sort of danger. They weren't, as it happened, in any
physical danger but they were completely distraught, and
especially my wife Debbie, for some Italian journalist had
told them that the children who had played the exhibition
match before the trouble began had been standing under

the wall when it collapsed.

Having seen the girls safely onto a bus I went in search of the Juventus coach to wish their players well and then returned to my team-mates who were standing on the running track inside the stadium looking in horror at the devastation around them. That running track must have saved more than a few lives that night and I shall never play at another stadium with the same facility without thinking of that ground and that European Cup Final.

I had seen for myself the failure of the police who, as the trouble began, had run away when a show of police strength could have headed off the holocaust. Now we were looking at the crumbling terraces, paper-thin walls, bent and buckled crush barriers and the trampled chicken wire fencing that would not have deterred a nursery group never mind drunken, violent, grown men with hatred in their heads and blood on their hands. Admittedly, Liverpool were going to have to bear the brunt of the blame, even after 21 years of successes in Europe, but some of it had to be shared by those who organised the Final, not just those in Brussels who ignored all the recognised guidelines, but also the UEFA officials who failed to spot the potential dangers of a stadium in such an ill state of repair.

There were not many people who emerged from that black Wednesday evening with much credit and I hope those who were responsible for the policing, the choice of the stadium and the selling of tickets, looked around that ground the way we did. They would have seen the area where the wall collapsed littered with hundreds and hundreds of shoes, children's, women's high heels, trainers and, as we left the stadium, the haunting sight of a little girl of no more than nine or ten in a pink dress with one shoe on and one shoe off, limping through the litter of shoes and discarded bags searching for who knows what, her lost shoe? a father? a brother? I wish I knew.

If only security had been as heavy before the game as it was afterwards, we could be talking about the football now. No one outside the Liverpool party could get near the two coaches as we climbed quietly aboard to join our wives and head out of the city to a dinner arranged for us by Liverpool's shirt sponsors, Crown Paints. It was hardly going to compare with the party in a country house in Rome 12 months earlier but who wanted to go back to a lonely hotel room with just memories for comfort? Some of the lads, not to mention the odd wife or two, tried to erase the events of the night in a sea of alcohol. For some it worked, for others it did not. In Rome we had partied and sung until dawn because we did not want the night to end. In Brussels many of the same players sang, danced, ate and drank until dawn again but this time without heart and only because it meant they did not have to reflect on what had happened earlier. Different people react in different ways. I could not join in. I couldn't drink, sing or dance and I scarcely touched the plate of food in front of me. I sat there thinking that if my mates had seen what I had seen they wouldn't have done so either. The quiet ones were those who had been out on the track when it happened. You could pick us out.

I tried to lift myself out of my deep depression on the way home that Thursday afternoon. With some difficulty I attempted to live up to my reputation with a little clowning around at Speke Airport in Liverpool but the heart was hardly in it especially after seeing sad Joe Fagan sitting at the back of the aircraft, completely devastated and still having to face the unrelenting newsmen hovering at the airport. He just wanted to get away from it all. What a way to end his brief reign as manager. My heart bled for him.

My mind was still in turmoil. When I had come out of Heysel Stadium after the game I went up to a friend and said: 'For God's sake get me away from this club,' and I meant it. As far as we knew, Liverpool people, so-called supporters of the club, were to blame and I did not want myself, my wife Debbie nor my little daughter Tahli connected in any way with the hooligans. Having heard Liverpool's respected chairman John Smith point the finger towards a group of National Front members who had confronted him at the Heysel and then hearing a friend from British Airways tell of the London, Scottish and other regional accents urging others to use the glass Coke bottles (actually on sale inside the stadium) as missiles as well as of an Italian in a green anorak directing operations through a megaphone, I began to revise my opinions – until I returned to my Liverpool house. I had always suffered in that particular street from young delinquents but on the day we got back they were the last thing I needed as a group of them wearing Everton's blue and white, stood outside the house chanting 'one-nil, one-nil, one-nil' and throwing stones at our windows. It sickened me. Not so much their actions and reactions but the very thought that this was the next generation of hooligan being bred under my very nose. The sort of young people my daughter would have to go to school with when she was older.

My depression was back, my urge to leave Liverpool began to grow again as I read in the newspapers and watched on television the dreadful follow-ups to the disaster. The memorial service at Liverpool Cathedral was a moving and upsetting occasion and I was ready again to quit football altogether, to go on holiday and then, perhaps, return home to Africa for good to find a new career. I played football for fun, not for money, and nothing could be further removed from fun. I felt so strongly about it that when I was asked by the *Sunday Mirror* to relate my version of what had happened in Brussels, I jumped at the chance to let my feelings be known and, despite what some cynics said, it had nothing at all to do with money as News Editor Tony Frost had already told me, even before he knew the strength of my feelings, that publisher Robert Maxwell had dictated no payment. That was my mood as I flew south with my family to Miami. I simply did not know what I was going to do with myself and my future and it was not until I read through the first pages of this book that my resolve began to strengthen and I decided that not only would I report for pre-season training with Liverpool but also that I would do whatever I could within my limited powers to try and make the game safe and happy again.

Of course, that is what every sane person wants and the world-wide reaction to the disaster proved it. We were banished from everything, with Liverpool themselves, striving to hold their heads high and maintain their dignity, voluntarily pulling out of Europe for the following season. In retrospect it was a hasty decision, an act inspired by the desire to take some of the blame but, in light of UEFA's indefinite ban on all English clubs plus an extra three years longer for Liverpool on the next occasion they qualify, it was a rather meaningless gesture. For me the UEFA ban was a bad decision. By all means ban the clubs with supporters who cannot behave themselves, Liverpool included despite their previous good record, but to kick clubs like Norwich out of Europe smacks of panic after all the building up to Brussels. My sympathy also went out to the international players of the blacklisted clubs, especially in the year before the World Cup, when they needed all the experience they could get. Even a criminal is deemed innocent until found guilty. Here everyone was found guilty by implication.

If UEFA's ban was hasty in view of the growing problem of violence then FIFA, the world governing body, behaved absurdly when they slapped a world-wide ban on all English clubs, stopping them travelling even to Wales, Ireland and Scotland. It was ludicrous, done without thought or consequence and though they as good as admitted their stupidity by withdrawing the ban before the new season began, a lot of damage had already been done with countries all over the world denied visits of top players from England as close and pre-season tours and tournaments were called off at the last minute doing nothing at all for the tarnished image of the game.

Without any sort of inquiry or inquest FIFA had used the iron fist to batter the reeling English game. They felt that they had to make an example, but why this time? Why not when one of their own World Cup matches in El Salvador provoked an outbreak of war? Or when, 21 years before Brussels, 318 had died and 500 were seriously injured in the worst sporting catastrophe of all time which took place at an Olympic qualifying match in Lima between the home country Peru and Argentina. That was caused by a refereeing decision, crowd violence and police panic. Seventy-four people died in Argentina, a regular scene of football deaths, in 1968 when Boca Junior fans threw lighted newspapers onto River Plate supporters in Buenos Aires. Even in Eastern Europe there is football fan trouble and it was only in 1982 that 69 died and 100 were injured at the end of a UEFA cup-tie between Moscow Spartak and the Dutch club Haarlem in the Lenin Stadium, home of the Olympic Games just two years earlier. Go through the records. Forty-nine died in Cairo at a friendly; 44 in Turkey; 22 in Greece during an Athens derby game; 6 in a Haiti-Cuba World-Cup qualifier at Port-au-Prince when police opened fire after a firecracker was thrown; 5 in Santiago before a Chile international against Brazil in a stadium used some years earlier to house political prisoners.

When the Brazilian-born President of FIFA, Joao Havelange, sanctioned that world-wide ban on English fans after a game he did not attend despite the fact he was in Europe, maybe he had forgotten about all those South American riots and acts of violence. It was only three years earlier that three had died and twenty-five were badly injured when police fired shots into an angry crowd in his own country after the home team San Luis had been beaten by Fortaleza. Because of the world-wide coverage, Liverpool's 1985 European Cup Final against Juventus will be remembered long after these other disasters, some of which were very much worse with far more serious crowd disturbance, have been forgotten and the name of the greatest club team in Europe since Real Madrid will permanently be tarnished and reviled.

12

From Paisley
to Dalglish

It has always been a major point of debate in professional football whether someone who is still playing the game at the highest possible level can manage his team at the same time. Trust Liverpool not only to fly in the face of convention but also to make sure that the appointment of Scottish international striker Kenny Dalglish would work by naming Bob Paisley, one of the all-time great managers, as his right-hand man. It took a great many people inside the game and even inside the club by surprise as it had always been the Liverpool custom to leak these matters well in advance so that everyone could become used to proposed change. There was plenty of speculation about the pending retirement of the then incumbent Joe Fagan, but it took most people unawares when Joe beat the club to an official statement about his retirement by holding an informal press conference for a handful of journalists in the team hotel after lunch in Brussels hours before the nightmare of our European Cup Final against Juventus. Kenny's name had been put forward by one or two newspapers but clearly only as guesswork, for others had mentioned our

English international full-back Phil Neal, our recently-departed skipper Graeme Souness, former boss Bob Paisley and the usual outsiders like John Toshack and Gordon Milne.

Not even the players knew anything official, which was a rarity in itself, but we had had an inkling of the appointment as early as our European Cup semi-final with the Greeks Panathanaikos when it was Kenny, rather than the new skipper Phil Neal, who seemed to be running the show in the absence of Graeme Souness. The rumours took on more substance on that same depressing night in Brussels as we went through the motions of an after-match party organised by our sponsors Crown Paints. Everyone that night seemed fairly convinced that it was Kenny who would be the new boss though at that stage no one knew exactly how much power he would wield and if his appointment was an apprenticeship one or merely a cosmetic one to allow Bob Paisley back into full power. One thing was sure and that was that Phil Neal had not been offered any part of the deal. You could tell just by looking at his face and it must have been one of the most unhappy nights of his life.

We had the entire summer to think about it and Kenny had the same time to prepare himself for the dramatic change in his professional life. I am told that when he first arrived at the club from Scotland hardly anyone, including his room-mate and fellow Scot Graeme Souness could understand his thick Glaswegian accent. It had clearly improved over the years but that broad edge remained and when he did speak it was usually to make a sarcastic remark or to tell one of his daft jokes. Everyone at Liverpool is quick to poke fun and clearly Kenny's big test was going to be how he handled the players in the first meeting of the season. Any hesitancy, stuttering or other mistakes and he would have been given a terrible time and his authority would have been instantly undermined. Kenny called us in for our chat and told us that off the field he was now the manager. He talked solidly for a couple of minutes without pause or embarrassment, leaving no room for doubt. He was positive and assertive. He was the new manager. Most of us welcomed his attitude though, inevitably, there were the odd one or two among the senior players who either could not see his ability or did not want to because of past differences.

If I harboured the slighted doubt over his authoritativeness it was soon dispelled when I had an indifferent beginning to the season and made one or two costly errors. Kenny Dalglish was not slow in letting me know that he would not tolerate slap-happy goalkeeping and made it abundantly clear that if it continued I would be 'on my bike' and looking for a new club. Some acquaintances may have been surprised that I took it so calmly. I did so because I have tremendous respect, firstly, for Kenny's extensive knowledge of football and, secondly, because he was basically right. I was not playing well and was costing the team goals and points. It had all begun quite well for Kenny and me with a solid two-goal victory over Arsenal but then, away to Aston Villa, a misunderstanding with Mark Lawrenson had led to a chain of events which finished with the ball going under my body and letting in Villa to score the first goal of the game. I held up my hands and took responsibility but afterwards Kenny told me: 'We cannot have you making the same mistakes week in and week out. Watch yourself.'

It happened again at West Ham when I was caught in no-man's land as the ball struck Alan Hansen on the heel. I was also faulted for the second. I could not accept that but, again, I had to admit that I could have done better on the first. It started to come to a head when I conceded a goal at Newcastle and Kenny told me that I was not in a strong position. By then I had suffered enough criticism and, for the first time, hit back. My argument, not just with Kenny but with the entire Liverpool set-up, was that I was a goalkeeper only on match days. Whether it was a legacy from Ray Clemence or even Tommy Lawrence I do not know but the fact of the matter was that I had arrived at Anfield as a goalkeeper and had developed into a fine five-a-side player! If I had been allowed to devote as much time to playing in goal as to scoring I would be a better goalkeeper now. To emphasise my point I banged my fist down on the treatment table sending the cups of tea flying around the dressing room. I had made my point but then spoiled it all at Oxford when, with just a few minutes remaining and Liverpool 2–1, I came a long way off my line and was beaten with a back pass from Alan Kennedy. Bob Paisley, as ever, offered his moral support but Kenny showed he was the boss and warned me about my future and the possibility of my looking for a new job. It put me on my toes and made me realise that I still had a long way to go if I was ever to achieve my ultimate ambition of becoming one of the world's best goalkeepers.

In those first few weeks Kenny had shown that he had both the physical and mental strength for the task ahead of him. When he is on the field and playing he asks for no more than to be treated as another player, participating in the usual verbal abuse that rages between players of the same team during a hard First Division game. But off the pitch he is boss. After that draw at Oxford he told players other than me that he was not happy with their performances. Some found it difficult to handle. Paul Walsh, who was challenging Kenny's place in the team, was told at half-time he was not trying. He turned on Kenny and told him what he could do. Kenny rounded on the Londoner and explained somewhat more directly that only one person would be leaving — and that would be Paul Walsh. No one makes a swear word sound quite so bad as a Glaswegian and Kenny really meant it. But Walsh worked hard in that second half and kept his place for the next game, before Kenny came back after injury. He had no hesitation in leaving out experienced, established players, selling full-back Alan Kennedy to Sunderland, keeping Phil Neal on the substitutes' bench for the local derby against Everton at Goodison Park, and naming Alan Hansen as the new captain instead of the expected Mark Lawrenson. One of the questions being asked at that time was whether Kenny could cope with pressures on the pitch as well as he could off it. He set about proving both his team selection and that his own form was at its peak by scoring a 20-yard stunner within 25 seconds of the start of the derby, though he later displayed endearing human fallibility by missing two open goals. Knowing Kenny and his demands for perfection, he probably warned himself about his own future after the game!

It would be unfair to judge Kenny Dalglish's abilities as a manager too quickly even though he has stepped into a job that most other managers dream about, a job that is backed by a team of top experts and a tradition that keeps the machinery well oiled. At least it certainly used to. Kenny was appointed at the most traumatic of moments in a climate that would have sent a great many players scampering for the cover of their nearest bank. Although Liverpool had finished second in the First Division behind Everton and reached the final of the European Cup, the previous season had been considered a near disaster because the club had failed to win a trophy for the first time in ten years. Worse still was that he took over in the aftermath of Brussels when English football, and Liverpool in particular, came in for world-wide criticism which culminated in that indefinite ban from European competition and was followed by a further three years for Liverpool when other English teams were readmitted.

So Kenny inherited a club with no international future, a club that was in decline according to its critics and, because of the attendant problems, a club that would find new players hard to attract. To make matters worse the City of Liverpool was also in turmoil with vast unemployment and an extreme left-wing council which was determined to fight Central Government regardless of the consequences. I have no doubts that the Anfield hierarchy had Kenny singled out as managerial potential well before his appointment but I am equally sure that they had anticipated Joe Fagan staying on a good bit longer than the two years he was in charge. What is more I am certain that it was originally intended that Kenny should eventually be offered the management of the club in harness with his old room-mate Graeme Souness. It can never happen now, of course, because Graeme stunned everyone when he returned from Sampdoria to take over Rangers in Glasgow. But I was not at all surprised when he took Scotland by storm, signing top players and matching Kenny by taking the double of Scottish Premier Division and Skol Cup in his first season, even though he had some problems with the referees over the border. The Scottish Football Association have come down hard on him but they may have to turn to him one day to manage Scotland. Both have an incredible will to win which dominates them. They want to be the best so badly that the feeling infects those around them. They also have a fierce loyalty to the club they are playing for as Souness showed when he went off to Sampdoria and soon inspired them to their highest-ever League placing and their first-ever Italian Cup victory. This attitude means that there are no favourites and if their best mates have to be dropped for the good of the team so be it. It was always obvious that Graeme had this hard ruthless streak in him and it needed only a few weeks for Kenny to display it too. Maybe it is something inherent within certain Scots for since Jocky Hansen was named as the new Liverpool captain he has displayed a tenacity and involvement that had not always been obvious previously. I have always thought that Hansen should be the best defender in Britain but, instead, that honour belongs to his fellow central defender Mark Lawrenson.

It may take a season or two but I have no doubts about Kenny's eventual success at Liverpool; after all he has a wonderful example to follow in his right-hand man, Bob Paisley, who is greatly esteemed by everyone at Anfield and not least of all by me. Bob Paisley is without doubt my favourite manager and that says a great deal in view of my admiration of Tony Waddington and my immense respect for Tony Waiters. Bob Paisley, as everyone with the slightest knowledge of football knows, is a down-to-earth, straight-talking man from the north east of England. He is not the most articulate of men but always makes sense when football is being discussed.

It was Bob Paisley who decided that I was the goalkeeper they needed at Liverpool and having persuaded me to leave Canada and, having led the lengthy and difficult negotiations before my transfer, he fully supported me through all my bad times. The story goes that when he went to Crewe to watch me for the first time, he stayed only long enough to see me go through my warm-up routine and the kick-in before the game to decide that I was worth following up. I am told that he left before the kick-off and I can believe it after our ultra-brief meeting in

Canada when all he wanted to know was whether I wanted to play for Liverpool. Once he was convinced that I did he allowed neither transfer nor work permit difficulties to stand in his way of taking me to the club. He backed me totally when I came in for all that criticism in my first couple of seasons and when it started again under Kenny he was behind me once more. He appreciated that I ideally needed a season or two in the reserves before taking over from Ray Clemence but when the moment came he had the confidence in my ability to plunge me straight in at the deep end and when I made my mistakes he would simply tell me that as long as I learned from the errors I made I would improve.

Some managers who have never been goalkeepers try to tell you what you are doing wrong and suggest how to put it right when it is blatantly obvious that they haven't a clue what they are talking about. Others do. Tony Waddington, for example, signed both Gordon Banks and Peter Shilton so he certainly knew the subject while Bob Paisley's arguments were so basic and full of common sense that you could not dispute them. He said that his one regret over me was that I could not grow older more quickly for he maintained that as I became more mature I would slow down and allow experience to override enthusiasm. He always claimed that I came off my line far too quickly. I hope to prove him right eventually. His greatest asset as a manager was being able to identify a problem before it developed and to do something about it. This was almost certainly because his knowledge of the game was so deep and his reading of matches so brilliant. He can still come in at half-time and, in a few words, explain a weakness in the opposition, how to exploit it and inevitably be proved right. He was able to capitalise on the opposition's mistakes and flaws. He and Graeme Souness seemed to have had an almost telepathic understanding and, in the end, Graeme was making the necessary adjustments before Bob told him about them.

Bob was very interested in my background and I suppose we also had an affinity in that we had both served in the army. He had been, by all accounts, a very brave soldier, serving in the tank corps in North Africa during the Second World War. I told him that he must have had the advantage in the desert of miles and miles of unrestricted vision while our visibility in the jungle was poor because of the trees and creepers. He quickly put me down by relating the story of a sandstorm so bad that he led an entire convoy of tanks straight into the middle of a German encampment. 'How,' I asked, 'did you get out of that one?' 'I just put my bloody foot down,' he retorted, 'What do you think I did?' However, he never put himself up on a pedestal, always remained down to earth and treated every player as an equal. He was very special and it was a sad day for all of us in 1983 when he decided he needed a break from the pressures of management and announced his premature retirement.

Bob had had an unenviable task when he took over the Liverpool reins from a legend named Bill Shankly. Bob had originally been nominated as a stopgap but did the job so well that he could have stayed on forever had he wanted. His secret lay in the way he allowed the great Shanks side to continue, making gradual changes until he finished with his own side which enjoyed even greater success than before. When Joe Fagan took over he decided to play it the same way, keeping Bob's team, and was rewarded at the end of his very first season by being named Bell's Manager of the Year after watching the team mop up the League Championship, the League Cup and the European Cup.

It was a just reward for a man who had devoted his professional life to the service of Liverpool Football Club, operating largely from the shadows of the famous bootroom before emerging into the full glare as manager. He was seen by the world as a marvellous, benign uncle figure who was always ready and willing to praise an opponent and underplay his own success. He was not like that all of the time, however. When he was angry he was not a very nice man at all as my room-mate Craig Johnston once discovered. Craig annoyed Joe with things he said and did and I am convinced that that is why Craig played so little for the team under Joe and why he did not realise his undoubted potential during those two seasons. It must be said that Craig deserved a lot of the treatment but he was and still is a talented footballer who simply needed a little help and guidance. Joe seemed unable to give it to him even though he would show his respect for Craig's football abilities by selecting him at crucial times for important matches. They had so many rows I could only imagine it was one of those unavoidable clashes of personality which sometimes occur. It reached a climax during one particularly bad run when Joe told the media that there would have to be changes at the back because of our leaky defence. Instead, when he read out the team for the next match, he left Craig and Jan Molby out of a midfield that had played well and named another midfielder, Kevin McDonald, at the back. At this I shouted out 'Who?' in an incredulous voice and quickly turned away to do up my shoelaces but when Craig discovered he had been dropped again he sighed and swore under his breath. Nothing was said to me but Craig was asked to stay back and, no doubt, they had another head-on collision.

However, I did have a difference of opinion with Joe that could have brought a halt to my Liverpool career. I would estimate that I came within five minutes of being sacked from the then European Champions. It concerned my unfulfilled desire to play international football at the very highest level and to help my country Zimbabwe to qualify for the World Cup finals. I did appreciate that Liverpool were my bread and butter and when I discovered that Zimbabwe's qualifying game against Egyptian Cairo was to be on the first Tuesday of the season I knew that the answer would be no and I was not prepared to take the issue to FIFA because of my respect for Liverpool. But, when I discovered that the midweek game was on a Bank Holiday Monday, I instantly applied for leave to play on Tuesday night in Egypt.

I was given a reluctant yes, providing I came straight back. I was delighted and, after playing against West Ham United at Anfield, I flew from Speke to Heathrow where I was to catch a flight early next morning. I arrived in Cairo in the late afternoon, as usual without a visa, because this time the Egyptian Consulate in London did not like the Israeli stamp in my passport. I was met at the airport by two Zimbabwean officials who were waiting for me and telling Egyptian immigration officials that no Grobbelaar meant no football match. It gave me a great lift to know they thought that much of me but nothing is ever as simple as that and no sooner had I arrived, with only three hours before the kick-off, than I was taken to the oddest team meeting I have ever attended. I was the only white man there with all the other players sitting on the floor while the President of ZIFA made a speech of welcome to me as I sat in one of the few chairs in the room. Having welcomed me he then turned to the players and said: 'We will now have a vote to see whether Bruce should play. If any player present feels for any reason that Bruce should not be in the team, he will not play.'

I sat there in amazement as the President looked around
the room and, seeing no hand raised, named me in the
team and told us all to go up to the eighth floor where,
would you believe it, the team witch doctor was waiting
for us. We were all required to strip naked and cover
ourselves with towels. Once inside the inner sanctum the
witch doctor rubbed some liquid on our faces, hands and
feet and then, when he had done this to everyone, we sat
naked in the bath, washed it all off and then put on our
match strips while still wet. Next it was the turn of our
boots and also, in my case, gloves to be treated. As I had
not had anything to eat for a while I asked if I could leave
my kit with the witch doctor while I had my usual
mushroom omelette. When I returned to the eighth floor it
was to find that some sort of animal flesh had been rubbed
in, leaving my gloves very greasy. It made me wonder just
whose side this lunatic was on and I had to sneak away
and clean my gloves before I could use them. No wonder
the local papers were predicting a ten-goal win for their
side.

The black magic must have worked for we had an
incredible game, hitting the crossbar twice and only going
down by a single goal. Even that was unlucky as a free
kick squeezed through our wall. Although I was unsighted
I somehow managed to scramble across my goalmouth and
push the ball against a post. Unfortunately I was the only
one on our side to react and every one of our team stood
admiring the save while their striker strolled up and put
home the rebound. But, despite that goal, we were ecstatic.
It was a tremendous performance that left us with a real
chance of beating Egypt in the second leg in Harare to
take one step nearer the finals. Our mood was matched by
people back home who were as convinced as we were that
the return match was a certain victory. I was looking

forward to the second leg as much as everyone else in the team and those back home in Zimbabwe.

With this in mind I left for Liverpool straight after the game as I had promised manager Joe Fagan I would. I got back so quickly and my enthusiasm was so great that I was even in Merseyside for the Wednesday morning training session having played in Egypt on the Tuesday night. Before I left I had full permission from the new Zimbabwe treasurer to make any arrangements necessary for the return leg which had been scheduled, thankfully, for a Sunday afternoon. There was a flight out of Gatwick at 8 p.m. on Saturday night and I could catch it if I could find a chartered plane to take me from Liverpool immediately after our game against Sheffield Wednesday. That organised and paid for, all it needed was Liverpool's permission.

Joe Fagan dashed all my hopes when he said that I had no chance, explaining that we had a European Cup game on the following Wednesday and that I could not be spared. I tried to explain that I would not even miss a training session and that I could be back on Monday. But he remained adamant. My mind was in turmoil as my professional instinct told me to forget it and get on with my job while my heart said to put two fingers up to Joe Fagan and Liverpool Football Club and go and play anyway. I reasoned that I could do it without anyone finding out and that as everything was timed to the minute there would be no problems. It was my chance to get to the World Cup finals and I was not going to throw it away. On the morning of the Sheffield Wednesday game I was wound up and by the time I arrived at Anfield I was positively euphoric. Suddenly Joe Fagan came up to me and casually remarked: 'By the way, who plays in goal for Zimbabwe when you are not there?'

I was amazed. It was as if he knew what I had in mind

and was testing me. I mumbled: 'Oh! It is some African named Lucky Dube.' 'Okay,' said Joe, 'that's all I wanted to know,' and with that he wandered off leaving me to wonder what the hell was going on. I carried on worrying about it for the entire game, going over in my mind what to do, knowing that if I were caught I would be in real trouble and almost certainly given my marching orders. Did Joe Fagan know of my plans? Was he guessing? Was it just a casual question? My concentration was shot to pieces.

The game was being televised all over Europe and in Britain as recorded highlights. I doubt that I will ever live down what I did that day when I ran yards out of my penalty area to intercept a through ball and then tried a clever little pass to Alan Kennedy. Instead I gave the ball straight to Imre Varadi who joyfully rolled it back past me and into the net. I have been involved in some bizarre incidents in football but none where I have looked quite as daft as that. We lost the game thanks to me and I could scarcely contain my anger as I quickly got changed and met a friend, Gordon Deardon, to go to the airport. We were scarcely five minutes from Speke Airport when I came to my senses and asked myself what the hell I thought I was doing. I was about to bite the hand that feeds me. I made up my mind then and there, went into the airport, cancelled the flight and returned to Anfield where I went to tell Joe Fagan exactly what had happened and to apologise for the stupid goal I had given away because of it.

He did not blow his top but said that he had known what I was up to and had I gone to Zimbabwe I would never have played for Liverpool again. Although I harboured a lot of bitterness over the episode there was no doubt that Joe was right and I was wrong. There was also an ironic twist to the tale for I discovered later that an engine on the aircraft I was due to catch at Gatwick had caught fire and that the flight was delayed while a replacement aeroplane was found. I only discovered this when some friends telephoned to say how unfortunate it was, while ZIFA also wrote to me saying what a pity it was that the plane had been unable to take off.

While accepting that I was wrong for even thinking about going behind the club's back, I still felt that Joe could have been a little more understanding over the situation especially when I heard how the match went. Zimbabwe had led for much of the match and looked favourites to go through after extra time. Then the Egyptians scored. What made it hard for me to swallow was that the goal had come eight minutes before the end from a 40-yard free kick! I am not saying that I would have saved it but I would have been very disappointed to have lost a goal from that distance. Just to rub it in the Egyptians went on to score another and World Cup dreams were gone again. I haven't played for my country since and because I now own a British passport I will not be able to play for them again unless they change their rules which state that holders of foreign passports cannot play for Zimbabwe. If they did I would be ready, willing and able to play for them providing, of course, I had my manager's permission.

Even so I had great respect for Joe Fagan and what he achieved with Liverpool. No one can take away that incredible treble of League, European and Milk Cup in his first season as manager while he was desperately unlucky at the start of his second season to lose the Club's most influential player, Graeme Souness. He not only lost a world-class performer but also a great leader, a player who was an inspiration to others. To make matters worse Ian Rush was absent for a large part of the early season campaign and the two factors together were a terrible setback. It is easy, with hindsight, to say Joe should have done this or that. If one of his experiments had worked he would have been hailed as a great manager but as it was he went through the card, trying seven players in Graeme's midfield position when maybe he should have accepted the loss and tried instead a different style using what players he had at his disposal.

I felt deeply for Joe at the end. It would have capped the marvellous career of a really decent, nice man if Liverpool had finished his last season by beating Juventus to win the European Cup. In the end no one, Joe or the players, cared who won the football match in Brussels. The events at the Heysel Stadium left Joe a broken man. He passionately loved the game and the club but that night a lifetime's work went sour on him and I will never forget his tear-stained face as he went to plead with the fans to behave themselves. On the aircraft back to Speke it was clear he wanted to be left alone and, since that day, I have scarcely set eyes on him.

When I arrived at Anfield Joe was one of the boot room team, which is part of the same exclusive group that had produced Bob Paisley before him. He was a happier man in those days, it seemed to me, and enjoyed the cut and thrust of his mates Ronnie Moran, Roy Evans, Tom Saunders, Reuben Bennett, John Bennison, Geoff Twentyman and, later, Chris Lawler. My particular favourite is Roy Evans, probably because he was my first real point of contact with the club when I arrived. He is the reserve team manager and has enjoyed huge success in that position, winning the Central League title almost by right. Evans was in charge of those first three reserve games I played and I am still convinced that his report of my performance against Bolton Wanderers was largely responsible for me starting the next season in the first team after the sudden departure of Ray

Clemence for Tottenham Hotspur. There always used to be considerable speculation that Roy Evans was being groomed for management, taking over after Bob Paisley and Joe Fagan, and I am convinced that he has the necessary qualities to make his mark if he ever has the chance. Maybe he lacks the mean, hard streak of Graeme Souness or Kenny Dalglish but he has a good knowledge of the game. He may have to wait for a long time for the opportunity but I can't see him going anywhere else in search of a job. He is Red through and through.

Ronnie Moran is just as dedicated and every bit as knowledgeable as 'Evo' but it would be hard to imagine him as Liverpool manager. There would be nothing but arguments and aggravation. 'Bugsy' Moran is a hard nut who is not afraid to tell anyone exactly what he thinks to their face, whether it is Graeme Souness, Bruce Grobbelaar, Kenny Dalglish or whoever. Sometimes he goes over the top and there have often been shouting matches with 'Bugsy' on the practice pitch and I have seen both David Hodgson and Jan Molby become so upset that they wanted to fight him. Ronnie didn't turn a hair, which is hardly surprising as he has even less than I do! I give him back as good as I get and on one occasion he rounded on me and shouted: 'You are not talking to someone in the jungle now, Grobbelaar.' I had the last word, replying: 'I wouldn't speak to a jungle man the way I speak to you. I have more respect for them.' People who don't know the Liverpool set-up and the man might wonder why he stays on. The answer, I am sure, is that his sharp tongue and aggressive attitude are deliberate ploys to get players 'at it', in other words to motivate us and start the adrenalin flowing. It is a bit like the detective films on television where you have one good, sympathetic cop working with a hard man who almost always plays the devil's advocate. Everything Moran does, every word he utters is for the good of Liverpool Football Club.

The key to Liverpool's success, something all the other 91 managers are constantly searching for, is simply the overwhelming importance of the team not just on the pitch where all players are equal, but also in the boot room and even upstairs where all the paperwork is done. This is the territory dominated by the Chairman John Smith, his General Manager Peter Robinson, better known throughout the game as 'P.B.R.'. They work extremely hard to keep Liverpool Football Club at the top and they must have suffered as much, if not more, than anyone else when the good name of Liverpool, which they have buffed and polished over the years, was forever tarnished by what happened in Brussels. Even if I wanted I could not think of anything bad to say about either of them for the limited contact I have had with them has always been conducted in the most proper and gentlemanly fashion.

My only serious negotiation with them after signing was when I renewed my contract after three years. I walked in to be greeted by PBR, Chairman Smith and Joe Fagan. They told me what was on offer, told me to think it over and come back later. As I consider it a privilege to play professional football, especially for Liverpool, I would have been happy to sign immediately and look at the contract later. This time I felt that maybe something was being asked of me so when I went back in and suggested that maybe they could help me with an annual trip back to Africa, it was then their turn to think about it and when they called me back it was to offer me a salary increase to cover my request which I could only assume was done because of tax purposes.

In every respect, it is a brilliantly-run club. The Chairman is one of the most respected sporting figures in Britain while PBR is, to me, 'Mr Liverpool'. They are both gentlemen but I would not like to be on the wrong side of either of them and I must admit to always feeling a little awed in their presence.

As far as I can tell they never interfere in the playing side with the dressing room being the manager's territory as are all affairs to do with the pitch. Although it is traditional now for the Chairman to say to every newcomer: 'The first 20 years are the worst,' and to follow it up by telling you on a Saturday afternoon or a Tuesday night that the first 90 minutes are the worst. He always tries to pop into the dressing room to wish us luck and I, for one, appreciate it.

The club is still run on the same day-to-day basis which can be traced right back to the time of the great Shankly. I should imagine that very little has changed since then as everything is checked against a big set of black diaries that are religiously kept up to date and checked against previous years by the boot room staff. The only ritual that has altered since I have been at Anfield is the regrettable axing of the daily club lunch. We still meet and change at Anfield before going by coach to our training ground at Melwood but in my first full season we would go back to the ground to change and then sit down together to chat and eat. It would only be something simple like a bowl of soup followed by a salad or steak and kidney pie. I thought it useful in helping to build club spirit. Now it's like every other club, change and home.

Liverpool are so professional in most things and yet surprisingly mean in other, small matters. A classic example is our training kit. Even at Crewe we had freshly-washed strip laid out every day but Liverpool just stick it in the drying room and you wear the same stuff until the end of the week. You can imagine what my gear is like after diving around in the mud on a wet day. Even if I wear it under the shower to get rid of the muck, it is still as stiff as a board for the following session. Friday is a dreadful day. Can you imagine the smell of those week-old socks?

Liverpool don't like physiotherapists either and, in fact, they are not too happy with players who get injured, particularly goalkeepers. Little matters like dislocated fingers and sprained ankles are not worth bothering with. When I started, if I wanted a tablet for a headache or an ointment for a sore limb, I would ask David Johnson who had earned the nickname of 'Doc' because he had more pills than the local chemist. The new dressing room doctor is Craig Johnston. His Australian connections earned him the nickname 'Roo' but I now call him 'Doc Roo' because he read tennis player Martina Navratilova's book and was impressed with all of her dietician talk of fibres, cholesterol and carbohydrates. He drinks water with every meal which invariably seems to be roast chicken. It reminds me of the day that I stood next to Bob Paisley watching Craig train. Bob turned to me, shook his head and said: 'I have just sold one headless chicken in David Johnson, and it is only right that I should sign another to replace him.'

Graeme Souness also had his own box of tricks, with his hairdrier, lotions, creams and his laxative tablets but then what else for 'Mr Perfection'. He was quite a character and he used to walk into the dressing room like some film star, always immaculate, reminding me of a Hollywood starlet who wakes up in the morning with perfect hair and all her make-up still on. We would take our tracksuits out of their wrappings with all the usual folded creases to spoil the line. Graeme's almost looked as if it were tailored. On the rare occasion he came in looking rough and unshaven he would brush aside all questions saying: 'Had too much sleep last night.' He could be arrogant and cutting but he had the total respect of everyone who played under him. He was an outstanding captain whose appointment was a stroke of genius by Bob Paisley, even though former skipper Phil Thompson was not too happy about it. It happened in a dressing room one half-time when Bob walked in and, in that blunt way of his, asked Thommo: 'What's the matter with you? The captaincy too much for you?' Phil gave a two-word reply and come the next game Graeme was the new captain.

Graeme looked super-smooth as he drove up in his smart BMW wearing his designer clothes. He was classy on and off the field but he could also be a very hard, mean man, and not just in matches but in training as well. But I did detect a weakness. He does not like the sight of blood, especially when it is his own! Once we were playing one of our usual fierce, five-a-side games and Graeme was driving players on and challenging for 50–50 balls as if it were the FA Cup semi-final. Suddenly I found myself in one of those situations where I could not have backed out even if I had wanted to with the ball falling between Graeme Souness and Kenny Dalglish who, as usual, were on the same side, and me. You will win no prizes for guessing who came out of the challenge with the ball but as I was sandwiched between the two Scots I was nudged off-balance by Dalglish and caught Souness on the bridge of his nose with my elbow.

He went down but appeared to be all right until he noticed the blood dripping off the end of his Roman nose. His legs gave way and he had to go off for a while. When he came back he looked at me and said quietly: 'I hope you did not do that on purpose, Bruce.' 'If I had,' I replied, 'you would still be lying there.' He believed me, or at least I assume he did, for I never got kicked back. Alan Kennedy was not so lucky – even though he was on the same side as Graeme when trouble flared up during a training session on a pre-season tour in Spain. Alan gave Graeme a terrible pass and when Graeme made the effort to give it back Alan did not try for it. Handbags were out instantly and before anyone could stop him Graeme had punched him. It turned out that he had waited four years to do that in return for something that had happened in the past.

It may sound a petty and vindictive act for such a highly respected player but it must be added that the two of them were drinking and laughing together after the training session. It was not often that Graeme came off the worst but he took a terrible beating in a Liverpool night club one night but it needed half-a-dozen grown men. Practice matches and five-a-sides were fiercely contested then and that, perhaps, is why Liverpool were always so competitive when it mattered on match days. It is not taken quite so seriously these days and I think our performances have suffered because of it. That is another reason why we miss Souness.

One place he was not missed at was our annual Christmas party at Tommy Smith's club in Liverpool. Every new signing has to get up at the party and do an act and I am reliably informed that the only act worse than mine was Souness's, who tried to do a smooth version of 'I left my heart in San Francisco', only to be shouted down and pelted with bread rolls and worse until he slunk off. I was thrown off when I played the violin. Those parties are a bit special and because they are strictly 'Stag' ones for the lads, the wives have become a little jealous and one year they arranged to meet for dinner on the same night and threatened to invade our party later on. We had bouncers on the door to protect us from our wives and girlfriends. The club have wisely always turned a blind eye to this one night when we let our hair down for it works wonders for the team spirit and the training staff get their own back next day.

The sort of fancy dress the boys wear to this special event confirms the character of this Liverpool squad. Everyone goes out of their way to be different and you would be amazed to see household names dressed in drag and worse. Traffic was once almost brought to a standstill in Liverpool city centre and to this day there are 'Scousers' who swear they saw Prince Charles going into Tommy Smith's nightclub for a private party. It is amazing what a latex mask, an evening suit and a pair of white gloves can do for a professional footballer! The majority of our parties invariably end in a sing-song, the most famous being after we had beaten Roma on penalties to regain the European Cup. It was a good job it was only photographs that were being taken, a sound mike would have dropped all of us in it. Gary Gillespie has proved himself to be an outstanding choir leader at these events which pop up in a variety of places around the world. It is quite remarkable the way the Liverpool players mix together when we are away, particularly when abroad. A good example was when we went to play a tournament in Swaziland and after playing on the Sunday we were told we need not report back until Thursday. I asked if anyone fancied a few days in South Africa and ended up hiring three five-seater planes to take us to Durban and the Sun International Hotel. The locals were amazed to see the entire Liverpool squad arrive and an old friend and ex-footballer, Alan Lazarus, invited the lads to be his guests and eat at his restaurant, which was called the Cattleman's Steak House. He did not appreciate what a united bunch we were and everyone turned up and tucked into the spare ribs, steaks and wine. We all enjoyed it so much that we went back again and again until Alan pleaded with us to give his staff a day off.

Our reserve goalkeeper Bob Bolder, now showing his qualities under Lennie Lawrence at Charlton, amazed everyone on that trip with his brute strength. I was sharing as usual with Craig Johnston, and when I returned to my room to change I found the door locked and no response to my knocking. We have all seen how in the films the cop puts his shoulder against the hotel-room door and bursts in on the gangster; well big Bob did not even need to do that as he just hit the door with both his hands and the whole thing came away from the frame, security chain and all. Craig thought it was the end of the world and I was totting up how much a new door would cost when Bob put it back, borrowed a shoe and nailed it back in place.

Steve Nicol, with whom I also occasionally shared a room, is often the butt of fairly harmless jokes but he takes them all in good spirit and bounces back. He is an excellent player and has still to reach his peak. He could even be as good as a Souness or Dalglish and that bodes well for Liverpool's future. I hope for his sake that he plays in the World Cup finals because I firmly believe that a player can only attain true world-class standard by playing in them. You may be an outstanding player, like George Best or any member of the Anfield squad, but it is the experience of a World Cup finals that polishes off the rough edges as it has done with Souness and Dalglish.

That was one of the reasons why I was so sorry to see Wales fail to beat Scotland in Cardiff because I would love to have seen Ian Rush perform at that level alongside Manchester United's Mark Hughes. For Rush particularly it would have been the icing on the cake. I am sure he would have been a sensation. I have not given up hope of getting there myself one day with Zimbabwe having been so close twice before when we went out to Cameroon and then Egypt. Even though I am currently banned from playing for my country, I will keep myself available in case they change their minds. Instead I will watch with some envy as my old Vancouver Whitecaps' manager Tony Waiters takes the Canadian team, featuring my old room-mate Carl Valentine, to the World Cup finals to play against the very best.

13

Looking Ahead

My life, and certainly my future, changed on 7 July 1984 when I married Devon-born, former air hostess Debbie Sweetland. It was a decision made if not on impulse then certainly very suddenly. Here at last was a woman who combined looks with a sharp brain, someone I could talk to about serious matters as well as laugh with. We hit it off straight away and, though I knew that confrontations would be inevitable over the years because we were both so much our own people, there was too much going for it to ignore it. The change in my attitude and style of living was confirmed when the marriage was blessed with our daughter Tahli. The responsibilities were not to be taken lightly for I had seen my father go through three marriages, and all the heartbreak involved, particularly after he died. I was determined at that moment to learn not only from his mistakes but from my own and those of my old pal Bob Scott whose marriage had also ended in failure.

I am not pointing the finger at anyone but I do have the enormous advantage of having done and seen so much in my short but eventful life. I see things from a different perspective than most of my age, having witnessed so much of life and death at close quarters. It meant changing, growing up and calming down by around 150 per cent on my previous wild ways. I would like to think that a large proportion of my future involves me playing football. After coming so close to quitting altogether after the Brussels disaster, I am now determined to follow in the footsteps of players like Dino Zoff and Pat Jennings who played football at its top level until well into their forties. I accept, however, that it is going to be increasingly hard to maintain peak condition, agility and clean handling. Once I had established myself at Liverpool I decided that I would not be able to accept playing at any lower standard than the First Division but, providing I still enjoy the game, I am not quite so certain now. I would not like to think that, towards the end of my career, I would have to play in the lower divisions because I needed the cash but, providing the challenge was right and my family were not dependent on my salary, why not? Certainly I feel that I am far too young to start thinking about coaching or management and indeed I am not yet sure whether I would be suited to it.

It would be out of character for me to stay at Liverpool for the rest of my life. I have always had itchy feet and boarding an aeroplane has become second nature to me. Maybe one day Europe will beckon as it has done to Graeme Souness, Ray Wilkins, Mark Hateley and others. It would appeal to my ego to be the first goalkeeper to leave England in search of success in somewhere like Italy, Spain or West Germany. I have never been able to understand why clubs are always willing to spend so much on strikers and midfield players and not on goalkeepers. A top keeper can be just as big a crowd puller as a goalscorer and I believe that the overall quality of goalkeepers is still far higher here than in the other European countries.

I would love to play in a stadium like Real Madrid's Bernabeau or Barcelona's Neu Camp; I would also love a chance to play at the Olympic Stadiums in Rome or Munich every week where the fans are football crazy and still go to games basically to enjoy themselves and not to spend the entire 90 minutes screaming obscenities. Maybe then I would change my style and, instead of being an auxiliary sweeper, I could concentrate on being a goalkeeper, producing reflex saves around my 6-yard box. Don't misunderstand me, I would still like to dominate my area, but without having to race 25 yards out of the goal, thus leaving myself open to errors and ridicule. I must say that, until Brussels, I enjoyed playing with Liverpool in the European Cup. I liked the colour, the excitement and the commitment and I will miss it badly. I always made an effort to be polite to my hosts by talking to them in their own language, even if the grammar was hopeless and I sometimes ordered a dish I did not want. It was always part of the fun. The European Cup Final in Rome seemed to do my reputation no harm at all and I was invited onto Terry Wogan's chat show after one of his researchers had seen some complimentary graffiti about me scrawled on a wall in a little Italian village. One of the popular 'girlie' calendars over there also saw fit to feature eleven topless girls and one topless Bruce Grobbelaar!

For as long as the top football-playing European countries hold a stimulating challenge I cannot see myself returning to Africa to play football, other than the international variety if ever Zimbabwe accept me and my British passport back into the fold. The football in Africa will never improve while they continue to have racial problems and I have no desire to become involved in that. Even if I did go and play in Europe I would like to think that I would return to England to finish my career. It would not break my heart if

I never left England for the game here still appeals enormously and it would be a challenge in itself to stay and try and stamp my name on the game. I would derive great satisfaction from proving wrong some of my critics, who have judged me on my formative years as a goalkeeper.

One advantage of staying in England would be that I could attend night school or further education college to read business studies. Although most of my savings are invested in pension schemes and endowment policies, I have now formed a limited company to take care of my finance. That isn't to say that I have any fancy ideas for investments but I hope it will secure my family's future with simple ventures such as endorsement of sports equipment. I can't imagine myself being as adventurous a businessman as I am a sportsman. One part of being a professional footballer that I dislike is that it restricts participation in other sporting activities. I can understand professional clubs like Liverpool not wanting to risk their expensive players, but I tried winter sports in Canada (without the Whitecaps' knowledge) and loved it while a dabble with sky diving when I was in the army whetted my appetite for that particular thrill. I also did a little flying during my two years' National Service and would love to take my private pilot's licence, but my contract prohibits me from pursuing that at present.

In the meantime I will be more than content to play my football for Liverpool. Despite the bans and the hooligans, it is still the greatest club in Europe by a long shot. I sometimes wonder whether the city deserves a club like Liverpool. When I arrived the supporters were fantastic; they were humorous, happy and appreciative. We enjoyed playing for them and the atmosphere they created was something very special. Most of them still are the same but, sadly, they are now the silent majority. It seems we have given them too much success for the most vociferous element's greatest delight now seems to be to harangue the players. Sometimes it is me, sometimes Kevin McDonald, and it has nothing to do with local loyalty for they even managed to get their knives into little Sammy Lee who is more 'Kop' than most of them. That lot think they know the game but they don't. If they knew how much they hurt Sammy or what they did to Kevin when they booed him off after he came on as a substitute in a Milk Cup-tie that we won well, they might think again. Kevin not only wants to do well as a professional but he loves the club and wants to do well for Liverpool. How can he give his best when his own supporters are giving him stick? It could only happen in football.

With the dreadful unemployment in Merseyside it is understandable why only 16,000 turn up for a Milk Cup-tie against a good Second Division side like Oldham, which brings a good many of its own supporters. I can also appreciate that those people without jobs are frustrated and bored. But why the hell do some go to football matches, pay the entrance fee out of their dole money and then have a go at people who are in jobs, trying to provide them with entertainment and trying to give an almost bankrupt city a little prestige and glory? Nobody in Liverpool, whether red or white by inclination, can accuse their footballers of giving them short measure. What is wrong with going to a football match to enjoy yourself? The London fans receive some criticism for their behaviour but when I went to West Ham recently I was once again amazed by their down-to-earth supporters. They are as patriotic as any in the country but they still accept that other teams can play football as well as theirs and they are not afraid to let you know it. At Anfield these days you have to have won the game before you run down the tunnel for the kick-off. Fortunately for the future of Liverpool Football Club the hard core remain as solid and partisan as ever.

This attitude could be a reflection of what is happening in the city. I know that footballers are supposed to be apolitical and read only the *Sun* and *Star* but you just have to live in Liverpool to feel the atmosphere and realise how the city has declined. Even my mother sensed it during the few days that she visited me. She was appalled that, having risked life and limb in the fight against Marxism, I was now living in a city seemingly controlled by it. There is a feeling of fear about the place and the already bad crime rate is on the up and up. It is time politicians on both sides woke up to what is happening in the city and did something for the real people of Merseyside instead of themselves. When the council was at war with Central Government, who suffered? It was the schoolchildren who were locked out and the old folk who could not fend for themselves.

If there is anything which would make me move out of Liverpool and into the country it is concern for my little daughter Tahli. I do not want her going to the sort of school where a caretaker can lock her out because he is on strike or where she comes home using the foul language that the kids use in front of my house. I wouldn't even feel safe letting her walk to the local church, 200 yards away, and that is a terrible indictment of the area. As a youngster I was an altar boy and a choir boy. Admittedly, in those days the financial rewards were an attraction but, though I have never been a regular churchgoer I do believe strongly in God. My faith was tested to the full when I was fighting in a war and in those days I went to church most Sundays when in the city and to impromptu services when in the bush. Religion became far more important to me than any political cause when fighting in the bush. I have kept my faith and I would like my children brought up in the church so that they can decide for themselves when they are old enough, as I was allowed.

Liverpool Football Club can count itself fortunate that at the worst time in the city's history, they have a man like Peter Robinson in charge. With the unemployment, the sad spirit of the inhabitants and the ban from Europe, the club could be facing a bleak future. If anyone can hold it together it is PBR who knows he will have the total backing of the management staff and the Board of Directors. European Cup revenue was counted on to pay the players' salaries and, but for his behind-the-scenes' manoeuvres, we would all be facing cutbacks. We will probably have to play games all over the world to make up for lost income until our re-entry into the European arena. That, if all of the conditions of the ban are fulfilled, could be a long time but providing our supporters realise that it is completely up to them I believe an appeal and our past record will see us back in action when the time is right. All three European competitions are devalued without the English clubs.

It is up to the true football supporters around the country to help bring the national game to life again. They can help us prove that the game is bigger than the hooligans who have tried to wreck it. They can treat the ruffians with the contempt they deserve and, when they see someone misbehaving and putting their favourite club and their favourite game under threat, they can point the culprit out to the police. It will then be up to the magistrates and the government to act on their promises after Brussels with firm action. I think even the hooligans were shocked by the deaths at Bradford, Birmingham and Brussels. They are not the bravest people in the world and they will gradually drift away if they sense danger to themselves or stiff prison sentences, then the game can return to the people it belongs to. For that to happen it needs co-operation between the authorities and the supporters to rebuild the game. It needs parents to come back to the stadiums with their children and for lads to bring their fathers as well. No father is going to get into a fight if they have their son with them and no youngster is going to be seen to be causing bother with his father standing next to him.

There is no reason at all why the game should not regain a great deal of its previous popularity and standing because, judging from what I have seen of football in all divisions, the standard of play and the entertainment value is extremely high. Maybe it is too high and the Football League would not be greatly harmed if they were to shed a few of the clubs and reduce the number of fixtures to a more sensible level. It is hardly likely when the moment fixtures were reduced by the unfortunate ban on English clubs, competitions were invented to take their place. If I were England manager Bobby Robson I would be despairing. The ban presented him with a wonderful opportunity to take a fully-prepared England squad to the World Cup finals, fresh, fit and ready for action. Instead his players faced a heavier programme than ever. As an outsider I found that sad for I happen to believe in the ability of both the England manager and his players at the present time and if they were given full rein there is no telling what they might do now or in the future. I am also convinced that a successful England football team would contribute towards a successful Football League. Yet few people connected with the game seem ready to help. They would much rather take a fee for criticising on a television programme.

But it seems that sport is a fair game for everyone these days, especially the politicians who take advantage of anything that can be brought within their sphere of influence, notably the Olympic Games. I, perhaps, feel it more strongly than most having been born in now isolated South Africa and brought up in Rhodesia where we were also excluded from international events because of apartheid. Sport has provided an easy option for the politicians without it ever involving economic hardship. Government ministers are not worried whether the Springboks play the Lions or the All Blacks providing the channels of trade and commerce are kept open. The only people hurt by sporting isolation are the sportsman and the supporters. I personally believe that sport is one way to break down every sort of barrier whether it is colour prejudice or religious sectarianism as in the case of Northern Ireland. The one time Ireland unites is through sport, such as when the country rejoiced after Mary Peters's Olympic success in Munich or Barry McGuigan's exploits in the boxing ring. South Africans, both black and white, feel pride when Zola Budd or Sydney Maree win races or set records on the athletic tracks.

Years of suspension from international sport have brought about mainly cosmetic changes but the dreadful bloodshed has suddenly forced the rest of the world into demanding more dramatic and effective measures. South Africa is a prosperous, wealthy country rich in natural resources. This has kept the door open for trade with foreign governments in chemicals for nuclear warheads, minerals for the multinationals and providing a centre in Africa for all the major banks. It was only when these were threatened that the rand fell to an all-time low. Foreign investments suffered and the politicians immediately acted to alleviate the financial pain.

There have been changes in South Africa over the years but they have been slow and not evident to the Western world. It seems incomprehensible to a European that coloureds and Indians have had the political door left ajar for them while the majority black population has been ignored. Yet it needed a tremendous amount of negotiation to get even this far. Unfortunately, bloodshed was inevitable after the fall of Rhodesia for South Africa is now very much alone, surrounded by hostile black nations. But I have been surprised and horrified at the level of death and the haphazard slaughter that has taken place. The white population, who seemed to be under great threat themselves, have stood back and watched black kill black. Worse still is that those that have been murdered by their own kind are those who have achieved status in the community. They are the very people who have increased the prospect of proper representation.

In some ways I can understand white South Africa's concerns as I fought for much the same thing and when Robert Mugabe was elected I feared the very worst. Ironically, he wanted to expel all whites from Zimbabwe but I have been back several times since and it seems that little has changed for the white population. They are getting on with their lives in very much the same way as before and the only significant alteration to their lifestyle is that they may now have a black family living next door. Robert Mugabe and his Government have clearly come to the conclusion that white expertise is needed to help the country develop.

My friends back home say that the country is going to flourish. Hotels are being built, tourism is on the increase and the general feeling is that the country will prosper and become one of the outstanding African nations. They have had the first-hand experience of seeing Uganda, Ethiopia, Tanzania, Mozambique, Angola and Botswana decline after being given their independence and they do not want to make the same mistakes. Malawi and Kenya provide far better examples of how countries can be developed to the best effect with stable governments. There is an abundance of natural resources in Zimbabwe. Until now it has been largely a farming community exporting tobacco to England and wheat and maize to countries like Mozambique and Botswana on its borders. Providing tribal trouble is kept to a minimum with Shono and Matabele living in harmony, which is a far more significant factor than black and white rivalry, the prospects are truly glorious.

I always supported Ian Smith but I have to admit that if he were still in power, the country would still be at war and white colonialism would have remained. Life has changed and the people of Zimbabwe have changed with it. I love going back and I always will. Once Africa is in your blood it is there to stay. It is a beautiful place.

14

The Double

I must admit that I had as many reservations about Kenny Dalglish as a manager as he had about me as a goalkeeper!

That may sound a daft thing to say after the man set what will be an unbeatable record of winning the 'double' of League Championship and FA Cup in his very first season, only the third team to achieve the distinction this century. What is more he did it in a way no manager did before or will do in the future — he scored the goal that won the League at Chelsea.

But to me that was not totally Kenny Dalglish's team. It also belonged to our previous manager Joe Fagan and the magical double was as much for him even though we had hardly ever seen him after he had left the game he loved in tears following the Heysel disaster.

Sadly Joe had finished his wonderful service to Liverpool as a three time loser, runner-up in everything and the everlasting mental scar of the night his dream turned into a nightmare in Brussels.

We were Liverpool without a trophy and Liverpool without friends. Liverpool with nowhere to go in Europe.

We could bounce back or we could sink into oblivion. No one was ever going to forget Heysel but what we had to remember was that the club was still great and that the players were not at fault and not to blame.

We owed it to Liverpool, we owed it to Joe. The critics helped us by writing us off, telling us our era was over. Liverpool were dead. Who was going to take over? Everton? Manchester United? Spurs? Arsenal? We decided no one. For a while it looked as though the critics might be correct when we dropped away points to teams like Aston Villa, Newcastle United, West Ham and Oxford but by the time we beat Everton at Goodison Park for our first away win of the season we were in second place and were never to be out of the top four again.

Our player-manager scored the opening goal of that game at Goodison in the first minute. It was one of only three he scored in the League all season but each of them had a great sense of occasion. Injuries and the pressure of the new job meant that his appearances were extremely rare and coming into the final phase of the season he had completed only half a dozen matches, starting in only eight games, and coming on as a substitute four times.

There was a period around the turn of the year when it looked as though our challenge would fade with only back to back wins against Watford and West Ham United keeping us alive in a sequence of 10 games without another win. Kenny brought himself back and played in all but two of our remaining dozen games and the only points we dropped were in a goalless draw at Sheffield Wednesday, one of eight clean sheets I kept in our final nine fixtures.

We went top on the last day of March and stayed there. Kenny scored only his second First Division goal of the season at West Bromwich Albion and then reserved his final strike for the day it mattered most, the final day when he volleyed the only goal of the game past Chelsea goalkeeper Tony Godden to give us the 1–0 win we needed at Stamford Bridge, pipping our great rivals Everton by just three points.

Did we make poor Everton pay that season! The team that were going to take over our role not only had to concede their Championship crown to us but then suffered what was literally a double blow when we beat them at Wembley to win the FA Cup. To be fair it was a poor reward for a wonderful season but we were not complaining. Hadn't we endured the same fate twelve months earlier?

It is drilled into us at Anfield that it is the League title which matters most and that everything else, even the European Cup, was gloss, a bonus to be enjoyed. However, there was huge satisfaction in that victory at Wembley.

How we enjoyed our day out in London and not simply because it was against the enemy from across Stanley Park. Liverpool had not won the FA Cup since 1974 which meant that a whole succession of players, not to mention managers Bob Paisley and Joe Fagan, had not experienced the unique thrill of winning one of the most glamorous competitions in the world.

Not that we had it easy, either on the way or once we were there. Little York City held us to a 1–1 draw before we beat them 3–1 at Anfield. A year earlier we had thrashed them 7–0 in a replay. In the next round everyone was ready to write us off again when Graham Taylor's well drilled Watford held us to a scoreless draw, at Anfield with their goalkeeper Tony Coton in magnificent form. It looked as though the gloomy forecasts were to be right this time when we lagged behind to a John Barnes goal and it was not until five minutes from the end that Jan Molby scored from a highly contentious penalty decision.

We were making hard work of it. In the previous round

York had not only held us to a draw on their own ground – when we also needed a Molby penalty – but took us to extra time before goals from Wark, Molby and Dalglish finished them off. This time it was the lethal Ian Rush who ended Watford's hopes in his own inimitable style, earning us a semi-final against Southampton at White Hart Lane and thus avoiding our neighbours Everton who had beaten Luton in a replay to earn a semi against Sheffield Wednesday.

We should have believed the Indian signs that this was to be our year for, although we were comfortably the best team against the Saints, Peter Shilton threatened to hold us up. Then the England goalkeeper clashed with his fellow international Mark Wright who was stretchered off, out of the tie and out of the World Cup, with a broken shin. It cast a damper on the game which went to extra time before Ian Rush ended speculation with two more goals. Everton had also won in extra time and there we were set for a repeat of the Milk Cup Final two years earlier. Merseyside were going to Wembley.

It seemed to capture the imagination of the whole nation, some feat considering that the Mexico World Cup was looming so close that the England squad left for their American training camp before we played. Fans told us that some had paid up to £1000 for a ticket on the black market—but I would bet that for everyone who had paid that much over the odds there was another Scouser who got into Wembley for nothing! I saw some risking their lives climbing up walls and fences to gain access to the ground.

Whatever they paid the 98,000 crowd had value for money. Gary Lineker was tipped as the key player. Not only was he about to depart for the World Cup finals where he was to become the tournament's top scorer but he was also on his way to Barcelona in a £2.75 million deal. Gary was the League's leading goalscorer with 30, seven more than our own Ian Rush and, almost inevitably, it was he who put Everton ahead. I was furious for I managed to get a hand to his first effort only to give him a second bite of the cherry. I even managed to get finger tips to that one but not enough to keep it out. I felt that if I had been more alert I would have saved it. Watching replays on television maybe I was a little harsh on myself but when you want to be the best you have to judge yourself by the highest standards.

That goal was a terrible set-back and knocked us for six. I reckon that if we had not won the League title a few days earlier we would surely have lost. But we were riding on a high and had nothing to lose. They might have scored more as we struggled but we held them off and Ian Rush stole in to equalise from a Jan Molby pass. I managed a good save to keep out a Graeme Sharp header and that proved to be something of a turning point as almost immediately our big Dutchman Jan Molby went through once more and crossed through a shattered Everton defence. Dalglish missed it but Craig Johnston did not.

Now, with Everton committed to total attack, it left us the sort of space we love and Molby and Ronnie Whelan combined to give Rushy his second goal. Should we have ever doubted our victory once Ian had scored that first goal? Liverpool had not lost in the previous 119 games in which he had scored!

We had done it! We had won the 'Double' and Bruce had added even more pots to his growing collection. But this time it was not the tangible rewards that gave me the most pleasure, it was the fact that I had survived the season at all. My name is down as part of football's history and folklore and no one can remove it.

A few tried that season. Considering I never missed a

game I had never suffered so much criticism in the course
of one season. Every single mistake seemed to be analysed
while my character and my ability were taken apart.
Everyone was joining in, managers picked me out as
Liverpool's weak point and former goalkeepers told
everyone I was no good. Every time I read a newspaper it
was to see who my successor was going to be as Liverpool
went on a nationwide hunt for a replacement. Some of it
dug deep particularly from people like Gordon Banks whom
I had always admired and respected. It was a nightmare for
me and my family.

Sometimes I felt that I did not receive enough protection
from my manager Kenny Dalglish. He was one of the few
people who knew the full truth of what I had gone through
that season, my worst ever in terms of injury. I dislocated
an elbow against York, flaked a bone in my ankle and
suffered a painful attack of shingles. I hated succumbing to
injury and when Kenny said he wanted me to play I was
not going to argue. Perhaps the biggest lesson I learned
that season was that once you pull on the goalkeeper's
jersey and cross the white line leading to the pitch, you
have declared yourself fit and there are no excuses.

Of course some of the criticism was justified, but it was
exaggerated beyond belief. I learned who my friends were
and there were not many who did not jump on that
particular bandwagon. A notable exception was television
presenter Bob Wilson who called on his experiences as a
goalkeeper with Arsenal and Scotland to mount a welcomed
defence for me. But, in the end, there was only one answer
and that was to do the business where it mattered most —
in between the sticks. I did in those last nine games when
only Craig Madden for West Bromwich Albion scored
against me.

To have won those two trophies after all the knocks was

sweet indeed and the Cup was the icing on the cake. The greatest satisfaction for myself and the team was winning the League, having being written off after Brussels. The FA Cup is a special trophy but luck and the draw can play such a big part in it while winning the best League in the world means doing it over 42 games in all conditions. Remember, too, most people had handed Manchester United the title when they went 15 games without defeat and left us trailing 18 points in their wake in the early stages of the season.

There was also further satisfaction in the wonderful behaviour of the Merseyside fans at Wembley, just as at the Milk Cup final two years earlier. Having had my say over Heysel, it has to be said that their demeanour and humour were exemplary, a credit to their clubs, the City of Liverpool and the country. It posed the question of exactly who was to blame on that unforgettable night of horror in Belgium. These were hardly the same people.

Naturally lavish praise was heaped on our player-manager Kenny Dalglish who was, quite rightly, nominated Bell's Manager of the Year but, as it always is at Anfield, the success was a triumph of team work on and off the pitch and as much credit to retired manager Joe Fagan and Kenny's consultant Bob Paisley. Bob kept out of the way when Kenny was not playing but had his invaluable say when our manager was involved in the action on the pitch. Some said Kenny should have hung up his boots when he took over the reins but he was brilliant when he performed towards the end of the season and was a major influence.

He continued as he started with me, pulling no punches and letting me know when he thought I was at fault. I understood and accepted most of what he said for I was a little larger than life, perhaps too much so in a club where it is continually drummed into you that no individual is bigger than the whole. But I like life too much to stop finding fun in the game and although I have grown up and calmed down a little I still find plenty of laughs in the game and consequently will always have running battles with managers like Kenny.

Having said all that Kenny still did a remarkable job. He had the courage to change the well tried and tested system, experimenting with a sweeper and other tactics which sometimes worked and sometimes did not. Often you could see the frustration building up in him because he knew what he wanted and the players could not always give it to him as he changed their roles.

One of the biggest obstacles was that often we did not know what the line-up was until we gathered in the dressing room before a game. Who am I to say what is right or wrong in that respect, but it was so different from what we had been used to at Anfield.

I harboured reservations about his ability as a manager despite that first season of success. Managing Liverpool has to be one of the most demanding jobs in football outside those odd exceptions like Barcelona. The club is so used to winning trophies that even relative failure comes hard.

I was even uncertain of my own future at the club at the end of that season. My contract had a year to run and no one seemed to want to talk about a new one. This time I was not just going to sign the first piece of paper stuck in front of my nose as I had in the past. In terms of my future this was going to be one of the most important contracts of my life and I owed it to my family to get it exactly right. I was unsure of how much Liverpool wanted to keep Bruce Grobbelaar. Had I outlived my usefulness?

The catalyst in the decision was, without doubt, a serious bid from my former Liverpool team-mate Graeme Souness who had returned from Italy to take on the task of player-manager for Rangers of Glasgow. Now here was a man I had always respected and I knew that whatever he did in football he would do with style and success even though I was never sure how he rated me.

But while Kenny turned his old rooming partner down flat and stated that I was staying at Anfield, there was still no offer of a new contract and neither was one mentioned until the following November. A lot of water had flowed under the bridge by then, not least of all the end of my proud run of 317 consecutive appearances.

I damaged stomach muscles and suffered a groin injury in the Charity Shield, the first serious game of the season, against Everton at Wembley on August 16 1986 and it meant that Bristol born Michael Hooper, bought from Wrexham, had his first taste of First Division football while I sat it out on the bench for the first seven league matches of the season. It was agony in more senses than one for while Mike played well enough to have kept his place I found myself treated like an outsider by my own teammates!

There was nothing malicious or new in the attitude. It was simply the way things are done at Liverpool stemming, I am told, from Bill Shankly's days when the great Scot hardly even acknowledged injured players. I travelled to all the away games but felt like a stranger at times. You have to win back your place to win back their respect. Maybe that is why I came back a little too quickly and played below my best form. I was lucky to keep my place after the way Mike had performed to help Liverpool into second place. I conceded three goals in my first game back against Aston Villa at Anfield.

Mike was destined to regain his place but not because of poor form on my part but because of yet another injury, this time one which could easily have finished my career altogether. I played until Easter Monday without undue problems and then, while making an awkward save, I fractured my right elbow against Manchester United in front of 54,103 at Old Trafford. I was in pain and knew that something was broken but although our substitute John Wark was asked how he fancied his chances in goal, I was asked to play on for the final 18 minutes. I conceded a goal to Peter Davenport after an error by Alan Hansen and made three further saves; fortunately all shots were to my good left side by the kind and sympathetic United forwards.

No one seemed to believe how bad the injury was and I travelled back the short distance to Merseyside from Manchester on the team bus, nibbling a packet of crisps and drinking a Coca Cola on the way. How I regretted that snack for x-rays confirmed my worst fears but there could be no operation because I had eaten. It was a bad, painful and sleepless night. Had I seen the pictures it would have been even worse because they showed it could have been the end of my professional career.

As it is I have to thank physiotherapist Paul Chadwick for insisting on rehabilitation after only three days. I staggered a friend of mine four days after the operation just before the local derby against Everton when I shook hands . . . using the damaged right arm! I don't suppose I will ever recover full range of movement and it was only decided to take out the metal pins because they were chiselling away the bone every time I dived full length. But at least it helped me reduce my golf handicap by three strokes and I have far greater control with my tennis now. Just call me Bionic Bruce.

I have often wondered since what would have happened to me if I had not signed a contract to keep me at Liverpool until 1991 a couple of weeks before my accident. Somehow

I think I might have been looking for a new club because the word was that I would be lucky to be playing again before the following Christmas if at all. As it was my long wait for contractual action ended in November when I was called upstairs and invited to talk terms. I wasn't too happy with the deal and telephoned my Canadian lawyer friend and advisor Ron Perrick to ask him what he thought. He studied the offer and came back to tell me that I could earn 80 per cent more playing in the North American Indoor League. What an eye opener that was. His advice was to keep talking and, in fact, he went one better and flew over to help me in my negotiations.

I had spelled out what I wanted and it appeared that we were still some way apart until another club showed an interest. This time it was Tottenham Hotspur who were reported to want to sign me, ironically to follow Ray Clemence yet again. I can only suppose that there was some foundation in the story for within a few days, the club and I had suddenly come together and I was only too happy to commit myself to Liverpool for a few more years.

That was an interesting season for me as, for the first time in my career, I was divorced from the action and was able to stand back and watch Kenny Dalglish in action as a manager. His playing appearances were few and far between as he concentrated his efforts on sorting out a team racked by injuries, not just to me but to players like Jim Beglin, Steve Nicol, Mark Lawrenson, Kevin MacDonald and Gary Ablett. There was some suggestion that Kenny was not coping too well. He had his problems with the media and came in for some very heavy stick. I knew just how he felt.

The injuries ate into the team and our confidence. While our rivals Everton had as many problems, they seemed to have the luck that we did not get. When I broke my elbow at Old Trafford it was our fifth defeat in six games and we lost our top of the table spot never to win it back again, eventually conceding the Championship to Everton by nine points. They had then turned the tables on us and gained their revenge for twelve months earlier.

Not only did we finish as runners-up in the league we also lost out in the cups, falling to Arsenal in the Little-woods final we should have won after a remarkable run that saw us score ten against Fulham and beat Everton away. The FA Cup defence never got off the ground and we went out in the third round in a blaze of controversy to Luton Town, losing 3–0 in the second replay on the plastic pitch at Kenilworth Road.

Having held them in the first game in Bedfordshire Luton let us, our supporters and football down by failing to arrive at Anfield for the replay. It was a disgrace. Our pitch was perfectly playable and not only were our supporters able to get to the ground, plenty of Luton supporters and even a couple of their directors reached Liverpool in the bad weather without mishap. But the team, who had cut things too fine, were stranded at the airport and never made it.

Their chairman David Evans admitted it was down to them. That should have been enough for the FA to boot them out as they would have done any other team in any of their other competitions and as would have happened in any other country. I felt it was disgraceful that they were given another chance – and said so at the time. I was punished for that but it did not change the facts nor my opinion.

That they did a job on us and gained a goalless draw at Anfield prior to beating us 3–0 on plastic has nothing to do with how I feel. Call it sour grapes. I do not care. It was wrong.

That was just another set-back Kenny had to suffer

during that traumatic season. The Littlewood's Cup final was another when we were the better side than Arsenal. We blew it on account of the old footballing adage of the side scoring the most goals wins. They scored twice through Charlie Nicholas and we scored once through Ian Rush. We would pick Wembley to end that remarkable run of never having lost a game in which Ian had scored.

There was another problem for Kenny. The club had already sold Rushy to Juventus for £3 million, an offer they could not turn down especially as they promptly loaned him back to us for the season because they had their quota of two foreign players with the Dane Michael Laudrup and the French captain Michel Platini. Naturally our crowd and particularly the vociferous Kop did not want to see their favourite player go and campaigns, petitions and meetings were organised in a vain bid to keep him.

It was all so different from the time when Kevin Keegan had gone to Hamburg. There was no rancour or bitterness aimed at Ian at all and neither should there have been as the irrepressible Welshman was the only player that season to complete all 42 League fixtures, a rare feat for a forward of his talents. He continued to produce the goods and the goals until the end and there is never going to be another like him. The nearest I have seen is Gary Lineker. Both have blinding speed and are natural goalscorers with Rush just earning my vote, although imagine them both in the same team.

Mind you, Ian had a rival in the 5-a-side games. Me. I was top scorer but he steadfastly refused to return the compliment and go in goal, saying all goalkeepers were lunatics. I can't understand that he meant.

But it was no joke to our manager for he knew that he not only had to replace the best goalscorer in Europe but also himself for he was clearly phasing out his own playing career. He was distracted in this effort as he had to plug the gaps left by the injuries. He was accused of buying players who were not up to Liverpool standards but that was unfair. Steve McMahon, Barry Venison, Nigel Spackman and Alan Irvine all played their parts with Spackman particularly underrated by my reckoning.

John Aldridge was the man bought from Oxford for a lot of money who had the unenviable task of replacing Rush. He may be a true Scouser and even similar in looks to Ian Rush but you need more than that. I know John was desperate to play in the team with Rushy but eight of his ten appearances were as substitute. The fact that he scored a goal in each of the two games he actually began became more significant next season when he started in sensational goal-a-game fashion.

Our manager at last began to get credit for his depth of knowledge of the game when he plundered the transfer market for John Barnes from Watford and Peter Beardsley from Newcastle. What brilliant buys those turned out to be. The lad Barnes is sheer magic and Peter Beardsley is not far behind him in terms of skill, although it took him a little longer to settle.

But by then Kenny Dalglish had won me over as a manager. I watched how he coped with the problems and was most impressed with his handling of something neither the public nor the press could see. After winning the double some of our players suddenly began to believe what great players they were and for the first time in my memory there were cliques being formed. Kenny not only saw it happening but sorted it out and brought the family back together.

I do not suppose I will ever convince him I am a great goalkeeper but he has convinced me that he is going to be as good a manager as he was a player and he is leading

Liverpool towards yet another golden era.

I will be more than happy to be a part of that. Happily the abuse and criticism seem to have tempered a little, although I have no doubt it will return apace as soon as I drop my next clanger. I hope that I make the vultures wait for I have changed both my attitude and my game.

I confess that I am much more inclined to look after number one these days. Because of the way Liverpool play I shall always be required to act as an extra sweeper, sometimes necessitating me coming out of my area but I have left far more responsibility to the defenders and now try to recover their mistakes rather than the other way round. Perhaps that is all part of maturing and growing up.

In 1991 I will be 34 and, by my reckoning, at my peak. My contract may finish at Liverpool then but whether they want me any longer will have no influence on my decision. Football will have to wait a lot longer to see the back of the Jungle Man.

BOB CRAMPSEY

JOCK STEIN
THE MASTER

Four days after Jock Stein's tragically sudden death,
every football game in Scotland at all levels held a
one-minute silence. That silence was echoed around
the world as a tribute to the greatest football
manager of them all.

JOCK STEIN was the most successful manager in
British football at club level. He led Celtic to nine
consecutive league titles and shifted the focus of
European football attention to Glasgow. He piloted
Scotland to two World Cup finals.

The best-known Scot of his generation is revealed as
a compassionate, humane and commited man in
this admiring but analytical look by someone who
has watched Stein's carrer from close quarters for
twenty-eight years.

POST A LITTLE HAPPINESS

Post·A·Book

A Royal Mail service in association with the Book Marketing Council & The Booksellers Association.
Post-A-Book is a Post Office trademark.

**GENE KLEIN AND
DAVID FISHER**

FIRST DOWN AND A BILLION

The guts, the glory, the drugs, the despair.

From the boardroom to the locker room the insider dealing of pro football .

'My two happiest days were the day I bought the San Diego Chargers and the day I sold the San Diego Chargers'
GENE KLEIN

In 1966, having made a fortune from nothing, Gene Klein bought the American Football team the SAN DIEGO CHARGERS.

FIRST DOWN AND A BILLION portrays two tumultuous decades in the National Football league and exposes the business battles between fellow owners, agents, players and the union. He hired and fired head coaches, drafted and traded players, survived the first major drug scandal in pro sport, and helped negotiate the largest television contract in sports history.

FIRST DOWN AND A BILLION is both an intriguing book for the businessman and a fascinating insight for the sportsman and will prove invaluable whether you're into fitness or finance.

NEW ENGLISH LIBRARY

MIKE BREARLEY

THE ART OF CAPTAINCY

English cricket's most successful captain of recent years, Mike Brearley was also the most thoughtful and articulate of captains.

Now he has written:

'The most perceptive book ever likely to be written on cricket captaincy'

The Times

'A masterpiece of its kind'

The Sporting Life

'No better nor more generously stocked brain has been applied to the writing of a cricket book'

Punch

'A fascinating study of leadership...he comprehensively illustrates the facts of decision-making in cricket while simultaneously dissecting his own batting ability and technique with refreshing truthfulness'

Time out

'Thoughtful, provocative, well-informed and readable... an essential companion'

The Journal of the Cricket Society

CORONET BOOKS

CHRIS BONINGTON

THE EVEREST YEARS

In 1985, at the age of 50, Chris Bonington fulfilled a lifelong ambition and crowned an already distinguished mountaineering career by reaching the summit of Everest.

This third volume of his autobiography is a marvellous blend of drama and reflection, a fascinating insight into mountaineering, revealing the great triumph of human endeavour. Culminating with his enthralling conquest of 'the roof of the world', THE EVEREST YEARS is an outstanding testimony to one of the golden ages of British mountaineering.

'Gripping...beautifully illustrated'

Daily Express

'Master climber and in this a master at describing himself and others in the sheer ice-white, frightening, often fatal world on the big tops'

The Sunday Times

CORONET BOOKS

CHRISTOPHER MARTIN-JENKINS

BEDSIDE CRICKET

BEDSIDE CRICKET is for people who have got beyond the stage of seeing cricket as a gentle and chivalrous game conducted ritually in the sunshine in beautiful surroundings.
The currency of this book is harder stuff altogether— beginning with pre-natal cricket and the eleventh hour race to make sure the boy is born in the correct county.

As the child becomes a man he meets the diabolical mysteries of club cricket, a world ruled by paunchy men with deceptive limps and yellowing sweaters. If he goes higher, he has to cope with the vagaries of the county game, perhaps reaching Test level. There it is his privilege to meet the greatest possible assortment of biased umpires, abusive spectators, eccentric commentators and pressmen-all in some way attached to the caravan of flannelled fools who tirelessly cross the globe in the cause of a game that people like Christopher Martin-Jenkins happen to think is the best and most sophisticated yet devised by man.

CORONET BOOKS

ALSO AVAILABLE FROM HODDER AND STOUGHTON PAPERBACKS

☐ 41425 1	**BOB CRAMPSEY** Jock Stein : The Master	£2.95
☐ 41844 8	**GENE KLEIN AND** **DAVID FISHER** First Down And A Billion	£2.50
☐ 41029 9	**MIKE BREARLEY** The Art of Captaincy	£5.95
☐ 41426 X	**CHRIS BONINGTON** The Everest Years	£2.95
☐ 32110 5	**CHRISTOPHER MARTIN-** **JENKINS** Bedside Cricket	£2.95

All these books are available at your local bookshop or newsagent, or can be ordered direct from the publisher. Just tick the titles you want and fill in the form below.

Prices and availability subject to change without notice.

HODDER AND STOUGHTON PAPERBACKS, P.O. Box 11, Falmouth, Cornwall.

Please send cheque or postal order, and allow the following for postage and packing:

U.K. - 55p for one book, plus 22p for the second book, and 14p for each additional book ordered up to a £1.75 maximum.

B.F.P.O. and EIRE - 55p for the first book, plus 22p for the second book, and 14p per copy for the next 7 books, 8p per book thereafter.

OTHER OVERSEAS CUSTOMERS - £1.00 for the firstbook, plus 25p per copy for each additional book.

NAME ....

ADDRESS ....

....